The Labor of Luck

The Labor of Luck

CASINO CAPITALISM
IN THE UNITED STATES
AND SOUTH AFRICA

JEFFREY J. SALLAZ

UNIVERSITY OF CALIFORNIA PRESS
Berkeley   Los Angeles   London

University of California Press, one of the most distinguished
university presses in the United States, enriches lives around the
world by advancing scholarship in the humanities, social sciences,
and natural sciences. Its activities are supported by the UC Press
Foundation and by philanthropic contributions from individuals
and institutions. For more information, visit www.ucpress.edu.

University of California Press
Berkeley and Los Angeles, California

University of California Press, Ltd.
London, England

Library of Congress Cataloging-in-Publication Data

Sallaz, Jeffrey J., 1974–.
  The labor of luck : casino capitalism in the United States and South
Africa / Jeffrey J. Sallaz.
      p.   cm.
  Includes bibliographical references and index.
  ISBN 978-0-520-25948-5 (cloth : alk. paper)
  ISBN 978-0-520-25949-2 (pbk. : alk. paper)
    1. Casinos—United States.   2. Casinos—South Africa.   I. Title.
HV6715.S25 2009
338.4'77950968—dc22   2009009190

Manufactured in the United States of America

18   17   16   15   14   13   12   11   10   09
10 9 8 7 6 5 4 3 2 1

This book is printed on Cascades Enviro 100, a 100% post-consumer
waste, recycled, de-inked fiber. FSC recycled certified and processed
chlorine free. It is acid free, Ecologo certified, and manufactured by
BioGas energy.

To my mother and father, Donna and Jan

Contents

Illustrations

Tables

Preface

Between 1999 and 2004 I lived a double life. Half of my time I spent in the world of academia as a graduate student and instructor at a large public university. The other half found me in the world of the casino as an ethnographer studying the global gambling industry. Academic life has its own mode and moves at its own pace; at the University of California, Berkeley, no one batted an eyelid if I arrived to class unshaven or unkempt, rumpled jeans and untucked shirts constituted the core components of my wardrobe, and tardiness was so taken for granted that classes regularly started at ten minutes past the hour.

Casino life could not be more different. My day began when the typical person's ends, at eight P.M., when I awoke to shower, shave, and get ready for work. I was a croupier—a casino dealer—and I passed my night in a dimly-lit pit handling cash, coins, and chips. My work was monitored by men in suits: pit bosses, themselves overseen by casino executives and surveillance cameras. Should I arrive at my table ten seconds tardy, or with a spot of ketchup on my tuxedo lapel, I could expect a tongue-lashing. Should I end my shift a few chips short from my table's bankroll, I could be fired. The university imagines itself as a world in which ideas circulate freely, but there is no such illusion in the casino, where hard cash is king.

By nature, ethnographic fieldwork produces in the researcher a divided psyche. He or she moves back and forth between two worlds, neither entirely comprehensible to the other. My colleagues at the University of California were intrigued by my casino study, but looked befuddled when I instinctively swiped my palms after paying for a cappuccino at a local café (dealers must "show clean hands" to the surveillance cameras after paying a winning bet—a hard habit to break.) My fellow croupiers in turn rolled their eyes whenever I pontificated on "gaming industry" politics. No time for such thoughts during a "lunch break" in the middle of the night, as you're gulping down one last cup of black coffee to get you through to the dawn.

Yet as different as the university and the casino may be, they do share some commonalities. Both market not material things but intangible services: education on the one hand, entertainment on the other. And both grew exponentially during the twentieth century. The worldwide expansion of institutions of higher learning has been well documented, and is generally believed to be beneficial for society.[1] The growth of legal gambling is less well understood and typically considered with consternation.

Consider that in the United States prior to 1978, one had to travel all the way to Nevada to gamble in a casino. By 2005, however, there were 680 casinos spread across 35 states. As a result, between 1960 and 2005, industry revenues grew from $800 million to $53.5 billion, while gambling losses as a percentage of all recreation spending increased 1,200 percent.[2] This, Eugene Martin Christiansen expounds, "is an awful lot of money: more than Americans [spend] on recorded music, movies and video games combined."[3] Thus, during the same decades that Americans moved greater and greater portions of their savings into the stock market, the gambling industry exploded.[4] Both trends reflected the emergence of a new economic order—aptly dubbed "casino capitalism"—in which individuals think of themselves less as hard-working savers than as risk-taking entrepreneurs. And while it remains to be seen whether the current financial crisis permanently tempers our tolerance for risky equities, the same is not true for slot machines, blackjack tables, and the other games of chance that produce profits for the famously recession-proof gambling industry. Casino capitalism may wax and wane, but the casino will likely be with us for the foreseeable future.

A plethora of works has appeared on bookstore shelves in recent years purporting to describe the new casino industry from various points of view. Politicians, we are told, strike Faustian bargains by easing restrictions on proprietors' strategies for "selling hope;"[5] shrewd gamblers devise ever-cleverer methods to "bring down the house;"[6] and pit bosses gamely patrol the "green felt jungle."[7] Largely absent from this literature, however, is the perspective of those front-line service employees who deal with and to clients. This inattention is curious, given the prominence of employment issues in larger political debates surrounding gambling legalization. While prohibition of gambling is typically justified in reference to the consumer (i.e., banning casinos deters betting), of late policy makers increasingly place rhetorical prominence upon the worker to promote the cause of casinos (legalizing gambling creates jobs for citizens). But what does the contemporary casino look like from the perspective of those in whose name its very existence is justified?

Studying casino workers can produce insight into not only this particular industry but the contours of the contemporary service society in general. It is well established that the ongoing displacement of agricultural and manufacturing industries by service enterprises has transformed the modal method of making a living in most countries. In the United States, for example, the proportion of workers employed in service occupations increased from 30 percent in 1900 to over 80 percent today.[8] The casino, because it sells what is essentially an intangible service (i.e., the opportunity to wager on events of uncertain outcome), is an excellent place to glimpse life and labor in the post-industrial workplace. (Some have even argued that it has supplanted McDonald's as the paradigmatic enterprise of the new economy.)[9] The casino industry today employs more than one million individuals worldwide, and the average U.S. worker is more likely to labor in a casino pit than on an automobile assembly line.[10]

Why are policy makers the world over opting to legalize rather than ban casinos? How do political struggles over gambling legalization play out in individual countries and states? And what are the consequences of these struggles for the growing number of people who make a living behind the tables? To address these questions, this book presents histori-cal and ethnographic data on the U.S. casino industry as it emerged in the state of Nevada during the twentieth century. But it also compares the United States to South Africa, a country with its own fascinating history of gambling regulation. During the dark years of apartheid, an illicit casino industry thrived in South Africa's infamous "homeland states." Although the puritanical apartheid regime frequently railed against America's "Sin City," in fact these casinos were—down to the smallest details—mirror images of their Nevada counterparts. And when apartheid ended, the new government not only legalized mass gam-bling but also passed new regulations designed to recreate Las Vegas in South Africa. My ethnographic research, however, reveals that these new policies have actually pushed South Africa's casinos away from the Nevada model. Their rhetoric may at times converge, but neoliberal and postcolonial modes of governance produce entirely divergent worlds of work and play.

The take-home point of the comparison of casinos in the United States and South Africa is a more general one: although states may imitate American-style leisure and tourism industries in an effort to find a pana-cea for their economic troubles, it is the balance of social forces in a given country that shapes systems for managing workers and clients "on the ground." (In fact, many features of the Las Vegas casino widely assumed to be general to gambling are actually unique to the American system for regulating markets of labor, capital, and consumers.) No less than their predecessors in the old, manufacturing-based economy, the service industries that are coming to dominate the new economy comprise pro-cesses that are social, cultural, and, above all else, political.

A work of this sort, a comparative global ethnography, is a labor of love, and a collective one at that. I would like to offer my gratitude to all those who shared their time, thoughts, and energy with me during the process of planning, researching, and writing this book. All credit for the insights contained herein I share with them; any errors or omissions are mine alone.

This project has its roots in a dissertation thesis written in the sociology department at the University of California at Berkeley. Among those who read and commented upon early iterations of the manuscript, I would like to thank Jennifer Chun, Eli Friedman, Gillian Hart, Tom Medvetz, Kim Voss, Loïc Wacquant, Chris Wetzel, and Michelle Williams. Neil Fligstein was a supportive mentor who challenged me to imagine casino law liberalization as a more general case of a political market-making project. Gil Eyal's seminar on the writings of Michel Foucault helped me formulate my ideas on deviance, criminal law, and the panopticon. Elsa Tranter, Linda Flores, and other "soc department" staff offered valuable administrative assistance. The dedicated employees at Café Milano provided daily nourishment and a cozy space to write and think. Special thanks go to Michael Burawoy, whose unflagging support and occasional doses of tough love sustained the project from start to finish. His devotion to his students is by now legendary; I don't know how he does it, but I am grateful to have crossed paths with Michael at Berkeley during those years.

My time in South Africa was spent among a remarkable group of scholars associated with the sociology of work program (SWOP) at the University of the Witwatersrand. Edward Webster, Khayaat Fakier, Bridget Kenny, Bongiwe Mncwango, Rahmat Omar, and other SWOP personnel assisted me with securing visas, establishing contacts, and formulating new ideas. As I conducted research on South Africa's gambling industry, Jacques Booysen, Edward Lalumbe, Sie Strauss, and Wolfgang Thomas took time to share their opinions and thoughts with me. Ann Champion, Patrick Heller, Mark Hunter, Kamau Kitchener, and Kevin Ntombela made sure I did not neglect the social life in the challenging but always invigorating city of Johannesburg.

During several research stints in Nevada, I encountered an array of scholars who shared a passion for understanding the workings of the state's gambling industry. Bill Eadington and Judy Cornelius at the University of Nevada's Institute for the Study of Gambling and Commercial Gaming were always generous and helpful. Su Kim Chung and David Schwartz at the University of Nevada, Las Vegas's (UNLV's) Special Collections library pointed me to a wealth of historical information on the early days of casinos. Also at UNLV, Al Balboni, Eugene Moehring, Hal Rothman, and William Thompson offered valuable feedback. Kelly Denton and Travis Stroud were fine tour guides of the cities of Reno and Las Vegas.

Conversations with Al Bergesen, Ron Breiger, Kieran Healy, Kathleen Schwartzman, and other colleagues at the University of Arizona honed the final argument contained herein. Sherry Enderle and other staff persons expertly organized logistics at various points in time. Danielle Hedegard, Amanda Lopez, and Zach Schrank provided assistance with the final editing. Yves Winkin offered his insights on Erving Goffman's "Nevada years." The research was funded by the National Science Foundation; Social Science Research Council; the University of California, Berkeley; and the University of Arizona. An earlier version of chapter 3 appeared as "The House Rules" in *Work and Occupations* 29 (2002): 394–427. Naomi Schneider, Caroline Knapp, and two anonymous reviewers at the University of California Press helped fine-tune the final manuscript.

Last but not least, I'd like to acknowledge my many coworkers—the dealers, pit bosses, and shift managers whose stories are told in this book but who for various reasons must remain nameless. I entered the casino by choice and could leave when I wanted; they sweat it out night after night in an industry for which few feel proud to work. One should typically be wary of gifts given by those who work for the house: casino "comps" are instrumental means to loosen up the gambler and his or her pocketbook. However, the generosity afforded me by my co-workers, which I can repay only with this cursory thank-you note, attests to the kindness of the human spirit found even in these otherwise voracious institutions.

Introduction

I was not the first sociologist to moonlight as a croupier. In fact, Erving Goffman, "the most famous of American sociologists," once worked behind the tables.[1] Goffman is remembered today mainly as an innovative social theorist, one who used metaphors drawn from the theater to depict everyday life as a series of dramatic performances.[2] But Goffman was also a devoted researcher who grounded his conceptual schemes in firsthand empirical observations of social life. Trained as an ethnographer at the University of Chicago during the early 1950s, at various points during his career he scrubbed dishes in a Scottish hotel, observed service station attendants at work, and even interned in an asylum for the mentally ill.[3] From this latter fieldwork came perhaps his most famous idea: that of the total institution, a "voracious" organization that seals the individual off from the outside world and remakes his or her identity.[4]

I

In 1958, Goffman accepted a professorship at the University of California and commenced studying a new total institution: the casino. He spent his summer sabbaticals in neighboring Nevada, observing the action in "the pits" by playing blackjack (a card game in which you compete against the dealer to reach twenty-one points). But playing cards all day was not a sustainable research plan—not on an assistant professor's salary anyway. Goffman thus studied "basic strategy"—a series of decision rules that minimize the "house advantage" on the blackjack table. He also consulted with the mathematician Edward O. Thorp, who had recently contrived a technique called "card-counting," through which gamblers, by tracking the cards played during the game, could actually swing the odds in their favor.

Ed Thorp would gain fame and fortune by making his method public in the best-selling book *Beat the Dealer.*[5] For Goffman, however, card-counting proved a bane to research. As his son Tom, who went along on his father's Nevada adventures, recounted: "Erving was a good counter, and eventually got blacklisted from all the major casinos for winning too consistently. You can do anything in Vegas except win too consistently."[6]

Banned from his research site, Goffman, like any good ethnographer, found another path of entrée. No longer able to beat the dealers, he joined them by training as a croupier and obtaining employment at a well-known Las Vegas casino. From this fieldwork came the books *Strategic Interaction* and *Interaction Ritual,*[7] writings in which Goffman refuted the classical contention that gambling is at root an economically irrational activity. Standing behind the tables, a deck of cards in his hands, he discovered the casino to be a world unto itself and each hand a suspenseful drama in which gamblers collectively made meaning of their worlds. They did not treat game outcomes simply as impersonal expressions of the law of probability. No, they experienced agency during the contests and sought to demonstrate character in the heat of the "action."[8] The overarching lesson, Goffman concluded, was that one must study both the material reality and the intersubjective meaning of gambling games—both "the management of fatefulness" and "the management of an affective state associated with it."[9]

I shared with Erving Goffman the conviction that interactions among real people in their everyday environments should be the starting point for sociological analysis, and thus that *participant observation* within the "belly of the beast" is the ideal method for researching organizations. In the spirit of what is known as an "ethnographic revisit," I followed in his footsteps.[10] I took up residence in Nevada and trained as a croupier. And I, too, obtained employment at a landmark gambling property, called herein the "Silver State Casino."

The goals of an ethnographic revisit are typically to return to the fieldsite of a past ethnographer, document what has changed, and explain these differences.[11] And there certainly have been changes in the U.S. gambling industry during the forty years separating our stints behind the tables. Goffman worked in what was then a typical Nevada casino: a small, upscale establishment secretly owned by an organized crime syndicate. My fieldsite, a huge gambling complex owned by a publicly traded corporation, in turn typifies the industry today. And while Nevada circa 1960 had a monopoly on casino gambling in the United States, today it faces fierce competition from other states (and even other countries).

Yet I was surprised to discover how little has changed on the Nevada casino floor, despite these radical transformations in the structure of the U.S. gambling industry. Dealing remains a craft; like Goffman, I learned to deftly shuffle cards and chips. Paternalistic pit bosses continue to treat the tables as their own private fiefdoms. And although slot machines now occupy a greater portion of the casino floor, the table games remain the lynchpin of organizational control. At Nevada casinos today, the tables department is the largest in terms of staff and payroll. It is the site of valued "high-roller" action, and most cheating "scams" take place there. In addition, interactions between dealers and gamblers at the tables remain the main point of firm-client contact. As a manager stated, "If you control the dealers, you control the industry. . . . They're the heart and soul of the place."[12] Why, I puzzled, has the Nevada casino pit remained essentially unchanged over the past forty years? How has it managed to buffer itself from larger structural transformations of the industry in general?

Upon tackling this initial puzzle, I found myself confronted with another, then another—like Hercules battling the Hydra. To know why dealers shuffle the cards in a certain way, it was necessary to understand the decision-making process of casino managers. But this entailed situating these managers within the larger leisure firm, and the firm within the larger field of politics in the United States. Before long, my focus shifted beyond the confines of a single Nevada casino to a comprehensive study of the constitution of the casino industry on a global scale. Throughout my research, I kept Goffman close at hand, and his writings proved indispensible for making sense of the interactions I observed and took part in. Blackjack players, then and now, engage in strategies of impression management as they battle "luck" and "fate" at the tables. But as my five-year ethnographic journey wore on, I increasingly found the sociology of Erving Goffman inadequate to capture the dynamics of this new and evolving global industry. Eventually, my own theoretical assumptions (along with the research questions and field data they engendered) led me to make three ruptures with the Goffmanian tradition. Summarized here, they also provide a concise overview of my findings and of the argument of this book.

First, *leisure industries such as casinos are constituted by both consumers and workers.* Goffman became a croupier only after being banned as a gambler. Work was for him but an alternate means to study consumption—to see, that is, how gambling constitutes the player's self in everyday life. But my own research revealed that dealers are not passive mediators between players and the house. On the contrary, they play an active role in determining game outcomes and structuring the gambling experience. The casino, in short, is not simply a world of leisure; it is simultaneously a world of work.

Second, *the U.S. experience of casino gambling (or anything else for that matter) should not be generalized to all times and places.* Based upon his study of a single Nevada casino, Goffman made general pronouncements about the immutable essence of risk taking, and thereby risked universalizing his own experiences (i.e., those of white, middle-class American men in the 1950s). To prevent such bias, I undertook systematic comparative research grounded in the principle of reflexivity. For reasons to be discussed below, I compared Nevada to another of the world's new "casino states," South Africa, where, following the fall of apartheid, the new government legalized Vegas-style casinos. I again worked as a croupier, this time at Johannesburg's "Gold City Casino," a carbon copy of my first fieldsite, Silver State Casino. Ethnographic immersion in the pits, however, revealed two very different ways of managing the same gambling games. The Nevada casino, I found, cannot be seamlessly picked up and replicated in a new national context.

Third, *differences in micro interaction orders must be traced to differences in social structures.* Goffman, the quintessential "sociologist of small-scale entities," never ventured beyond the casino floor to make sense of his ethnographic findings.[13] But to explain the differences between Silver State Casino and Gold City Casino, I had to extend out to the larger societal context of the United States and South Africa. Drawing upon new approaches in economic and political sociology, I show how state systems for regulating service industries structure the production and consumption of the gambling "product." The labor of luck, far from being universal and invariant, plays out differently in different countries as managers, bureaucrats, and other actors struggle to legitimize mass gambling within the political field.

The remainder of this introductory chapter elaborates upon these three points: seeing the casino as a world of work, situating the Nevada casino in a global context, and moving from situations to structures.

THE CASINO AS A WORLD OF WORK

We typically think of casinos as spaces of leisure in which individual consumers purchase entertainment from "the house." Erving Goffman overturned common sense by depicting the casino floor as a social microcosm wherein serious contests are played out over meaning and character. He did not go far enough, however. He systematically studied gambling from the perspective of players, but not from those of workers and managers. It is thus necessary to develop a framework for understanding the casino as not simply a space of leisure but also a place of work for its employees. Drawing upon the work of Michael Burawoy, another Chicago School ethnographer, I argue that the casino constitutes a "service production regime" in which the house must manage not only gamblers but workers, too.

A casino offers an opportunity to wager money along with a legal guarantee that winnings will be paid. In return, it grants itself a small statistical edge on each game—called the *hold percentage*—to cover expenses and make a profit.[14] The task of administering the games, and thus of extracting this "fee" from clients, however, falls upon front-line service workers, such as dealers. Moving inward from the set-up of the casino as a whole to that of the individual card games, we may gain a sense of the parameters within which casino work is performed.

Consider the design of the casino complex itself. Its purpose—given that the house comes out ahead of players in the long run—is to establish an emotional footing for this transfer of money. Casino architecture thus entices visitors to both commence and continue gambling. Table games and slot machines are often arranged in maze-like formations in order to preclude a clear line of sight across the casino floor. This creates the illusion of a crowded, exciting gambling environment. Walls lack windows to avoid reminding gamblers of passing time, while restrooms are located in the rear of the building so that visitors must meander through banks of slot machines before and after relieving themselves.[15]

Management also precipitates and prolongs play by providing clients an array of wares. While most service enterprises offer both physical goods and immaterial services, in a casino the latter are primary: food, drink and accommodation are discounted and sometimes even free. Complimentary goods ("comps"), ranging from cocktails to penthouse suites, are prototypical "consolation prizes" used to "cool out" losing gamblers, allowing them to rationalize their losses through the illusion of bargains received during their stay in the casino.[16]

The table games themselves are grouped into oval-shaped formations known as pits. A dealer is stationed at each table, floorpersons (also called inspectors) each monitor several tables, and a pit boss watches over all of the action in the pit. Watching all of the pits are shift bosses: senior managers who patrol the casino floor. Shift bosses are supervised

Figure 1.   Bird's-eye view of a blackjack table. © Nik Wheeler/Corbis.

by the tables manager and the casino manager. All casino personnel are in turn monitored by surveillance specialists manning an extensive network of video cameras.[17]

This study focuses upon blackjack. Known as "the king of table games," it remains the most popular casino game in the world.[18] A blackjack table is topped with a semicircle of felt (see figure 1). Players perch upon stools along the rounded edge of the table, while the dealer stands at the flat edge. In front of the dealer is a tray holding the table's "bank" of plastic gambling chips. Each player receives two cards and attempts, by drawing more cards if needed, to get as close as possible to a total of twenty-one points without going over ("busting"). Aces count as either eleven points or one point (at the choice of the player); tens, jacks, queens, and kings as ten points; and all other cards are worth their face value. Gamblers play not against each other but against the dealer, who also receives two cards played out in accord with a set of predetermined rules.

Given the general setup of the casino floor and the table games, there are a range of strategic decisions to be made on the part of gamblers, dealers and the house. We consider each in turn, beginning with Goffman's seminal argument concerning the interactive construction of meaning by gamblers themselves.[19]

The hold percentage, introduced above, is a useful starting point for grasping *the player's point of view.* If the hold on a particular game is 10 percent, we may envision the gambling transaction thus: for every dollar a player wagers, the dealer hands back 90 cents. Industry advocates in fact often evoke the language of economics to describe this exchange. The 10 cents lost is here the price voluntarily paid for the entertainment of playing: "[Gamblers] trade off the probability of winning for entertainment value derived through extended playing time."[20]

To anyone who has spent long chunks of time in a casino, however, this characterization of the gambling experience could not be more at odds with the observed behavior of patrons. Most gamblers hope to win and do not rationalize losses in terms of the sheer enjoyment (i.e., the expected utility) of wagering. Consider a survey of U.S. casino patrons finding that three in four gamble for the express purpose of "winning a really large amount of money."[21] The gambler's mind-set is well summarized by a longtime Nevada casino operator: "I sure as hell don't gamble for the gay, mad ecstasy of it. I want to win and I expect to win!"[22]

Gambling is best understood by starting not, as the economic approach does, with each individual hand, but with the full succession of plays constituting a player's gambling session. Assuming a hold percentage of 10, along with a constant bet size and a sufficiently large (though finite) number of plays, we get the theoretical distribution of wins/losses per session depicted in figure 2. Taking the session as our unit of analysis illuminates gambling's lure: some portion of sessions (shaded area in figure 2) will witness the player leaving the casino with more money than he or she came with. "The pot," explains Jerome Skolnick, "is not all pain."[23]

The above figure assumes that the size of the bet remains constant throughout the session. But gamblers often change their betting patterns as games progress, behaving as though the middle range of the

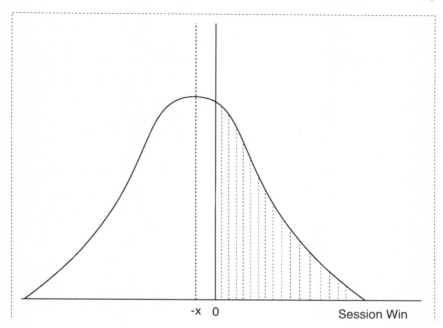

-x 0   Session Win

Figure 2. Theoretical frequency distribution of gambling session outcomes.

distribution is unsatisfactory. They seek the far right end even at the risk of accumulating large losses. In the words of a tables manager I interviewed, "Nobody leaves here with what they came with. They try to win big and would rather lose big than break even. They're greedy."

Two common betting strategies illustrate this tendency. One is *doubling*. Here the player, after a successful hand, "lets it ride" by betting all of his or her winnings on the next hand. This tactic can, when repeated, increase winnings exponentially rather than linearly. Conversely, a player may *chase* losses, essentially doubling in reverse. Here a gambler in the red increases the bet to an amount equal to the total sum lost during the current session. If this bet wins, the player is now even. If it loses, the player is doubly in debt, and the next bet must be twice the previous one. Chased losses pile up exponentially, and their emotional consequences are not hard to imagine.[24]

Doubling and chasing illustrate the fundamental problem with economic theory: it assumes gamblers purposefully purchase entertainment. In fact, the underlying "truth" of the gambling transaction—the loss to the house of a set percentage of each bet—is collectively misrecognized by players.[25] This is the "opposing truth, that defines the full truth" of the exchange.[26] Having witnessed firsthand over the course of my research tens of thousands of gambling hands, I can pinpoint two general processes through which the statistical reality of gambling is misrecognized and meaning is created on the tables.

On one hand, wins and losses are rarely treated as objective expressions of statistical probabilities. Rather, players tend to assign *agency* for game outcomes: credit for wins and blame for losses. Agency may be attributed to immaterial entities such as God ("Please, Lord, let me win this one!") or chance ("Oh well, Lady Luck wasn't on my side."). Gamblers may externalize and objectify rationality itself, usually through reference to the "handbook" of basic strategy ("How could I have lost? I did just what the book told me to."). Nor is it immediately apparent who should be deemed responsible; hence, there may occur a struggle among participants to claim credit or displace blame.

On the other hand, accompanying the assignment of agency is an appropriate *emotional display*. In general, credit begets appreciation and gratitude, while blame begets anger and retribution. As with agency, the creation of consensus as to the proper emotional display is often a process of struggle. Nor do such attribution contests involve only players themselves. Dealers may be perceived to be responsible for players' wins and losses, and so may have a stake in the contests too. It is thus to *the workers' point of view* that we now turn.

Casinos, like all leisure enterprises, are simultaneously spaces in which everyday concerns are suspended for clients *and* the workaday world of employees. Upon a few square feet of felt two lifeworlds intertwine: that of the gambler on holiday, for whom winning a jackpot is a once-in-a-lifetime experience, and that of the dealer, for whom the deliverance of such miracles is a quotidian work task. Players, we have established, misrecognize the economic reality of gambling through agency attribution and emotional displays. What stake do dealers have in this process?

If Erving Goffman overturned the commonsense view of gambling as inconsequential play, he provided little guidance for understanding the casino as a world of work. We here turn to another Chicago School sociologist, Michael Burawoy, who demonstrated that even the most monotonous of jobs can be experienced as enthralling forms of play.[27] He studied factory workers, who, like gamblers, transform a banal economic transaction (the daily exchange of their labor power for a wage) into a meaningful contest: a "game of making out." To "make out" was to each day produce a number of parts above a set minimum yet below an implicitly agreed-upon ceiling. This goal was problematic insofar as it required skill and ingenuity. And it was consequential, too, insofar as making out led to valued outcomes such as status within the workgroup and relief from the drudgery of factory labor.

Burawoy labeled the pattern of game-playing and control characteristic of a given workplace a "production regime."[28] And although this idea was originally used to describe manufacturing industries, it can also, I argue, be fruitfully applied to service industries.[29] As a profit-oriented enterprise operating in a competitive market system, the modern casino can be analyzed as a "service production regime." Games, furthermore, are an apt analogy for understanding dealing work. On the tables, croupiers play their own game, one that overlaps with but does not fully graft onto the official gambling contests.

Let's explore this idea of using production regimes to analyze dealing work further. First off, labor relations in the service sector are more complicated than in manufacturing industries. Factories contain but two parties—management and workers; service jobs, in contrast, are characterized by a triangular pattern of conflict and cooperation among managers, workers, and consumers.[30] On a blackjack table, for instance, we find a conflict of interests between clients and management: players seek to "beat the house," while pit bosses "sweat" a player on a winning streak. The interests of dealers, however, are ambiguous; they officially represent the casino, but do not necessarily benefit when it wins.[31] Service industries are also unique in that managers seek to control not only workers' physical effort, but their emotional labor as well.[32] Casino dealers, for instance, are often required to imagine themselves as performers spreading good cheer on the floor.

Given these complications, what sorts of "games" do service workers such as dealers play? The short answer is that it depends on the costs and rewards workers associate with various outcomes, as well as their ability to effect these outcomes. The incentives and skills characteristic of a particular work game, however, are ultimately under the control not of workers but of management. "The games workers play are not, as a rule, autonomously created in opposition to management. . . . [Management] actively participates not only in the organization of the game but in the enforcement of its rules."[33] To round out our picture of the casino as a world of work, then, we must thus consider *management's point of view*.

Managerial decisions concerning how to organize the casino are made in line with three objectives common to all service industries: speed, service, and security. Managers seek to increase the number of hands played in a given period of time by maximizing workers' speed; they try to enhance the quality of the product by creating good customer service; and they guarantee the security of the gambling transaction. Furthermore, they seek a particular balance of speed, service, and security by specifying a "procedure" for dealers to follow.[34] Though many elements of procedure are standard globally, managers make choices at four key points of the gambling encounter.

The first stage, that of "squaring off," involves readying the game equipment for play.[35] This is the point at which players exchange cash for the plastic chips that serve as currency on the tables. For example, when a player sets a hundred-dollar bill on the table, the dealer retrieves twenty $5 chips from the tray and "cuts out" and "proves" them, building four stacks of five $5 chips and spreading one of them along the felt. At this moment the dealer has created a "picture" for supervisors who, with a glance, can verify that there are twenty chips on the table. The placement of every finger at every moment of the entire process is specified to maximize speed and security. Official procedure for this stage is standard worldwide, with variation mainly in the degree to which it is monitored and enforced.

Gamblers now place their bets. To ensure security, dealers must mentally note each wager so that players do not later surreptitiously increase ("press") or decrease ("pinch") their bets. Some casinos allow gamblers to place a side bet on their hand for the dealer. These are conditional tips.

Figure 3.   Randomizing, by hand, six decks of cards. Photo by the author.

If the player loses, both bets go to the house. If the player wins, the dealer pays both bets but collects and keeps the dealer bet and its winnings. Managers may, however, forbid tip-bets entirely as a potential security risk (i.e., due to concerns that dealers will help players win in order to secure a tip).

Squaring off next involves shuffling. Because the casino's hold percentage assumes that the ordering of the fifty-two cards in each deck is random, shuffling ensures security. Tension exists, though, between security and speed, because after the first hand is played, those cards are removed from play and the distribution of cards in the deck becomes skewed. Reshuffling after each hand, however, would slow down the action. Managers must thus organize the procedure for disorganizing the cards.[36] Most importantly, they must decide whether or not to automate the task. Traditionally, dealers shuffled cards by hand, and they often still do (see figure 3). But in 1992, a Las Vegas company introduced the first shuffling machine, a small box that sits next to the dealer.[37] "Shufflers" not only maximize security, but speed up the games by up to 60 percent. Nevertheless, as of the year 2000, only 35 percent of casino tables worldwide featured shufflers.[38] The main reasons cited for not installing this technology are cost (purchase price plus maintenance fees) and a perceived consumer distaste for shufflers.[39]

After squaring off comes the "determination" stage of gambling, as the dealer delivers cards to gamblers, who then play out their hands. If a player's first two cards are an ace and a card with a point value of ten, the hand is a "blackjack" and the player is paid, usually 3 to 2, immediately. Otherwise, each player either "hits" (takes another card) or "stands." Next comes the moment of "disclosure, " as dealers reveal their cards and play out their hands in accordance with a preset formula (usually, they must hit until their hand totals at least seventeen or until they bust). Then comes the "settlement" phase, during which dealers pay winning bets and collect losing ones. Throughout these final three phases, managers face myriad decisions concerning how strictly to enforce procedure and whether to use technology to monitor the transactions. All else being equal, each of these choices represents a tradeoff between guaranteeing security, maximizing speed and keeping down operating costs.

There is, in sum, more to a casino than meets the eye. In placing their wagers, gamblers do not simply purchase entertainment; they seek a meaningful chance at a big win. Rather than passively facilitating the games, dealers strategize to control the distribution of blame and credit on their tables. And to produce a world of leisure for consumers, managers must first structure a world of work for employees. The end result is a complex configuration of actors and interests: a *service production regime.* And as such complexity suggests, it is highly unlikely that casinos operating in different national contexts will feature identical service regimes. Indeed, diversity rather than homogeneity in the global gambling industry is precisely what my ethnographic research uncovered.

LAS VEGAS IN SOUTH AFRICA?

Erving Goffman's underlying sociological project was to discover that which is general to the human condition.[40] He was surely a comparativist, but his brilliance lay in his ability to compare seemingly disparate cases and highlight their commonalities. In his hands, boarding schools and concentration camps became but two instances of the same phenomenon: the total institution. And in his gambling essays, Goffman deftly drew upon an array of examples—from the work routines of trapeze artists to the dynamics of craps tables—to distill out the universal essence of risk taking. Any differences between tightrope walkers and casino gamblers were in turn judged irrelevant, noise to be filtered out.

But should we assume that the fundamental nature of gambling remains unchanged regardless of the time or place in which it occurs? Could Goffman's findings on the dynamics of blackjack games not have been unique to Las Vegas in the 1950s? In fact, the Nevada casino at mid-century represented a peculiar institution, one sequestered away in the Mojave Desert, far from the public eye. But in the decades since, this former pariah has become a paradigm for states around the world as governments opt to legalize rather than ban commercial gambling. Furthermore, they often explicitly model their new casino industries explicitly on Las Vegas. Why and how did this happen? To answer such questions requires that we examine not the universal essence gambling, but the specificity and historical origins of the Nevada casino model.

History, of course, reveals not only widespread demand for gambling—the "world's second oldest industry"—but social condemnations of the activity as immoral and destructive.[41] Governments, in turn, typically took a middle ground. They would officially label gambling a vice (to appease conservative constituencies), then grant small-scale monopolies to nonprofit organizations on the condition that they use revenues for "good causes" and not "overstimulate demand."[42] (That the churches and charities advocating prohibition ended up with monopolies has provided rich fodder for social critics through the ages.) When commercial casinos *were* first permitted, they were heavily regulated to protect citizens, usually by restricting patronage to the wealthy. A good example is the (recently repealed) British model, in which casinos were private clubs open only to members who paid dues and visited during evening hours.[43] The private club model characterized all of the world's major casino jurisdictions in the mid–twentieth century (Monte Carlo, Havana, etc.), save one.

Nevada legalized casinos in 1931, and over the succeeding decades, the state honed a "wide-open" gambling policy. Consumers could gamble as much as they wished, minimal restrictions were placed on proprietors, and regulators favored operators who could maximize revenues (and thus tax dollars).[44] The results of this wide-open policy were striking: between 1950 and 2000, Nevada casino revenues grew 2,500 percent, from $40 million to $10 billion. And they inspired a slew of imitators. To create jobs, stimulate economies, and attract tourists, governments in Europe, Latin America, Asia, and Africa have legalized Nevada-style gambling over the past several decades.[45] By the year 2000, casinos worldwide grossed revenues of $300 billion.[46]

The globalization of the casino industry offers an ideal opportunity to see how a seemingly simple activity such as gambling can be structured and experienced in different contexts. Even when other jurisdictions explicitly attempt to recreate the Las Vegas casino, it does not follow that the worlds of leisure, work, and management within these new gambling houses will be identical to the original. And so it was that, following an initial stint of fieldwork in Nevada, I investigated possible cases for an international comparative study. In 2000, I spent a semester as a visiting scholar at the University of the Witwatersrand in Johannesburg. I knew that South Africa had a bustling casino industry (in the top ten globally in terms of gross revenues; see table 1), but even I was shocked to see how thoroughly the country was attempting to recreate the Nevada experience. Government officials openly proclaimed their ambition to build a veritable "Vegas on the Veld." In fact, I discovered that a South African leisure company, "Empowerment Inc.," had recently built, only a few kilometers from the university, a shiny new gambling palace which I will call "Gold City Casino." My first visit confirmed for me that this was a perfect comparative case, for the casino was an exact replica of my first fieldsite, Silver State Casino! The décor, the blackjack tables, the gaudy tuxedo uniforms the dealers are required to don—all were identical. Later, after I'd begun fieldwork there, the Gold City Casino manager told me that he carries in his wallet photos of the two casinos. Few friends, he boasted, can tell them apart.

This discovery was a fortuitous coincidence, but could a systematic

Table 1 Top Ten Casino Countries in 2000

Rank	Country	Gross Casino Revenues (US$ in Millions)
1	United States	35,000
2	Canada	2,430
3	France	1,820
4	Macao	1,670
5	Australia	1,500
6	Germany	930
7	United Kingdom	840
8	South Africa	610
9	The Netherlands	590
10	The Philippines	590

SOURCE: Global Betting and Gaming Consultants, *Global Gambling Comes of Age: 2nd Annual Review of the Global Betting and Gaming Market* (West Bromwich, UK: Global Betting and Gaming Consultants, 2002).

comparison be made between the United States and South Africa? The latter, after all, had recently undergone a dramatic political revolution, while the former has had a stable democracy for over two hundred years. But further research revealed several important similarities between these two cases, parallels that convinced me that the countries could be fruitfully compared.

First, the casino industries in the two countries exhibit similar historical trajectories. Scholars such as Anthony Marx and George Frederickson have documented general parallels between the United States and South Africa regarding the colonization of indigenous peoples, the codification of legal segregation, and subsequent movements for racial equality.[47] Yet no one had yet documented the role played by gambling industries in these processes. In both countries, casinos were initially legalized as an economic development strategy by what were, in essence, "fictitious states." On one hand, Nevada had been granted statehood in the nineteenth century only as a political ploy to ensure passage of the Fourteenth

Amendment. Sparsely populated and lacking a sustainable resource base, the state was soon controlled by outside interests.[48] All that local elites could do was to try to exploit America's prohibitory vice laws by luring tourists with casino gambling. On the other hand, the apartheid South African government (controlled by the arch-conservative National Party, dedicated to preserving the ethnic heritage of white "Afrikaners") had granted statehood to several black "homelands" to buttress the political project of apartheid. The homeland states too were underdeveloped and isolated, in response to which local leaders legalized casinos to take advantage of the puritanical vice laws of South Africa proper.

Second, South Africa and Nevada today share a similar regulatory philosophy regarding gambling. The African National Congress (ANC), upon winning the country's first democratic elections in 1994, faced a dilemma. During the political uprisings against apartheid, an illegal casino industry had sprouted up in South Africa's cities. Plus, apartheid's end entailed the reintegration of the homelands into South Africa, thus raising the question of what to do with their casinos. Considering the turmoil of the transition era, the gambling question loomed large in the public sphere. In fact—as was the case in the United States—the issue served as a proxy for larger debates concerning the national good. Many South Africans advocated banning gambling, or allowing only a limited amount. Considering the poverty and lack of education among the populace, such a cautious approach would not have been unwarranted.

The ANC, though, chose a different course: competitive corporate casinos. Party leaders framed the new nation's problems as fiscal in nature, and touted the Nevada casino model as the proper panacea.[49] Casinos, it was argued, would create jobs, empower "previously disadvantaged individuals" (PDIs), and produce "painless taxation" for the state. In the new province of Gauteng—home to Johannesburg and Pretoria, the financial and political centers of the country—the admonition to "go Vegas" was fully embraced. Government officials in the province granted gambling licenses to large corporations, favoring those who promised to build American-style casinos (hence the reason why Gold City Casino was designed to mimic the famous Silver State Casino). By 2002, Gauteng, like its prototype Nevada, was the largest gambling market on its continent. And like Nevada, where taxes culled from casinos constitute half of the state budget, Gauteng today garners over 40 percent of its tax revenue from casinos.[50]

Nevada's Silver State Casino and Gauteng's Gold City Casino look exactly alike. Both are operated by publicly traded "gaming" companies in competitive urban markets. Both employ primarily persons of color (recent immigrants to the United States versus black South Africans) and cater to a diverse working class clientele. We may even say that the two establishments constitute a quasi-natural experimental setup for a comparative ethnography. Contra Goffman, who saw only similarities across disparate cases, here was an opportunity to uncover differences between highly similar cases. How would the games played by workers, consumers, and managers at Silver State Casino compare to those at Gold City Casino? What can this tell us about service labor in the new economy? What can we learn about work and politics in the United States and South Africa?

My central finding—to be described in detail in the following four chapters—is that service work is structured very differently in the two countries. In Nevada, dealers are minimum wage employees who must hustle tips to survive (over 80 percent of their income derives from tips).[51] To do so, they act as independent entrepreneurs behind the tables, playing a "work game" of making tips. Every player at a dealer's table is quickly classified as either a "George" (a tipper) or a "stiff" (a non-tipper). Dealers seek to assist the former with their hands (for instance, by surreptitiously offering strategy advice)and try to force off the latter by withholding service (smiling or smirking when they lose, for example). The end result is an experience of agency, of being able to control the action and interactions on the dealer's own table. (The game of making tips also allows Nevada dealers to shrug off displays of anger from losing gamblers—insults hurled at you from an irate stiff are but a swan song from a disgruntled tenant you've evicted for not "paying the rent.")

This image of the Nevada dealer may seem suspect to those who have visited Las Vegas as a tourist. To the casual observer, the Nevada casino does indeed appear a "total institution"! But in fact, Nevada managers make organizational decisions that allow dealers to bend the house rules. Most blackjack games are dealt by hand, allowing dealers to time their shuffles to influence game outcomes. Video surveillance, in turn, does not function like an omniscient gaze. The cameras scrutinize high-action play more closely than "grind play," allowing workers to develop a practical feel for the logic of monitoring. As a coworker explained: "The cameras? Most of the time you don't even think about them. But the moment someone slaps down a hundred-dollar bill, you can feel them zooming in." As for pit bosses, they are former dealers who informally sanction dealers' entrepreneurial game. As long as the hustling stays "soft," the tip system keeps the games moving and is satisfactory for regulating work.

Having mastered Silver State Casino's game of making tips, I stepped onto the floor as a croupier at Gold City Casino. Mere minutes into my first shift, the contrast between service work in the two countries could not have been more striking. South African casino managers seek to maximize control. They deskill dealing work by deploying shuffling machines throughout the pits. They prohibit dealers from accepting tips. They even affix microphones to each worker so that surveillance personnel can monitor their words as well as their movements. And perhaps most ominously, a "zero tolerance" policy rules the pits; no offense is to go unnoticed or unpunished. As a result, while Nevada dealers act entrepreneurially to make tips, the lifeworld of the South African dealer is dominated by disincentives. Any inkling of intervention could convince players (or management) that the dealers were responsible for their losses. This is a game of effacement, in which dealers must downplay their own agency on the tables.

There is, in short, no universal experience of working (or wagering) in a casino. The decisions made by managers at Silver State Casino and Gold City Casino regarding task routinization, surveillance, and remuneration produce two very different regimes of service labor (summarized in table 2). This leads, though, to the question of *why* service regimes differ so dramatically in the two countries. Addressing this issue requires making one final break with the sociological tradition epitomized by Erving Goffman.

Table 2 Two Worlds of Service Work

	United States (Nevada)	Republic of South Africa (Gauteng)
Technology	Minimal, craft-like	Extensive, deskilling
Surveillance	Decentralized	Centralized
Remuneration	Tipping	Flat wage
Workers' Game	Entrepreneurialism	Effacement

FROM SITUATIONS TO STRUCTURE

Goffman was notoriously obstinate in his refusal to situate his findings on the dynamics of face-to-face interactions within larger social structures. In the book *Frame Analysis,* intended to be his magnum opus, he stated:

> This book is about the organization of experience . . . not the organization of society. I make no claims whatsoever to be talking about the core matters of sociology—social organization and social structure. . . . I personally hold society to be first in every way and any individual's current involvements to be second; this report deals only with matters that are second.[52]

But to explain the differences between service regimes in South Africa and the United States, I had to leave the casino floor and investigate the social, economic, and political forces that shape work, management, and play.

Linking, in a systematic yet parsimonious way, the "micro" and the "macro," interaction orders and institutional fields, is the holy grail of most research traditions. Structuralist theories concede that local dynamics are important, yet typically treat firms and other organizations as "black boxes."[53] Ethnographers, meanwhile, when in the midst of research, tend to bracket questions concerning the larger environment. Their fieldsites are like worlds unto themselves. It is possible, however, to treat organizations as neither black boxes nor self-contained social worlds. Through

focused, primary research in several locales, one can document and
demystify the external forces that shape one's fieldsite(s).[54]

This is precisely what I attempted to do. Following my stints on the
tables, I moved on to the world of management. I exchanged my gaudy
dealer tuxedo for a staid business suit, interviewed casino managers, and
even briefly worked as a pit boss in each country. Then I traveled further
up the ethnographic chain, to the level of the state. I combed archives
to unearth policy histories, analyzed parliamentary and congressional
debates, interviewed lawmakers, and observed officials as they went
about their own work of regulating the industry.

To order comparative data obtained across multiple levels requires
a theoretical framework. Burawoy's theory, introduced above, provides
just such a lens. It argues that while employees' games are ultimately
structured by managers' choices, managers are themselves constrained
by laws, rules, and regulations. In other words, production regimes, be
they factory floors or casino pits, are always shaped by the larger political environment.

Production politics theory specifies two general "governmentalities"
that structure workplaces in patterned, predictable ways. On one hand
are laissez-faire states, in which officials are unwilling or unable to regulate firms, while employees have few legal rights and minimal job security. Such free-market systems tend to give rise to *despotic* management
strategies, wherein obedience is secured through direct supervision and
harsh punishments. On the other hand are states that regulate firms'
labor practices and assure employees various rights and protections.[55]
In such systems, work should be organized *hegemonically*, basically the
carrot to despotism's stick. Managers grant workers autonomy, tolerate
some rule-breaking, and structure incentives to "manufacture consent"
to the firm's goals.

Viewed through this lens, Gold City Casino—with its invasive surveillance and "zero tolerance" discipline—appears a despotic workplace,
and Silver State Casino—where dealers are permitted to act as entrepreneurs—seems a hegemonic one. How, though, do these divergent service
regimes fit within larger systems of governance in South Africa and the
United States?

In fact, systems of industrial regulation in Gauteng and Nevada run counter to common stereotypes. It has long been taken as a truism that countries in the Global South—especially those in southeast Asia, Latin America, and Africa—grant workers few legal rights, and that states in the Global North—especially those in Europe and North America—will protect workers. Such a broad generalization, however, misses many important nuances. Nevada, for instance, is an extreme case of a business-friendly, anti-labor state. All Silver State Casino workers must sign contracts ceding any claim to job security; guaranteeing employers the right to fire workers without cause is a basic pillar of U.S. labor law. In South Africa, in contrast, the governing ANC is allied with the country's trade unions and communist party and has passed a plethora of laws to ensure "economic empowerment" in the workplace.[56] Employees are guaranteed unionization rights, protection from arbitrary dismissal, and assurances of affirmative action. Furthermore, South African casino dealers are represented by COSATU, a powerful national service union, while Nevada dealers do not have union representation at any major firms.[57] Paradoxically, hegemonic control at Nevada's Silver State Casino results from a *lack* of state regulation, while despotic control at South Africa's Gold City Casino derives from *effective* regulation of the service enterprise. Why do neoliberal and postcolonial forms of governance have these unexpected effects? Deciphering this puzzle—and, more generally, the complex relationship between political fields and service regimes—is the goal of this study.

THE STRUCTURE OF THE ARGUMENT

Part I describes in detail two very different ways of organizing the global casino. The comparative ethnography commences in Nevada (chapters 1 and 2), where I expected to labor inside a panopticon of total control. Yet Nevada managers trust their dealers and allow them to act as independent entrepreneurs on the tables, even if such behavior is not always in the immediate interests of the house. Chapters 3 and 4 describe the casino industry in contemporary South Africa, where I also worked as a croupier. Dealing in South Africa could not be more different from dealing in Nevada. Managers do not trust their staff and automate all facets of dealing, essentially transforming service work into estranged manual labor.

At this point, the book departs from convention. Social scientific narratives typically unfold chronologically, from cause to effect and from independent to dependent variable. Part II, however, moves backward in time to explain *why* service regimes differ so profoundly in South Africa and the United States. It explains the puzzle highlighted above: why it is that in Nevada, the quintessential neoliberal state, workers retain skills and act autonomously, while postcolonial regulations to empower workers in Gauteng paradoxically produce an employment system in which dealers must erase their own agency.

Chapter 5 provides the theoretical scaffolding needed to craft a solution. It argues that standard academic accounts rely upon a rudimentary vision of the state and of management. States are not, as realist theories of politics assume, unitary entities; nor are managers rational actors, as economic theory would suppose. Drawing upon Goffman's friend and contemporary, Pierre Bourdieu, I advance a conception of states as complex fields of action characterized by economic and also symbolic struggles, as well as of managers as embodied individuals whose biographical trajectories influence their strategies for controlling workers and clients. Like gamblers themselves, politicians and proprietors pursue material resources (taxes, profits, etc.) but also engage in symbolic strategies of impression management. And although they may draw up detailed strategy plans (policy documents, mission statements, and the like), frequently, in the heat of action, they must follow their gut instincts.

Chapter 6 resumes the empirical analysis by documenting a remarkable historical convergence: that casinos in the United States and South Africa were once mirror images of one another. In both early Nevada and the apartheid homelands, state leaders granted casino licenses to operators of dubious moral character and left them free of regulatory oversight. And in both cases, casino managers operated in line with what I call a traditional managerial habitus: they used personal networks and ascriptive criteria (especially racial stereotypes) to recruit "trustworthy" workers. The result in both cases was hegemonic service regimes in which casino workers were allowed to play entrepreneurial games on the tables.

Chapter 7 addresses the question of why the systems for managing service workers in the United States and South Africa diverged. It situates casinos in relation to the evolving political fields in the two countries. In both cases, gambling industries moved from the margins to the center of national politics when prominent political actors moved to outlaw casinos. These prohibition attempts focused not on the immorality of gambling, but on the character of the operators (crime syndicates on the one hand, apartheid collaborators on the other) and their labor market practices (especially institutionalized discrimination against workers of color). Clean, modern countries, critics argued, can not countenance such repugnant business practices. But regulatory responses to these "legitimacy threats" were mirror opposite. In South Africa's postcolonial political field, industrial stigmas were overcome by "cleaning up" the labor market, while leaving ownership untouched. In the neoliberal field of the United States, casinos were purified by cleansing the industry's capital market, while managers' authority over the labor market went unchallenged.

Chapter 8 explains further *how* these new regulations produced divergent service regimes. It elucidates the worldview of contemporary casino managers in each country. In Nevada, casino control remains decentralized in the person of the pit boss, who continues to recruit dealers based on networks and stereotypes. The pit, as a consequence, remains as it did in Goffman's time: a private fiefdom in which managers trust their dealers and organize work hegemonically. In South Africa, in contrast, weak capital market regulations have allow entrenched managers to centralize control of the firm. Casino managers experience new labor regulations (especially affirmative action) as a forced substitution of distrusted ethnic groups, and so organize service work despotically.

The concluding chapter summarizes this study's implications for understanding the general process whereby neoliberal casino capitalism disseminated across the globe during the final decades of the twentieth century, as well as its fate in the face of the economic crisis jolting the world at the beginning of the twenty-first century. In the process, I try to rescue Goffman from the critiques levied thus far by extending his theory (especially through synthesis with the sociology of Bourdieu). The end result is dubbed a politico-performative perspective. As opposed to neoinstitutional accounts, which emphasize apolitical processes of diffusion and the decoupling of models and practices, it demands that we examine ethnographically the strategies of local agents as they maneuver within a consolidated global field of meanings and values. A short appendix then discusses the challenges and opportunities encountered when performing comparative ethnography in line with the principles of reflexive science.

PART ONE

Behind the Tables

ONE Nevada

LEARNING TO DEAL

The contemporary casino represents a potential panopticon. Like those "observatories of human multiplicity" pioneered by the English Utilitarian Jeremy Bentham and documented by the French historian Michel Foucault, the casino offers those who operate it total control. The video cameras dotting its ceiling relay images to a central control room from which managers can see everything without being seen themselves. This is a power of surveillance both "visible and unverifiable."[1] Supplementing the electronic monitoring is a pyramid of supervisory personnel. Corporate managers monitor shift managers, who monitor pit bosses, who monitor inspectors, who monitor dealers; they are "supervisors, perpetually supervised."[2] The action on the casino floor is in turn strictly standardized by casino "procedure."

It was argued in the introductory chapter, however, that the realiza-

tion of this panoptic potential requires a series of concrete choices on
the part of managers. At Nevada's Silver State Casino, the landmark
gambling house at which I conducted participant observation research,
there was no decision to structure the casino as a panopticon. Managers
eschew shuffling machines, choosing instead to let dealers work by hand.
Surveillance cameras, workers learn, actually leave the majority of play
unmonitored. And dealers act autonomously on the tables in order to
procure tips (referred to in industry parlance as "tokes") from gamblers.
The end result is not a despotic service regime but a hegemonic one,
while the very experience of dealing in Nevada may be conceived as an
entrepreneurial "game of making tips." Chapter 2 describes the experience of playing this game, while this chapter offers a firsthand account
of the process by which one becomes a Nevada casino dealer.

THE CASINO LABOR MARKET

As of the year 2005, there were 274 casinos in Nevada, ranging from
billion-dollar spectacles with hundreds of gambling tables to roadside
"joints" in rural towns.[3] Altogether, Nevada's casinos employ approximately 25,000 dealers to staff the state's 6,000-plus gambling tables. But
how does one enter this particular labor market? How does one become
a dealer?

The requisite first step, I found as I embarked upon my study, is to
obtain a vocational degree in dealing. Prior to the 1970s—during those
years in which Erving Goffman worked the tables—aspiring croupiers
learned the trade from a friend or associate. Today, they must train at one
of the state's ten or so "academies" licensed to teach the craft (as must
workers in other semiskilled services, such as manicurists, bartenders,
and barbers). Therefore, I perused the local phone book and paid a visit
to the school nearest my apartment, the "Sure-Thing Dealer Academy."

The Academy is located in a storefront in a roadside shopping plaza.
It consists of a single large room crammed full of old blackjack, roulette,
and craps tables donated by local casinos. Paula, a white woman in her
fifties, has been the director of the school since it opened in the early

1990s. A self-described "firebrand" with "extremely thick skin," she previously spent twenty years dealing at a large casino in town. But Paula eventually grew weary of the stress and the smoke-saturated pits, and so accepted an invitation to direct the Academy. She hired instructors Cathy and Tex, both veteran dealers whom she had known from her dealing days. Cathy had immigrated to the United States from Hong Kong fifteen years prior. Shortly after arriving, she herself attended dealing school and found employment at a "locals casino" (one catering to city residents rather than tourists), where she works to this day. She likes it there, she says, because the tips are decent and steady. Plus, she has a good relationship with the pit boss. He gives her the same three days off each week so she can teach blackjack and roulette at the school. Tex, in turn, specializes in craps. With his cowboy boots and handlebar mustache, he looks like he just stepped out of a Western movie. He, too, works at a nearby casino, teaching here three days a week.

Though I already planned to enroll, on my initial visit to the school I listened to Paula's sales pitch for prospective students. It's a good one. To get a dealing job, she tells me, you must know one game well and be on the way to mastering a second. The average student can master a game in four weeks and begin applying for work within a month of enrolling. The fees are steep, though; a standard course costs $800. As Paula explains why this is money well spent, I can easily imagine her behind a casino table calling out to passersby. Though you put a large amount down, she says, it's a sure thing that you will recoup your investment: "I guarantee you 100 percent that you'll get a job, and could guarantee you 200 percent if you enrolled twice. You see, the owners of this school are real bigwigs in town, and I can't keep up with the need for good dealers. They're callin' me every day, and I can barely keep up." As I pull out my checkbook, Paula looks surprised. Most new students put the tuition on a credit card, she tells me, with the intention of paying it off over their first few months of work.

The student body at the Sure-Thing Academy is diverse. Among my two dozen co-enrollees, men and women are equally represented. About half are recent immigrants, mainly from east Asia and Latin America; the rest are either recent arrivals to Nevada from California, like myself, or local residents seeking to break into or move up within the industry.[4] Unlike me, however, they've all enrolled for one reason: to make money. Casino dealing is the *crème de la crème* of jobs in the Nevada service economy, mainly because of the tips one earns behind the tables. As Manny, a twenty-four-year-old Filipino man currently busing tables in a steakhouse, explains: "You can make okay tips when you're waiting tables, but dealing is where the real money's at." Rosales from Mexico concurs, adding, "Learn as quick as you can. Dealing's a good place to make thirty or forty thousand a year, lots of it in cash."

Upon arriving for my first day of instruction, I am given an overview of the curriculum. There are no regular classes, Paula explains. New students receive a quick tutorial from an instructor, after which they practice dealing to other students, while the instructors move from table to table offering feedback and advice. Everyone starts off by learning blackjack, by far the most popular game in the state. Instruction progresses from basic skills such as "cutting out chips" to specialized moves such as dealing from a shoe.

I soon discover that while dealing is officially classified as semiskilled labor, mastering even the most rudimentary aspects of the job is not easy. Consider the procedure for running a single-deck blackjack game. The dealer must hold a deck of cards halfway down the palm of the left hand; the pointer and middle fingers must be clasped together to conceal the front of the deck; the thumb must cover the upper left corner of the top card; the forearm and deck are held close to the body, at a 45-degree upward angle. To then deliver cards, the thumb and index finger of the right hand pinch the side of the top card, while the middle finger is placed along its side. In one motion, all three fingers are extended, causing the card to fly in a spinning pattern across the table. This "pitching" of the cards must be perfectly accurate, so that they land lightly in front of the correct player. And during this entire process, only the dealer's fingers may move. Wrists and forearms remain locked in place, and the dealer rotates his or her shoulders to deliver cards to different players. (Not surprisingly, repetitive stress injuries such as carpal tunnel syndrome are a common affliction among veteran dealers).[5] I recorded in my field notebook how alien these postures felt:

I'm tense trying to do all of this, all these tasks, body positionings. And at the same time keeping track of the value of the hands. I grip the cards too tightly and begin to sweat. I constantly say to myself, "Forty-five-degree angle, thumb in place, fingers together." I suppose that through practice and repetitions it will become second nature. But for now I have to find a way to make myself relax.

The instructors' pedagogical practice consists primarily of proffering suggestions for making these movements feel natural. They direct us to go slowly and perfect our form—speed will come, they say. And we are advised to keep in constant contact with the casino equipment. Cathy recounts that when she was learning to deal, "I kept that deck on me all the time. I slept with it in my hand. You must hold it always too." Tex advises: "Don't just sit there on the couch at home. Pitch your cards into a soup bowl while you watch TV." The instructors also offer simple heuristics to help us retrain our reflexes: "You must make this deck a part of you." "One day you'll be standing there looking out the window, and suddenly everything will click." Trainees learn that with practice, basic procedures will become so natural as to require no thought. For instance, dealers, when making change, regularly reach into their money tray to retrieve twenty chips (e.g., a $100 player buy-in requires twenty $5 chips). On my first day, I instinctively look down to eyeball twenty $5 chips before picking up a stack. "No, no!" Cathy scolds. "Just reach in and grab. After not too long, you will pick out twenty every time."

As a student masters the nuances of dealing blackjack, the instructors begin to talk about sending him or her out for an "audition"—a live job interview on the casino floor. At this point, informal talk at the school makes it clear that students have been sorted into two categories. In one are those possessing some flaw that puts them at a disadvantage on the job market. Tim, for instance, is a white male in his late twenties with strong dealing skills, but with a felony conviction on his record.[6] Such a black mark means that rather than auditioning at one of the main entry-level casinos, he will have to "break in" at a small casino at least an hour's drive from the city. Muhammad, a Pakistani man in his late fifties, is also at a disadvantage. After his small business closed in Los Angeles, he relocated to Nevada and enrolled at the school. While he picks up the games quickly, his chances of landing a good job are slim, we are told, because major casinos rarely hire new dealers over the age of thirty-five.

Then there are those acknowledged to be in a strong position on the job market. Carmen, a twenty-three-year-old woman from Venezuela, currently works as a hostess in a casino restaurant. Her job prospects are good because, as Paula tells us, "She already has shown she is a good worker in the casino. They will see she is dependable." In addition, it is understood that Asian dealers are in demand. Prospective dealers of other ethnic groups often complain privately that casino managers have a "fetish for Oriental women." Later chapters will explain why employers "queue" workers in this manner.[7] At the time, however, I was puzzled by why, of all the possible criteria for evaluating job candidates, technical aptitude was overlooked. I had dedicated myself to training with all the zeal of an ethnographer in the field for the first time, and within six weeks, both my blackjack and craps games were acknowledged by all to be the strongest in the school. Yet the instructors, when discussing my job prospects, referred not to my skills but to my *personality*. During my first week of school, I had asked Paula what the key was for landing a dealing job. "Personality," she had responded. "If you go in with a sour puss, you're not gonna make a good impression. But with you, that shouldn't be a problem." Later I overheard Cathy and Tex chatting about my chances: "He has such a nice, charming personality. They'll love him behind the tables." My initial audition would confirm that casinos prioritize personality as a hiring criterion.

THE BIG AUDITION

In Nevada, new dealers typically obtain their first job at a small- to medium-sized casino known as a "break-in house." As they gain experience, they seek to move up the hierarchy of casinos toward the "high-end joints." It was at this point in my research that I caught a break. I was sent to audition at Silver State Casino, one of the largest and most well-known properties in the state. Though its management only rarely auditions break-in dealers, it was late spring and they were short of blackjack dealers for an anticipated early summer busy season. They had contacted Paula, and I was one of three of the school's top students who was sent for an audition. Before describing this process, I will provide some background on Silver State Casino and "Upstanding Inc.," the company of which it is a part.

The history of the Nevada casino industry is typically divided into three periods: the 1930s to 1950s, during which casinos were small, individually-owned enterprises; the 1950s to 1970s, during which organized crime syndicates took over the industry; and the 1980s through the present, a period in which publicly traded corporations dominate.[8] The roots of Upstanding Inc. are in the second period, while its subsequent history illustrates the subsequent evolution of the U.S. casino industry.

The firm was founded in the 1960s by an eccentric businessman. While considered a visionary in terms of casino marketing, he was a heavy gambler under whose watch a crime syndicate infiltrated one of his main properties. With help from regulators, the syndicate was expunged, and the firm grew rapidly by catering to the burgeoning market of middle-class vacationers. In the 1980s, Upstanding Inc. went public and became an industry leader in securing funding from mainstream lending sources on Wall Street. It built dozens of properties throughout Nevada, at one point becoming the largest employer in the state. Today, the company operates casinos across the United States and is often heralded by the industry press as an innovator in keeping production costs low while offering a high-quality gambling "product."

My fieldsite, Silver State Casino, was built during the late 1970s as one of Upstanding Inc.'s signature properties. In fact, it soon became an icon of the state's casino industry as a whole. About ten years before my research, its original facilities had been upgraded and expanded so that, with over 2,000 hotel rooms, it became one of the new generation of "super casinos": properties so large that they take up an entire city block.[9] Its primary market remains middle-class vacationers, though it draws a fair share of both working-class locals and upscale "high rollers."

The process through which I secured employment at Silver State Casino begins with a phone call to Paula from one of her contacts at the casino. Two fellow trainees (Samuel and Melissa) and I are told to leave school immediately and head over to the casino's human resources (HR) department. We drive over together and find in the rear corner of a parking garage the small, sparsely decorated room that serves as the HR office. There we are handed job applications requiring our basic personal information (name, address, phone number), credentials (I feel a sense of pride as I fill in my dealing academy certification), and prior work experience. As I hand mine to the woman behind the desk, a young Hispanic woman runs up and asks "how old do you have to be" to work in the fast food restaurants in the casino. "Still sixteen," the HR woman says, rolling her eyes as the girl turns away. Turning her attention back to my application, she points out periods unaccounted for in my job history.

"Oh. I was in school, or living with my parents," I explain.

"Well, then, write it down. You have to account for every day. No gaps."

When we arrive back at school, Paula pelts us with new directives. "Come in tomorrow wearing your black slacks and a white dress shirt. And shave off those sideburns, Jeff! They can call you in for your audition at any time, and you have to be ready." Every morning for the next week, upon arriving at school, we are asked if we've received "the call" from Silver State Casino. As the days go by, I become increasingly nervous, especially after Sam and Melissa don't show up for school on Tuesday and I find out it is because they both had auditioned the evening before and were starting their first shifts that night! "Don't worry," Cathy consoles. "It's a busy weekend coming up. They for sure will call you." Sure enough, while practicing my craps game on Thursday afternoon, the phone rings and Paula yells, "There's someone who wants to talk to you, Jeff!"

I pick up the phone. It's the HR woman from Silver State Casino, who says simply, "Can you come right in for an audition?"

"Now?"

"Now."

"You betcha," I reply before hanging up and rushing to grab my things. The other students yell encouragement: "Your game's strong, don't worry." "Knock 'em dead!" Paula offers one final piece of advice as I jog out the door: "Remember to smile!"

At 4:50 P.M. I arrive in the main pit at Silver State Casino for my 5 P.M. audition. I glimpse Sam, from dealing school, behind a blackjack table, and he flashes me a grin. The pit boss—a tall woman in a black business suit—walks over to me. "Excuse me," I say to her, "I'm here for—" "Your audition," she finishes my sentence for me, pointing me toward a "dead" blackjack table in a back corner of the casino.

Soon I am joined by two other aspiring dealers. Maria, in her late forties, had come to the United States from the Philippines twenty years before to "make [her] fortune." She had previously dealt blackjack for seventeen years at another large casino, only to discover upon returning from a medical leave that she had been laid off. "No heart," says Maria, in her typically brusque yet incisive manner. Alex, from Iran, came to Nevada five years ago with his two brothers. He currently works as an instructor at a community college, but wants to boost his income by breaking into the gaming industry.

Eventually, a middle-aged man ambles over to the table and intro-duces himself as Rick, the shift boss. He explains that Silver State Casino makes its hiring decisions based on applicants' personalities rather than their dealing ability:

> We're looking for people people. Those who can carry on a conversa-tion. We can always teach technical skill, but we need people with good personalities. As a matter of fact, we hired a gentleman recently who didn't even know how to deal, but was so outgoing and fun that we had to hire him. And we did and we trained him and now he's the best dealer in the house.

With this introduction, the audition begins. We take turns dealing while Rick acts as a tourist, asking us a series of canned questions: "I'm from out of town, can you recommend somewhere good to eat?" "So where're you from, Jeff?" Paula had forewarned us that the interviewer would ask such questions, so I had prepared short responses, to which Rick now nods enthusiastically. And my "game" (as a dealer's general prowess is called) is strong tonight. No screw-ups, at least!

When Maria's turn comes, she takes her place behind the table. In response to Rick's questions, she basically just repeats the answers I had given, to which Rick murmurs, "Mm-hmm." But her game displays her two decades of dealing experience. The cards fly from her hands while she gracefully picks up chips, pays out winners, and swipes up losing cards in a single motion. My game looks decidedly amateur in comparison. At one point, another manager walks by and recognizes Maria. "Are you working here now?" he shouts over, with a wave and smile. "She has this job," I think to myself.

Now comes Alex, who is obviously quite nervous. He repeatedly touches the cards after they've been dealt—a big no-no. And at one point he mistakenly pays a losing bet. Completely flustered with the physical aspect of the game, he is unable to form a coherent sentence in response to Rick's canned service queries. I feel bad for Alex, and am relieved when his audition finally ends and we three shake hands with Rick and leave the casino. Though he didn't get this job, I saw Alex months later dealing at another casino and waved to him, though I don't think he recognized me. Nightmarish audition tales are a favorite component of occupational lore, and I hoped Alex had put his behind him.

LICENSED TO DEAL

For me, "the call" came the following morning. I ask about Maria, and am relieved to hear that she was hired as well. "Your employment status is provisional until we do your credit and drug tests, but we need you to start tonight," the voice on the line says, "which means you got a lot to do today."

I rush back to the HR office, where a fresh mountain of paperwork awaits. After filling out the standard tax forms, I am told to sign a release authorizing Silver State Casino to check my credit and finances. "Always on the lookout for those with a champagne appetite and a beer income," explains the HR rep. Then comes a one-page contract affirming that I understand Nevada's "employment-at-will" doctrine, according to which I may be fired at any time and for no reason, nor shall anything the company provides me—not employment handbooks, raises, or promotions—imply the existence of a permanent employment contract.

"What happens if I don't sign this?" I ask, with a fake air of naiveté.

"Well, then, you're back on the streets," the rep deadpans.

Having signed away any claim to job security, I head off to my second stop: the city's police department, where I must, by law, submit to another thorough background investigation. I join a motley crew as I queue up behind a blonde exotic dancer, an old Italian casino "host," and a muscular bouncer. While waiting in line, we begin filling out a stack of forms collecting information on our criminal records, child support obligations, scars, tattoos, and so on. When my turn comes, my fingerprints and picture are taken, and I am handed a temporary employee identification card (so I may begin work while my background checks are completed).

On my way out, I run into Maria, and we exchange hugs and congratulations. "Your game is so smooth!" I say. "But I did not know how to answer those questions. You knew just what to say," she replies. Maria, too, is rushing around to get ready for work tonight, so we say goodbye and I head off to my final stop: the drug-testing clinic.

Located in a suburban office park, this clinic contracts with casino firms to perform drug tests on new employees. Like bad finances or a criminal record, illegal substance use can disqualify you from casino work.[10] After processing my paperwork, a nurse escorts me to a private exam room and begins inspecting my head and neck. "Not enough there," she says in reference to my short crew-cut. "Looks like we'll have to do a urine." (To translate, my hair is not long enough for a chemical analysis of dead hair cells. This is preferred to a urine test, which only evidences drug use during the past month versus the year-plus window a hair test provides.) I am handed a small vial and directed to the restroom where I fill it up, directing the overflow into the commode. Upon completion I reach out and flush the toilet, which brings the nurse scurrying into the stall. "You're not supposed to flush!" she exclaims. "We have to make sure you don't tamper with the sample."

"I'm sorry," I say.

She grabs the vial and quickly affixes to it a small thermometer. "Well the temperature is fine, so you're okay. It must have been a reflex."

"Yeah," I answer. "After twenty-five years of flushing it's hard to stop cold turkey."

She laughs and tells me my sample will be sent out to a California laboratory. The results will not be known for a week, but in the meantime, I am cleared to start work. As my urine is loaded onto a truck bound for Los Angeles, I head home to catch a quick nap in preparation for the "graveyard" shift, which starts at 9 P.M. It is going to be a long night's journey into day.

TWO Silver State Casino

ENTREPRENEURS AT WORK

Before my first shift at Silver State Casino began, I wrote a research memo detailing my expectations for fieldwork. On one hand, the invasive background tests suggested the lengths to which Nevada firms will go to maximize security—why not take the final step of structuring the pits themselves as a panopticon? On the other hand, Rick's emphasis on "personality" during my audition suggested a more gentle, service-centered workplace. But I would discover neither a panopticon nor a Disneyland. Rather, casino management grants dealers considerable freedom to act as independent entrepreneurs on the tables. This autonomy is not absolute; indeed, it is carefully measured and regulated by the house in accordance with the financial status of the player. Nonetheless, it has important consequences for structuring dealing work as an exciting and consequential game. Silver State Casino, in short, is a hegemonic service regime.

The House Rules

New dealers are required to report to work an hour before their first shift begins for an informal orientation session. At 8 P.M., Maria and I meet Rick in the main pit and follow him into his office. He informs us that all new dealers at Silver State Casino are classified as part-time workers. As such, we will receive no health benefits and are guaranteed no minimum number of hours per week. The criteria for achieving full-time status, meanwhile seem vague, for they are based not on seniority but on an undefined notion of "job performance." (In fact, only 10 percent of current Silver State Casino dealers are full-time employees.)

Rick next explains that while we may possess the requisite physical skills to deal, we must also master the interactive aspect of the job. He tosses us handbooks outlining seven golden rules for handling players. First, when a novice player sits down at your table, you are required to deliver a quick lesson on how to play the game. By doing so, you both create new customers and ensure that neophytes do not hold up the action. Second, this education must involve only the rules of play. Although the casino recognizes that many dealers know the principles of basic strategy (the rules for when to hit or stand), they mustn't offer any sort of strategy advice. Third, dealers should act as security guards at the tables, reporting any unusual player behavior to the pit boss. Fourth, all game-related communication between dealer and players must be signaled visibly, so management can monitor the action from afar. Fifth, to prevent inter-employee cheating schemes, dealers may not "carry on unnecessary conversations with other employees" on the floor.[1]

While these first five rules related to speed and security, the last two spoke to service. In order to make players feel like guests, we are instructed to "introduce yourself to each player" and "show a general interest in your players." We may not "display body language that could be interpreted as unfriendly" or "ignore a player." Finally, it is forbidden to "hustle tokes." We may not "imply that a player should tip," nor give "differential treatment [to] players who tip." The house, in sum, officially organizes our interactive labor to maximize speed, security, and service.

The First Sixty Minutes

At twenty minutes to 9 P.M., Rick's secretary scurries into the room and says, "We gotta get these two to wardrobe." Maria and I are herded down a set of stairs and into that area of the casino known as the "back of house." The contrast with the casino itself is striking: from plush carpets and speakers blaring Celine Dion to unpolished concrete and the hum of heavy machinery. Hurrying, we follow the secretary through a labyrinth of halogen-illuminated hallways to the wardrobe department, where we are issued our dealer uniforms. Both men and women wear white tuxedo-style shirts, the sleeves of which are exceptionally tight. To cover our black slacks, we are given aprons to wear. This attire is designed for security, not comfort: the constricted cuffs ensure we do not slide chips up our sleeves, and the aprons prevent us from accessing our pockets while on the tables.

By now it's five minutes to 9. "Hurry!" Maria shouts as I finish buttoning my collar. We leave wardrobe and merge into a stampede of dealers rushing up the stairs and across the casino floor. I take note of the blackjack tables. Two or three feature shufflers, but the majority of games are hand-dealt. When we reach the main pit, we line up at the podium and are greeted by the pit boss, Anne. She calls out our table assignments. "You, the new guy, you'll be on BJ-1–12 [i.e., the twelfth blackjack table in pit one]. Since it's your first night, we'll have someone watch over you. Joanne's been here for almost ten years. She'll take good care of you."

Joanne grabs my arm and escorts me to my table, where three middle-aged men sit awaiting their cards. Because of the intensity of their work, dealers work in eighty-minute units: sixty minutes of dealing, then a twenty-minute break while a relief dealer takes your place. Just one hour, I tell myself. No problem. As I step up to the table, though, I realize that the adrenaline has worn off and I'm terribly frightened. This is not like school. These are not fellow students using play money, but real people with real cash. And they are smoking like chimneys. Is the air conditioning working? It feels 100 degrees in the casino, and I begin to perspire profusely. Slick hands can be a major problem when dealing, and I fight the reflex to wipe my palms on my pants (dealers are not to touch their clothing while on the tables). Instead, recalling a piece of advice given by Cathy, I rub them on the table's green felt surface. Much better; they're dry for the moment.

I pick up the deck, shuffle, and begin pitching the cards. So far, so good. I'm concentrating on following procedure, and the first few hands fly by in a blur. As I find a rhythm, my tunnel vision dissipates and I become aware of the gamblers in front of me. Two of the three are winning consistently, but no one is making any tip bets for me. I smile and make small talk anyway, as Rick directed. Joanne whispers to me: "Listen, kid, your attitude sucks. When they're winning but not toking, you ain't supposed to be nice. Dummy up and deal. Get them outta here." Needless to say, I right away cease all small talk.

As the hour progresses, the players stay hot but still do not tip. I can feel Joanne squirming uncomfortably next to me every time I bust. She finally directs me to adjust my shuffling technique: "Take a third from the top or shuffle an extra time. It doesn't matter. Just do something different." I'm not quite sure what I'm doing wrong, but I do as I'm told. When my sixty minutes are up, Joanne and I walk back to the employee break room together, and I ask her what was wrong with my shuffle. "Nothing. Your dealing is great," she tells me. "A little slow but that'll improve. But you gotta learn. They were winning, but they weren't tipping. You gotta change the flow of the cards, try to break them up a bit." Though I was unaware of it at the time, I had just been introduced to the two main tactics Nevada dealers use to make tips: controlling one's emotional offerings and influencing game outcomes. As I would soon discover, mastery of these tactics is a serious and collective endeavor.

Meet the Dealers

On their twenty-minute breaks, dealers head to the employee cafeteria. It is here that I first meet my coworkers. Of the approximately 100 dealers on the swing shift, around two-thirds are women and two-thirds nonwhite (see table 3).

These workers vary greatly in terms of age and experience. At one

Table 3 Race and Gender Composition of Silver State Casino Dealers (percent)

	Caucasian	Asian	African American	Hispanic/ Other	All Dealers
Female	19	33	4	9	65
Male	18	12	2	3	35
All Dealers	37	45	6	12	100

extreme are the "break-ins" like Sam, Melissa, and me. At the other are more experienced workers, most in their forties and fifties. For many of them (like Maria), employment at Silver State Casino represents a downward trajectory insofar as they have recently been forced out of better positions. It is standard knowledge in the industry that casinos routinely purge veteran dealers, who are more likely to have full-time status.[2] For instance, early in my fieldwork I met a dealer named T.J. She had worked at the upscale "Paradise Casino" for many years before quitting and applying to Silver State Casino. She explained her decision to resign in the following way:

T.J.: Well the company brought in some hotshot new management, and they really cracked down on us old dealers. They watched over us constantly and criticized everything we did. It got so bad that I had horrible stomach pains, and the doctor said I was developing an ulcer from the stress. And then they called me into the office to say my dealing was too slow. I thought, after twenty-five years of dealing, I have to go through this? Then I saw this sheet on his desk that had all us old-timers on it, and I knew we were who they were out to get. And you know how they ask you on job applications whether you ever been fired? Well, if you check yes, a casino won't hire you. So I called in one night before my shift and said, "I quit." So now on applications I can say I've never been fired.

AUTHOR: So why do you think they were after all the old dealers?

T.J.: Cuz we made eight dollars an hour, not minimum wage. And plus we were full-time and had benefits.

AUTHOR: So now you're here at Silver State Casino. Are you full-time
           here?
  T.J.:   No.
AUTHOR: No benefits?
  T.J.:   Oh, no.

The first thing I learn about the occupational culture of my new work-
group is that it is saturated with food and drink. Because of our tight
time schedules, we are permitted to cut to the front of the food line and
have reserved for us several large tables in the front of the room. The
cafeteria itself features a 20-foot long buffet, from which we can eat as
often as we want—as if we are being "comped" by the house! And the
food isn't bad either. Besides the standard fare, a cook is available to fix
us sandwiches or mix a milkshake. Most workers, I learn, fast all day
long, come into work a little early to gulp down a big meal, eat snacks
and drink sodas throughout the night, and then gorge themselves again
when their shift ends to hold them over until the next evening. As a
researcher, I soon fell into this habit. After ten hours in the pit, three
hours of writing field notes, and then six hours of fitful sleep in the bright
light of midday (I had not yet learned the trick of taping aluminum foil
over my bedroom windows), it was only too tempting to forego cooking
until my shift began again. (Of course, when my fieldwork ended and I
returned to Berkeley twenty pounds heavier, I regretted having coupled
such culinary lassitude at home with dietary turpitude at work.)

While drinking coffee and munching on BLT sandwiches, dealers
talk nonstop about two topics. One is management's scheduling practices. On busy nights, we are regularly told that we must work overtime,
while on slow evenings we are given "early-outs" (EOs). The former
practice disrupts transportation, child care, and sleep plans; the latter
affects anticipated earnings. Overall, on only one of every five shifts am
I released at the scheduled time. As the weeks go by, workers also voice
concern about the slow season that invariably accompanies the late, hot
summer. Part-timers, I am told, should begin job-hunting soon because
many will be laid off. And because layoffs are not based upon seniority,
an air of insecurity pervades the casino's backstage areas, especially

among older dealers. Maria and I live nearby, so we often ride to work together. One early August morning, she shares with me her concerns about the upcoming year. She is worried about getting sick someday and not being able to pay the bills. Silver State Casino will not make her full-time, she knows, but what else can she do?

No job security, no benefits, long hours. Why would anyone want this job? In a word, tips. On any given night you might encounter a high roller on a winning streak and walk out of work with hundreds of dollars—in cash—in your pocket. Tokes thus constitute the second, and by far most common, topic of conversation. Indeed, the lingo and logic of the occupation revolve entirely around them. Workers, for example, classify casinos according to the tips their dealers bring in on an average night. We make $60 to $100 nightly at Silver State Casino. Better casinos are "two-buck" joints or ones where dealers have a "buck-seventy-five job" (nightly tokes are $200 or $175, respectively). And someone always seems to know someone at a nearby casino where dealers pulled in a big score last night of $300 or $400. (Dealers furthermore rank potential employers in this way: who wouldn't forgo a job at a "classy" resort full of light-tipping retirees for one at a dilapidated "store" where the regulars "know how to take care of you"?)

As is standard in the U.S. casino industry today, Silver State Casino utilizes a shared tip structure. All tips earned by dealers on the swing shift are pooled and divided equally at the end of the night.[3] The fact that tips are shared affects workplace culture and conversation. Throughout their shift, dealers are expected to keep one another updated on the tokes they are taking in. And they do so with startling accuracy. If a table is tipping well, the dealer will rush into the break room and announce: "Two hundred and thirty bucks in my first three hours!" Stories of big "drops" in fact serve as energizing "interaction rituals" for the work-group.[4] As I recorded in my fieldnotes:

> It is about three hours into the swing, and I'm on break. Cid, a craps dealer, rushes into the cafeteria and announces that his table has a high roller and they have dropped [received as tips] $720 in the past hour, and maybe as high as $2200 for the shift. Everyone is whooping and clapping. "They better not give me an EO tonight!" someone

shouts out [if a dealer is given an early out, their tip earnings for the night are pro-rated]. We all laugh.

In turn, a dealer having a bad tip night will look visibly upset and even promise to make amends in the future: "I can't make anything tonight," Mitch announces to the room, "My players aren't toking and I keep pulling up nineteens, twentys, twenty-ones every time. Wait till this weekend, though. I'll drop 150 or 200. I always do."

The shared tip structure induces dealers to discipline coworkers perceived to not be "pulling their weight." Katie, a young dealer from Vietnam, labels Salvador "a stick in the mud," pointing directly at him. "He don't say nothing. He just smile." As we walked up the stairs following a break, someone would invariably yell out, "Okay, people, talk to them!" I catch a healthy dose of such discipline one July morning. I am on my second hour of forced overtime; my stomach aches from all the coffee imbibed during the night. During a break, I cross my arms and put my head down on the cafeteria table. Whack! Someone has slapped me on the top of my head—hard! I look up and see Tessie, a petite woman from Cambodia. "You shouldn't be partying the night before you work," she scolds. "You have to be well rested so you can smile, talk a lot, and make us some money!"

The occasional slap upside the head notwithstanding, as an ethnographer I find the shared tip structure to be an invaluable tool for gaining entrée and establishing rapport with my coworkers. Because the most experienced dealer depends on the tip-making acuity of the greenest, tyros to the trade are "taken under the wing" and made privy to the "tricks of the trade." For instance, after my first few nights of dealing, I become worried that I am not making adequate tips. Though I'd quickly mastered the art of withholding service from non-tippers, when offered a tip bet, I always seem to win the hand (and so lose the tip). Calculating my average tip earnings at the end of my first week only confirms my fears; although I'd contributed about $40 each night, my share of the collective toke pool had averaged $75. Not wanting to be perceived as a free-rider, I keep quiet as dealers chat about how much they've brought in so far that evening. Finally, though, while we're sitting at a crowded table, Maria asks me directly how much I have made so far tonight. All eyes turn my way.

"Twenty-five bucks all lousy night!" I blurt out. "I don't know what to do. They never bet for me and when they do it always loses. I'm going crazy here!"

To my immense relief, my confession is met by laughter. "Don't worry," Maria says. "New dealers are always hot like this."

"Yeah," concurs Katie. "It takes a while to learn how to lose."

Learn how to lose? What Katie was implying was that dealers must master their own game, one that overlaps with but does not completely graft onto the official games. To make tokes, Nevada dealers take an active role on the tables and control the associated distribution of emotions (e.g., blame and credit). And although I describe this game as a formal typology of tactics, it must be emphasized that, in practice, workers learn the game not through explicit instruction but through dramatic and often humorous stories of individual tippers, hands, and moments. In the words of Michel De Certeau, dealers, like all those subcultures lacking in official power, communicate by

> Tell[ing] each other about the hand they had to play the night before. . . . The stories could be formulated in a special code, thus making it clear that every event is a particular application of the formal framework. But in replaying the games, in telling about them, these accounts record the rules and the moves simultaneously. To be memorized as well as memorizable, they are *repertories of schemas of action*. . . . Moves, not truths are recounted.[5]

A GAME OF MAKING TIPS

Classifying Players

Nevada dealers categorize players into two broad types: tippers and non-tippers ("Georges" and "stiffs," respectively). The ideal table is one at which tippers occupy all seven seats and are winning, and thus tipping, frequently. When a new player sits down, however, the dealer does not know which category the player falls into, so embarks upon a process of information gathering. A new player, for instance, can announce that he or she is a tipper:

> "Win me a couple hands, buddy, and I'll be a generous fellow."
> "All right, pal, let's make us *both* some money!"

In addition, an unspoken protocol of tipping exists on the tables. After a series of wins (typically three to five), table norms dictate a tip. A "blackjack," though, offers a special test of a player's tipping status. Because these wins pay 3 to 2, the gambler will often receive a silver 50-cent piece as part of his or her earnings (e.g., a $15 bet will earn a $22.50 payoff). This coin, literally "small change" (both in terms of monetary denomination and its size relative to the larger plastic gaming chips), represents a perfect opportunity for even a moderate tipper to get on the dealer's good side. Too small for use as a cocktail waitress tip or slot machine token, it can easily be bet as a potential $1 tip for the dealer.[6] A player who pockets the 50 cent piece or, far worse, uses it as part of the next bet (referred to invidiously by dealers as "putting the silver on top") immediately betrays his or her status as a stiff.

Often though, a new player will be "cold," losing game after game. Since even the most generous George rarely tips during a losing streak, dealers can use jokes or stories to discern a player's true colors; they can, that is, slyly "hustle" an initial tip:

> While riding home with a fellow dealer, we talk about how to get players to start toking. She says she doesn't wear her wedding ring at work because it gets dirty from handling money. "Once, while I was dealing, a man asked me if I was married. 'Yes, yes,' I said. 'Well, where's your ring?' 'Oh, we can't afford one right now, but we are saving up to buy one.' 'Did you hear that?' he says to the table, 'C'mon, let's put some tips up for her.'" We both laugh.
>
> A middle-aged woman is playing at my table and asks me what I make an hour. "Minimum wage," I respond.
>
> "So how do you make your money?"
>
> "From our tips."
>
> "Oh."
>
> I take advantage of the opening and say softly, "Hint, hint." She laughs, catching my humor, but doesn't tip.

A dealer elaborates upon the mind-set of a new gambler: "Most novice players think of the dealer as part of the 'house,' disciples of the casino . . . they want me to lose; hell, they're probably paying these guys mint anyway."[7] When such a player does offer an initial tip, the dealer's demeanor changes dramatically, from indifference to active engagement. As a dealer explains, "Once people see the amount of service that a George is getting and they are not getting, they usually figure it out on their own."[8]

Communicating Information

Information on tippers is not only collected, but shared. During relief changes, workers utilize a complex but informal code communicating customer tipping behavior—a veritable service semiotics. When relief arrives, a dealer must finish the current hand and inform the table that he or she is leaving. Through this act of saying goodbye, however, the exiting dealer communicates to the incoming dealer vital information, such as who's tipping, how much, and how frequently. This code has a long history; it was documented by Diane Arness, an anthropologist who worked undercover as a blackjack dealer in the 1970s:

> Dealers have developed rituals and codes which communicate to the incoming dealer what types of players are at the table. A smiling dealer who thanks the table at-large tells the incoming dealer the players are *nice tippers*. When he says, "good luck" but does not thank the players, it usually means they're *nice stiffs*. If he adds, "Take care of them, they're just learning," it means "Find a way to start them toking. ". . . A grim dealer with narrow eyes indicates to the incoming dealer that there are bastards on the table, even though the dealer may curtly thank a *tipping bastard*. When a dealer pointedly thanks individual players, he is saying, "These are the tippers, the rest are stiffs."[9]

When I broke in as a dealer, however, I had to piece together the code myself, through experiences such as the following:

> I am relieving Juan tonight. As I am finishing a relief break, three new players come to the table with about $200 each and begin playing $25 hands. After their first hand, Juan comes back, and I move on. When

I return in an hour to relieve him again, the three players are now all laughing and have about $500 each in front of them (signifying that they have been winning). Yet there are no tips behind Juan's tray. As Juan turns to leave, he says nothing to the players but gives me an exasperated look and says, "Good luck, Jeff." I've never had a dealer wish *me* good luck, I think. It is not until I have already dealt out my first hand that I realize what he was implying. He wants these stiffs to lose!

Improving Tippers' Luck

When dealing to Georges, Silver State Casino dealers seek to "improve their luck." The two most common tactics for doing so are to proffer advice on basic strategy and to selectively time your shuffle. A couple points must be made about such tactics. First, while a "sharp" dealer may "palm cards" or "deal seconds" to guarantee a win for a George, the average dealer bends rather than breaks the rules to tilt a tipper's odds. Much like the casino, dealers play the percentages; over time and with sufficient volume, such minor alterations pay off. Second, while assisting a George allows him or her to play longer, win more often, and continue tipping, a dealer must also display to the table his or her capacity to influence the games in order to impart a sense of gratitude. In brief, on the tables, dealers both act and appear efficacious.

The typical casino employee understands better than the casual gambler the principles of basic strategy, and will attempt to bring the play of Georges into line with them. For instance, in blackjack, if a player's first two cards have the same value, the player may split them, playing each card as its own hand. With certain combinations, it is wise to do so; with others, it is not.[10] Splits thus represent key opportunities to offer advice:

> Sam and I are talking after work about helping out players who are tipping. Sam says, "If they try to split tens, I'll say, 'Are you *sure* you want to do that?'"[11]

More generally, dealers can advise players whether or not to hit their hands:

I tell Sam that I do this too. "Like when I can see that a person has fourteen and my up-card is a six and they start to swipe (signal a hit), I'll go, 'Now, be careful here,' and then wait for them to give the hit signal again."[12]

It was also common for players to ask directly for assistance when confronted with a difficult decision: "I don't know, Jeff. What do you think?" "What does the book say to do here?" Savvy players may even let you, the dealer, decide whether to hit those hands upon which they have placed a tip-bet. To offer such assistance, though, the dealer must first see the player's cards. At about half of Silver State Casino's tables, house rules require players to hold their cards in their hands (rather than laying them open-faced on the table). A dealer may here crane his or her neck to catch a glimpse of the player's cards, ask the player directly for this information, or allow the player to verbally or visually convey it:

> It is late in the night, and I am dealing to Troy, an outgoing salesman from Los Angeles. He is a tipper and "puts me up" [i.e., makes a tip-bet for me] frequently. But I soon realize that he is not the savviest of gamblers, and so help him out as best I can. He begins flashing me his cards when he receives them—so I will be able to see his hand—and giving me ambiguous hit signals. I respond by doing everything I can to assist him, practically playing the hands for him. "We're good there," I say. "That thirteen's gonna need some help." Eventually, the pit boss notices and strolls over and tells Troy to stop exposing his cards, casting me a dirty look as well. While this reprimand would have scared me early in my fieldwork, I now merely tone down my assistance. The exchange of tips—dollar chips for helpful hints—continues, albeit more covertly.

Dealers will also monitor a George's bankroll to make sure that the player is adequately stocked in the currency in which he or she is tipping. If, for example, a player typically wagers a green $25 chip along with a red $5 chip bet for the dealer, the dealer will occasionally pay a winning bet with five reds rather than a single green.

The second tactic for helping tippers involves paying attention to the cards that have been played from the deck and timing the shuffle to better the player's chances. The basic principle behind card counting is that the higher the proportion of tens and aces remaining in the deck, the more the odds favor the player. In fact, if a deck contains enough ten-valued cards, the odds will actually favor the player. So while procedure dictates that the deck be shuffled exactly two-thirds of the way through, dealers may engage in rudimentary card counting and "break the deck" (i.e., shuffle) accordingly. Thus, if after the first hand the deck is disadvantageous to a George (i.e., a high number of tens have been played), the dealer may shuffle early. Conversely, the dealer may shuffle later than procedure dictates when the deck is favorable to the player.

(It should be noted that one danger with this strategy is that, in pushing a good deck to its limit for a George, the dealer might use up the entire deck before the hand is finished. The dealer then must call over a pit boss, who will not be pleased. Veteran dealers tell stories of having had to "sweat it out" as players drew card after card while the deck grew smaller and smaller. These stories culminate with the dealer finishing the game with but one card left in his or her hand.)

Recent developments in table game design have augmented dealers' ability to assist tippers. For instance, as slot machines have grown in popularity, table game designers have attempted to adorn traditional games with slot-style "bells and whistles."[13] One common innovation is a "side-bet" on a standard blackjack game. These award gamblers a prize if their initial two cards represent a certain combination. For instance, Silver State Casino featured several "Royal Match" tables on which gamblers win a small jackpot if their first two cards are a king and a queen. Because these jackpots nearly always result in a tip, dealers have an incentive to track the kings and queens, and shuffle accordingly:

> Kim tells me during break, "When I'm dealing Royal Match, if they put a tip-bet down and I notice the queens and kings are out, I'll reshuffle right away."

And in "21 Madness," a player's' side-bet wins a mini-jackpot if he or she receives a blackjack:

> Maria and I are talking in the cafeteria during our break, and I tell her that I'm on Madness tonight. "Well, the trick to dealing that game," she tells me, "is to watch how many aces come out on the

first hand. If none do, someone is sure to get a black jack on the next hand." When I return to my table, I notice after the first hand that not a single ace has come out. So I say to the table, "I strongly encourage y'all to bet the madness, and when it hits I want a commission." Sure enough, two players get blackjacks on the next deal, and I play it up. "See! Now what would you do without me?" Each plays a tip-bet for me on the next hand.

As would be expected based upon this discussion of dealers' discretionary shuffling, the tables in the casino featuring a shuffling machine or a six-deck shoe (which requires a reshuffling only once every twenty minutes or so, versus the three- to four-minute cycle of a single deck) are unpopular among croupiers:

> On my first break tonight, I run into Juan. Always good for a laugh, tonight he looks depressed. "What's up?" I ask.
> "I'm on the shoe tonight and I hate it . . . because you can't ever fix a bad deck."
> "What do you mean by a bad deck?"
> "You know, where the dealer keeps winning. You can't reshuffle or anything."

So these are the techniques used to improve a George's luck: strategy secrets and selective shuffling. Although they are often used in tandem, one or the other could be more appropriate for certain types of players. A novice gambler may understand nothing about how the timing of the shuffle affects his or her chances, but will be extremely grateful for advice on what to do with a twelve when the dealer's up-card is a nine. Conversely, a basic strategy player will have no need for such advice, but will take note if you break the deck early when the count is a negative five (i.e., advantageous for the house).

A Note on Agency and Credit

Attempts to assist tippers, as the preceding examples demonstrate, entail not simply the physical labor of altering the odds, but the interactive work of conveying this agency to players in order to invoke what can be called a norm of reciprocity.[14] Dealers, in short, must make clear that tips are not mere gestures of generosity, but a fee for a service rendered. They whisper advice to players, to emphasize that strategy hints are technically against the house rules. Gamblers may play along with such insinuations, referring to their tips as illicit kickbacks: "Maybe we can bribe him." It is also not uncommon for dealers to stretch their presentations of self beyond the bounds of the possible. Players, for example, often request a specific card: "Hit me, my thirteen needs an eight!" A dealer can dramatically slap down the next card and, on the one in thirteen times that the eight does appear, really ham it up: "There you go! See the magic I can work for you?" If the card is a six or seven, agency can still be claimed: "Sorry, I was out of eights, but that should get you close enough to win." Though I doubt many gamblers believed we could magically make certain cards appear, such playfulness usually drew smiles and maintained the ongoing interactive construction of dealers as agentive participants in the games.

All these strategies of agency-construction work fine when tippers are winning, for they allow the dealer to claim credit and demand gratitude for game outcomes. But what of those moments when Georges are cold and suffering losses? It is tempting in these situations to deny agency, for players may grow angry and abusive, screaming and calling the dealer every name in the book. When I first began dealing, I reflexively did just this. For instance, after the dealer shuffles a player is chosen to cut the deck with a yellow plastic "cut card." When I found myself hot, I would say, "Who cut this mess? I'd better reshuffle." Such techniques of agency denial are at times useful, such as when the dealer senses that a player's anger has reached the boiling point. But dealers must learn to suppress such reflexes to maintain consistency in their agency-construction, even at the cost of accepting blame for tippers' losses.

To manage blame while maintaining agency, several tactics are available. If, despite all attempts to the contrary, a dealer is "hot," the dealer can emphasize that he or she is in fact on the players' side and as much a victim of bad luck as they are. Consider this excerpt from my field notes:

> After work tonight, I take $50 of my tip money and go to play
> blackjack at a neighboring casino with a coworker. We immediately
> make our status as tippers known, and the dealer, a young Asian

man, responds by cracking jokes and laughing with us. He keeps turning up blackjacks and twenties, however, so our tip-bets go into the chip tray (to the house). I see that he is continually breaking the deck early, but to no avail. With each winning hand, he looks increasingly distraught and says apologetically, "I'm trying! I'm trying!"

If all else fails, dealers can simply accept the blame for players' losses:

Tonight I again play blackjack at another casino after work. The dealer is "hot," and I lose all but five dollars within minutes. On my last hand, I turn up a blackjack, and upon leaving the table, hand the dealer a tip. She looks shocked and remarks, "I don't deserve this."

Serving Georges

Nevada dealers attempt to increase their tip earnings not only by influencing game outcomes, but also by providing good customer service. We can view this as an exchange of financial capital for emotional capital, the most basic unit of which is the smile:

I am talking before work with Teresa, a rather shy dealer. "To make tips," she tells me, "you have to please the customer."
"Well, how do you do that?" I ask.
"You smile at them."

Richer forms of emotional capital are generated by personalizing interactions. A dealer can address Georges by name, inquire where they're from, what they do, and so on:

Two women sit down at my table, and I casually greet them. After a couple hands, one of them puts a tip-bet out for me. As that hand is being played, I ask her name—Amanda—and where she's from—Texas. And I find myself with each tip asking the tipper more and more questions: "What do you do?" "What brings you to town?"

Dealers furthermore "read" players in order to customize the emotional capital offered. Customization occurs along two axes. One situates the current hand within the player's entire gambling session. Smiles, for example, while generally appropriate, could be misinterpreted by a cold player. As Cathy explained to us one afternoon. "Sometimes when you smile, [the player] will look at you and say, 'Look at her. She is so mean. We are losing all our money and she is happy.'"

The second axis of customization differentiates tippers into "relaxed" versus "serious" gamblers. The former tended to be female and/or young players seeking informal and "fun" service. Experienced dealers constantly offered me advice on procuring tips from such players. "Flirt!" many said. "Bullshit with them." "Laugh at their jokes, even if they're totally dumb." Dealers can also provide these players general entertainment. New dealers, in fact, regularly visit other casinos in town for the express purpose of picking up witty jokes, calls, and routines. Over time, I developed a working repertoire of humorous commentary for the games:

> I begin my shift at a table on which the players tip occasionally but are really sedate. I am in top form, though. After calling for insurance and checking my hand when my up-card is an ace, I give the players a sorrowful expression so they will think I have a blackjack.[15] When they all go, "Awww!" I say quickly, "Oh calm down, I'm just pulling your legs." This gets lots of laughs. And after the game is briefly interrupted by a tray fill, I say to the players, "And now back to the regularly scheduled blackjack game."[16] Soon the table is in an uproar, and they are offering toke bets practically every hand. In fact, when my shift ends, the woman at third base hands me a $5 chip and tells me with a big, genuine smile, "You were fun!"

In contrast, older players and men playing alone typically expect deferential and status-enhancing emotional capital. As a veteran dealer explained, "A good dealer [gives this] player what he or she most desires—recognition, the VIP treatment. 'Hello, Mr. D. How are you? I heard you were in the hotel. Did you bring the wife?'"[17] And during the game you "take care of them" by watching and learning their basic game strategy:

> "All players have a system," Tex explained to us one afternoon at dealing school. "A guy sits at home all week figuring out how to make a profit on his game. If he's a smart man and pays us our

commission now and then, we're gonna pay attention and learn his system and do the work for him."

A dealer can also build up a player's status by making his or her play seem central to positive table outcomes. For instance, if there is one George at a table full of players, the dealer, upon busting, can say to him, "Good play, sir. That'll get everyone paid," even if his play had nothing to do with breaking the dealer. At a table full of players, all following the game closely, the difference in a dealer's treatment of a tipper relative to others is conspicuous to all.

Forcing Off Stiffs

While they pamper Georges, dealers aspire to force "stiffs" off their tables as quickly as possible. Dealers are landlords, I was told, and stiffs are tenants who don't pay the rent:

> "You know how some players be sitting there for three or four hours at a time but never put down a bet for you? You go to break, come back and they're *still there.* No offense. Sit down and play a few hands, but don't be taking up that seat all night long if you ain't gonna pay some rent." .

Dealers try to "walk" these players. On the most basic level, this can entail "working to rule," that is, following procedure by withholding the assistance one normally grants even a modest tipper. The dealer merely says nothing when the player splits tens or doesn't split eights, while responding to requests for advice with, "That's a tough call . . . are you feeling lucky?"

Compliance with procedure is rarely considered adequate, though, given the intense animosity stiffs invoke. A veteran dealer expressed this sentiment vividly one hot July evening. After helping a table full of novices win their bets without receiving a single toke in return, she hissed to me, "Not one goddamn cent. My checks are starting to bounce from all the smiles and thank-yous I've been depositing." In this situation, a dealer can become more proactive, bending the house rules slightly by altering the shuffle (i.e., dealing sooner or later than procedure dictates) in order to reverse a bad run of cards (here, one going well for the stiff). And once the dealer finds a good run of cards (one going poorly for the player), he or she can concentrate upon dealing rapidly, knowing that, after all, the odds are in the dealer's (and the house's) favor. In the words of Sue, a veteran dealer, "Just find a sweet spot in the deck and wipe 'em out."

Antagonizing Stiffs

To further force off non-tippers, dealers may withhold service. On one particularly bad tip night in early August, eight dealers assembled at a table in the cafeteria and complained as follows:

> Kim brings up a Silver State Casino regular notorious for engaging dealers in endless conversations yet not tipping. "Just talk, talk, talk and no tip. I don't want to talk, mother. I am tired. Put up a dollar here and there and I will talk, but no money and I am tired." Phil launches into a diatribe against the most despised of players: those who look well-off and are on a winning streak but don't tip. "I love to take those people's money. To dummy up and deal. I hate 'em."

Two of my coworkers went even further, explaining how they openly antagonize non-tippers:

> "Sometimes I'll piss them off on purpose, 'Oh, you lost again, sir, too bad'" [all laugh]. "Yeah! Or just smile a little when they lose. That usually gets to them."

That dealers view service as a form of capital possessing an exchange value is revealed by an old joke among tables staff: ""If those damn stiff players would have put a nickel in my slot, they would have seen a god-damn smile. I'd light up like a nickelodeon."[18]

On the casino floor, the various tactics for dealing with and to non-tippers were often exercised in tandem, and their overall effect could exert considerable pressure on a player. When I encountered a non-tipper who was also verbally abusive, I did all I could to force him off my table:

> A man is playing by himself at my table, and terribly at that. He is not tipping but I can tell he is very intoxicated and in a bad mood, so I

decide to play it safe by not directly antagonizing him. He loses on a nineteen after I pull up a twenty. As I take his chips, I try to distract him by asking about his Oakland Raiders T-shirt, but he just hisses at me, "You piece of shit." I laugh it off, but feel angry. From then on, I pay attention to the number of aces and tens left, breaking the deck early if too few come out on the first hand. And when he hesitates on a tough decision, I squeeze my mouth closed, and the minute he makes the slightest hit signal, I whack the card down. Eventually he loses four hands in a row and staggers off.

Ideological Effects of an Entrepreneurial Game

To be an entrepreneur is to think of oneself as independent and self-employed. It is in this sense that to play the game of making tips is to adopt an entrepreneurial identity. On the tables, dealers act in their own interests, systematically identifying with neither the house nor players. At times, they may side with the casino to drain the bankroll of a (non-tipping) player; at others, they may side with a (tipping) player wishing to win big. But in the final analysis, Silver State Casino dealers think of themselves as independent actors. As usual, Maria gets right to the heart of the matter: "Hell, if a player's tipping, who cares if he's winning? It ain't my money I'm giving away!"

Independent interests mean little, however, absent a capacity to pursue (and occasionally realize) them. A second dimension of entre-preneurialism at Silver State Casino is thus an experienced agency of work. Although, as I pointed out above, shuffling selectively and offering strategy advice can only nudge the hold percentage a few points one way or the other, these tactics feel like powerful tools on the tables. As Sam remarked one night, "I swear, it feels like you can will people to lose. It's like there's an energy in you and you can make it happen." Much as clients misrecognize the statistical reality of the gambling transaction, so do dealers their own agency. Nor is such misrecognition peripheral to the working of the larger service labor regime; indeed, it is essential to it insofar as it produces two effects.

The first effect is *the mollification of vertical conflict between workers and management.* Dealers, for instance, regularly blame stiffs, not the company,

for their low wages. The entrepreneurial game also conditions workers
to what is by any standard dreary and monotonous work. "Hands where
no one is tipping are boring," dealers would often complain. "With tippers, at least you care about what's going on." The desirability of having
a stake in the action is demonstrated by those instances of a conflict
between dealers' material and game-playing interests. I found that when
players offer a choice between a direct tip and a toke bet, dealers nearly
always request the latter: "Play it for me." Though an economically irrational decision insofar as workers are forgoing a definite one-unit gain
for a less than 50 percent chance at a two-unit gain, it illustrates well the
lure of becoming an active game participant.

A second outcome of the entrepreneurial work game is *a lack of commitment to the company.* Because Silver State Casino largely lacks internal
opportunities for promotion, dealers seek to increase their earnings
through lateral moves across firms—they "chase tips," in the occupational lingua. This is in fact one of the reasons Nevada dealers have been
unable to sustain unionization drives. In the United States, unions are
organized at the enterprise level, not the industry level. The frequent
movement among casinos engendered by the tipping system thus hin-
ders attempts to organize workers (a subject explored further in Part II
of this book).

REGULATING AUTONOMY

We now consider the role played by floor managers in regulating service workers' games. The hallmark of a hegemonic labor regime is the
absence of direct, despotic managerial control. Such autonomy, however,
is not necessarily an expression of worker power, insofar as it is granted
and can be revoked by managers themselves. This is precisely the case
at Silver State Casino. Dealers are permitted to play their tip-making
game when "grind" players are on the table, but when a high roller sits
down, the house's panoptic power is unleashed. Pit bosses play the key
role in regulating the boundaries between these extremes of autonomy
and control.

Floor Managers and Their Fiefs

Of the fifteen pit bosses who regularly worked the swing shift during my fieldwork, seven were white men, three were white women, three were minority men (two Asian, one Hispanic) and two were minority women (both Asian). They, not the camera crew or upper management, performed the majority of routine surveillance at Silver State Casino. Trusted by the house to keep order on the floor, these managers treat the pits as their own private fiefs. And though they are salaried representatives of the casino, they are also all former dealers who act as "middlemen" between workers and the house. In fact, on unexpectedly busy nights it was not uncommon to find a floor manager dressed in "black and whites" rather than a suit and tie—that is, dealing rather than supervising.

On one level, floor managers tolerate workers' tip-making tactics because they themselves benefit from them on those nights they deal. Consider the time I arrived at work to find Robert, a notoriously finicky and dour inspector, dealing blackjack. My initial snickers turned to consternation when I realized I was scheduled as his relief dealer. Would his temporary demotion precipitate particularly bitter invectives towards me? To my surprise, though, as I tapped him on the shoulder to relieve him, he smiled broadly at two of the players on the table: "Thanks guys, good luck to you." Of course he was merely signaling to me that these are Georges; but this was the first time I've ever seen him smile, and so he mistook my look of astonishment for a novice dealer's ignorance of the relief code. "Talk to them," he hissed before departing for the break room.

More generally, pit bosses' interests are well served by allowing dealers to play their entrepreneurial game. While official house policy directs dealers to maximize simultaneously speed, security, and service, floor managers recognize that this is largely impossible. They concern themselves with ensuring a smooth flow of play in their pits and preventing losses on particularly large wagers. Given these preferences, as well as their own necessarily limited surveillance capacities, floor managers categorize players not as Georges and stiffs but as low rollers and high rollers, with different logics of control imposed for each. For low rollers—the vast majority of patrons—the tipping system regulates the action just fine, even if security and service are somewhat sacrificed. For high rollers, however, security and service are strictly enforced.

The Nightly Grind: Autonomy for Low Rollers

Low rollers constitute around 90 percent of Silver State Casino's clientele. Floor managers want to maximize the overall volume of these players' small-stake wagers, and they consider the tipping system ideal for doing so. Because dealers understand that the more hands they deal, the more tipping opportunities present themselves, they spontaneously maximize their speed. In fact, not once during my fieldwork did I witness a pit boss direct a worker to deal faster. On the contrary, players would often gripe about the pace at which we dealt, plaints to which we would invariably respond, "Sorry, can't help it. The hand is quicker than the eye."

Upper-level management also allows dealers to act as entrepreneurs. After my first night of work, I never again saw Rick, the swing shift boss who had auditioned Maria and me. And during my entire employment, I only saw the casino manager once, during one of his perfunctory visits to the employee break room. At 6 feet tall and weighing 300 pounds, he would have been hard-pressed to sneak up on us anyway. Neither did the video cameras systematically monitor grind play. Referred to as "saturation targeting," the logic of electronic surveillance is neither comprehensive nor random. Rather, it focuses its gaze upon high rollers and players on winning streaks.[19]

With experience, dealers become cognizant of when and where they are under observation. For instance, I at first assumed that my dealing was being watched continuously by the surveillance cameras. Yet I found that although I often forgot to show clean hands when leaving my table, no one reprimanded me. About a week into my fieldwork, I had the following revelation:

> Tonight I accidentally pay a woman on her bet when we both have eighteen (ties are a standoff). Even worse, I pay and collect her $1

tip-bet too. At first I panic. What if the cameras saw that? Will they fire me? But then I rationalize it, telling myself that this place is so packed tonight, while the players at my table are playing such small bets. What are the odds that two or three guys in surveillance, monitoring all the action on all the tables, saw one little mispay? And sure enough, the night ends without anyone in management having noticed.

In addition, although the cameras can potentially *see* all the action, they do not capture any audio. As long as they are out of earshot of the pit boss, dealers can proffer insults and hints with impunity.

In contrast, the cameras closely monitor high-stake action. Through experiences such as the following, I became aware of this fact:

The three men at my table are playing relatively large sums ($100 per hand) and winning—and tipping—big. Robert is the floor manager, and I can feel him behind me, watching the game closely. After my first hand, he comes over and corrects my procedure, telling me to spread the cards better when laying them out. I find this odd, as he has never said anything about this before. But he explains, "Do it like this. The camera has to see the cards in this situation." Robert also orders a player to be more careful when handling the cards so as not to bend them: "Look, I got a camera to deal with."

I talked about this episode with Joanne later in the evening. She said that she, too, often makes minor errors on the tables, but usually doesn't worry much about them. When a high roller is playing, though, it's a different story: "The moment someone slaps down a hundred-dollar bill, you can *feel* [the cameras] zooming in." As Joanne's quip conveys, dealers are able to routinely breach procedure through the cultivation of an embodied sense of the casino's logic of surveillance.

Floor managers do not simply tolerate dealers' tip-making tactics, they at times actively encourage them. Consider official norms of service. While corporate discourse equates players with guests, pit bosses more often compare them to dishonest scam artists:

Frank, the pit boss, comes to my table and tells the man sitting at first base not to bend his cards. [A rudimentary player cheating strategy is to bend certain cards in order to mark them]. I hadn't even noticed that he was bending them. When my next break comes, Frank calls me over and explains: "These people just aren't honest. They bend the corners of the aces or tens. Just tell them in a serious tone to not bend them while you straighten out the cards. . . . Believe me, there's a cheater inside this casino every night."

Dealers are also allowed to violate service norms when confronting slow—typically inebriated—low rollers. Here, too, floor managers deflate the status of the casino's "guests," thereby granting dealers the right to ignore or even antagonize them:

Two middle-aged men are among the six players at my table. They are drinking Budweisers as fast as the waitress can bring them, and the man on my far right is so inebriated he keeps passing out at the table and spilling his beer. He somehow manages to keep putting up bets, though, so I must deal to him. But he is too drunk to read his cards or make the proper signals. "Would you like to hit, sir?" I must repeatedly ask, and then interpret his garbled response. The other players are getting annoyed, and Larry, the pit boss, is now standing permanently at my side. Larry nags him. "One hand on the cards." "Keep your beer behind your bet." "Sir, look up, it's your turn." Eventually, the two drunk guys get the hint and stumble off. "If they're slowing you down like that, you gotta get on their case, bug 'em, get 'em outta there," Larry tells me.

Floor supervisors direct dealers to discipline suspected cheats and force off slow players. Dealers comply, and in return may withhold service from low-rolling non-tippers. Although this arrangement is implicit, floor managers will, when pressed, acknowledge its existence. This was revealed through a conversation I had one early morning with Deb, a pit boss. "Our dealers know they have to treat everyone with respect," she told me. But after a moment of reflection, she added: "Of course, they'll find a way to get in a dig [i.e., an insult] for a stiff. As long as they're subtle about it, well, then, of course they get away with it. It's part of the game, really."

Floor managers monitor grind play mainly to make sure that dealers do not cross the line separating a subtle "dig" from a hard "hustle." I quote at length a former dealer's memoirs, for they illustrate not only the nature of this informal agreement, but also the fact that the line between a dig and a hustle is situationally contingent and open to negotiation:

> All the talk in the dealers' room was about money or, more precisely, the lack of it. What happened? . . . We were getting lazy too, and angry. When a stiff landed on our games, we fired cards at his hands as if we were trying to drive nails, aimed for his knuckles and let fly . . . Where were the Georges? . . . One morning in the middle of July he walked in and landed on Caroline's blackjack game. . . . Caroline's tongue could turn small talk into money. She saw those hundreds, and the gab started flowing. . . . He was as lame a player as any who'd ever walked into a Strip casino. . . . When she paid him time and a half for a queen-ace [blackjack], he tried to give half the money back, two hundred and fifty dollars to be exact. Caroline glanced over her shoulder at Jimmy, a boss, who was a nice enough guy, but when money hit the layout, he turned into the biggest sweater in the joint. Bob said Jimmy was such a sweater that his DNA was two-thirds angora wool, one-third cotton yarn. Caroline noticed beads of sweat forming on Jimmy's brow and knew it wasn't a good time to hustle a toke. But this was the summer of our worst drought. She smiled . . . and said, "It's yours unless you want to give it to me."
>
> When she came off the game for her first break, Jimmy grabbed her and demanded to know what the hell that was all about.
>
> "About feeding my kids, Jimmy. If you had kids and needed money, you'd understand."
>
> Jimmy had to bend. Times were that tough. . . . Besides, he'd been there in the good old days when the dealers laid off a few tokes on [i.e., bribed] the bosses. Two or three Ben Franklins in an envelope had compromised the virtue of more than one sweater. Jimmy had gotten his share, had drunk and gambled a lot of it away, but he'd looked the other way when it was to his benefit. We knew it, and so did he.[20]

Floor managers permit dealers to bend the rules regarding not only service but security. They emphasize that dealers are not, as official policy proclaims, passive mediators between players and the casino, but active game participants able to improve the house's edge:

> Melissa and I are sitting in the cafeteria waiting to clock out. Chuck, a pit boss, saunters over to our table and sits down. "You two are new," he says. "And so there's something I want to tell you. When

you're dealing, pay attention to how many tens are out of your deck.
If they ain't coming out [recall that the player's odds are improved in
proportion to the number of ten-valued cards in the deck], break
your deck [i.e., shuffle sooner than procedure dictates] and we have
the advantage again. Just something to think about."

While such requests would be honored when facing a stiff or a high
roller, dealers would use these same techniques to the opposite end for
low-rolling Georges. To finish the anecdote:

Melissa and I nod intently while Chuck is speaking. "Sure, sure,"
we both say. As soon as he leaves, though, we both begin laughing.
"Whatever," says Melissa.
   "If he's tipping, I ain't gonna push him off," I say.
   "Yeah. As long as no one's behind me [i.e., I'm not being watched]
I'm gonna help the man out."

As my fieldwork at Silver State Casino neared its end, I felt embold-
ened to ask a pit boss directly about this implicit license to assist low
rollers. "Well, most of the time you can say, 'The book says to do so
and so,'" Anne responded, "But if it's a very big bet, don't think about
it." In other words, when a high roller is playing, it's a whole different
ballgame.

To Protect and to Serve: Tight Control for High Rollers

About 10 percent of Silver State Casino's clients are considered high
rollers. For such players, pit bosses seek to ensure maximum security
and proper service. As a consequence, dealers' latitude to play their
tip-making game is sharply curtailed. The passage from autonomy to
control is audibly marked by the procedure for announcing the arrival
of a high roller. Upon seeing a player put down a "high-action" bet such
as a purple $500 chip, a dealer must yell, "Purple plays!" and wait for a
floor manager to come to the table before dealing.[21]

   Though this procedure slows the action, the immediate presence of a
supervisor not only prevents dealers from treating a (non-tipping) high
roller rudely, it also allows the pit boss to perform personalized service

by greeting the player or offering a complimentary dinner. "You have to know how to treat someone playing five grand a hand, whether or not he's tipping," a pit boss explained to us. Managers' orientation to security changes here as well. A pit boss staring down a $5,000 wager—insofar as it alone can significantly affect the table's and even the pit's win for that shift—wants to win at all costs:

> This is the first time I have had to deal to a high roller, and I am extremely nervous. Robert, a notorious "sweater" and the least forgiving manager in the place, is standing at my side. And I of course pick this moment to pitch a card onto the floor and knock over a stack of chips. Nonetheless, I am hot and wipe out the high roller's bankroll within twenty minutes. As I leave the table for a break, I prepare for a tongue-lashing from Robert for my foul-ups, and sure enough, he calls me over to the podium. "Sorry about that," I say in advance. "No problem," he replies. "You took their money, right?"

Punishments, in turn, are enforced when high rollers are on the table; the only two dealers fired during my time at Silver State Casino were accused of assisting high-rolling Georges.

SUMMARY

My initial hypotheses concerning labor in the contemporary Nevada casino were not borne out. Despite the powerful technologies of control available to management, the casino was not structured as a despotic panopticon. It is true that dealers must submit to invasive prehire screenings, possess practically no job security, and have few legal rights vis-à-vis the casino firm. Nevertheless, dealing remains organized as a craft and workers are permitted to accept tips from gamblers, while surveillance is decentralized to floor managers. Dealing, as a result, is experienced as an entrepreneurial game of making tips.

We must resist, however, the temptation to end the analysis at this point, content with having documented the skill and ingenuity with which workers circumvent the house rules. This is the reason I label

Silver State Casino a hegemonic service regime: worker autonomy is itself regulated according to the larger prerogatives of management. It is furthermore a central tenant of production politics theory that workplace regimes must be situated in their larger context. One way to do this is to do a genealogy of the site, to discover how it originated and how it has changed over time. This is what we will do in Part II. However, a second way to contextualize one's fieldsite is to compare it to a similar one located in a very different environment. Hence, in the following chapter, we consider the curious case of contemporary South Africa. Following the fall of apartheid, policy makers commissioned a new casino to be built in the city of Johannesburg. This new "Gold City Casino" not only allows us to contextualize the case of Nevada, it raises important questions about work and politics in the new South Africa. Though they deal the same games on the same tables, South African dealers experience a vastly different regime for regulating their service labor.

THREE South Africa

It was after mastering Silver State Casino's entrepreneurial game of making tips that I took my place behind the tables at the "Gold City Casino" in the fall of 2002. During an earlier stay in South Africa, I had interviewed several executives at "Empowerment Inc.," one of a handful of firms licensed to operate casinos in the country following the fall of apartheid (the appendix provides a detailed account of how I gained access to casinos in both the United States and South Africa). These executives agreed to let me deal cards in their new Johannesburg casino. The "game of work" played by South African croupiers, however, could not have been more at odds with the one I documented at Silver State Casino.

This new environment revealed not a hegemonic service regime, but a despotic one. Gold City Casino managers use technology to fully deskill

dealing work, deploy extensive video and audio surveillance throughout the complex, and forbid workers from accepting tips. Rather than
adopting an entrepreneurial orientation toward their work, dealers in
turn play what I call a game of effacement. They seek to obscure their
own power on the tables, so as to deflect both suspicion from management and anger from players. My own experience of habituating to this
despotic service regime demonstrates that the dispositions of workers in
the United States and South Africa are not fundamentally different, leading the former to act entrepreneurially and the latter passively. Instead,
interactive tactics of effacement are a natural response to life in a panopticon. To be a dealer in South Africa is to learn to deny one's own agency
(though as with all forms of "shadow labor," such effacement requires
great skill and ingenuity).

In this chapter, I first describe how Empowerment Inc. (a company
with possible links to the recently deposed apartheid regime) acquired
a new casino license by pledging to empower "previously disadvantaged individuals" (PDIs) as dealers and pit bosses. Instead of feeling empowered, however, these new employees experience work as
iniquitous and enervating, an issue explored in the second part of the
chapter. I conclude by describing in detail the inner workings of the
panoptic system of surveillance at Gold City Casino. Floor managers
are here deskilled "tokens" who spend their time doing data entry,
while the "camera crew" relentlessly monitors dealers for security-
related infractions.

THE ROOTS OF THE GOLD CITY CASINO

During the apartheid era, several South African leisure firms operated
casino resorts in the region's quasi-independent black states (including
not only South Africa's notorious homelands but also the countries of
Swaziland and Lesotho). These industries were largely unregulated,
allowing managers to routinely discriminate against black patrons and
to staff their casinos with white croupiers recruited from the United
Kingdom. When apartheid ended, a consortium of executives from the

homeland casino firms formed a new company—Empowerment Inc.—
and applied for a casino license in the new province of Gauteng. They
soon came under criticism for their actions during apartheid—especially
for the practice of importing British croupiers in light of the poverty and
unemployment that plagued the homeland states.

To counter such critiques, and to symbolize that Empowerment Inc.
was a forward-looking, modern, and, above all else, global company,
executives proposed to build a "Vegas-style" casino in an industrial
suburb of Johannesburg. The well-known Silver State Casino (my first
fieldsite) was chosen as a model. In an interview, Empowerment Inc.'s
development planner offered the following account of Gold City Casino's
origin:

> To brainstorm the idea, I called [name omitted]. I'm sure you've
> heard of him; he's a quite famous architect who's helped plan more
> than a few of the major Nevada properties. Well, we flew off to
> Vegas and holed up in a hotel room for a long weekend to make a
> plan. We had sketches and drawings everywhere, but I was stuck. It
> was late at night that it came to me. I was looking out the window
> and saw Silver State Casino. That was it. It was . . . perfect.

The architecture, design, and theme of Gold City Casino were thus all
modeled directly on Silver State Casino.

In addition, Empowerment Inc. executives promised to rectify problematic labor practices. Gold City Casino would serve as a showcase
service enterprise for the new South Africa, one exemplifying the principles of social equity spelled out in the country's new constitution. To
give flesh to these commitments, the firms submitted a Black Economic
Empowerment (BEE) plan specifying concrete targets for hiring previously disadvantaged individuals as workers and managers. When I commenced research there, three years after its opening, Gold City Casino
had in fact made significant progress toward incorporating PDIs into
most strata of the organization (see table 4).

Two aspects of the process through which Empowerment Inc.
recruited PDIs to staff the Gold City Casino are salient for understanding how service work has subsequently been organized at the casino.
First, workers were, for the most part, recruited *de novo*. The casino's

Table 4 Labor Empowerment Plan, Progress at Gold City Casino
(percent of PDIs)

	Five-Year Target	*Progress after Three Years*
Senior Management	42	25
Supervisors	50	82
Front-Line Staff	88	95

1,400 initial job openings were filled mainly with black workers who lived in the immediate area, nearly all of whom had no prior experience. Second, the entire process was done under intense time constraints. Upon being notified by the Gauteng Gambling Board (GGB) that they had been granted a license, executives rushed to be the first to open a casino in the province. They were seeking a temporal monopoly, and even erected adjacent to the construction site a large tent into which they crammed several hundred slot machines with which to "tap" the local market until the casino proper opened.

Managers today recall that, because of these regulatory and time constraints, the screening process for new workers was far from perfect. Over 15,000 job applications were received during the week following the announcement of the casino's opening. These were screened by human resource officers operating out of a trailer in the construction site parking lot. The applications had included basic verbal and mathematic tests, which were used to narrow the initial applicant pool down to around 4,000. Final hiring decisions were then made based upon a twenty-minute phone interview. Applicants were asked scripted questions, most of which dealt with issues of security and theft. "If you observe a coworker stealing money from the cash register, is it proper to report him to the supervisor?" was a typical question. Management today believes this to have been the best process they could have come up with at the time. But they also feel that the "smoothest, fastest talkers," and not necessarily the ideal casino workers, did best in the interviews and were thus hired.

So these were the demographics of the initial cohort of dealers at Gold City Casino. Eighty percent of these 220 new employees were classifiable as PDIs. Although the precise definition of a PDI in South Africa can vary greatly depending on the context, as we will see repeatedly throughout this study, at the time it was understood to denote black men and women from nearby townships (segregated, largely poor communities on the outskirts of South Africa's cities). Indeed, the labels "PDI" and "township black" are used interchangeably by managers. It is important to note, however, that a full 20 percent of new dealers were not PDIs. These were mainly young whites from local blue-collar families. Comparing their experiences behind the tables to those of the PDI dealers (see the following sections) will help us to see the power a rigid work organization has to override pre-existing status differentials.

All newly hired dealers attended a training school run by the company in a nearby warehouse. At the conclusion of the two-month program, they were rushed over to the casino just in time for its grand opening. There, they took their places behind the tables and commenced delivering cards to a clientele of gamblers that was—based upon my own visual surveys—about three-quarters white and one-quarter nonwhite (black and Asian, mainly).[1] The relative demographics of employees and clients at Gold City Casino were thus roughly similar to those at Silver State Casino: workers of color serving a mainly white, working-class clientele.

Today, Gold City Casino runs an "in-house" training school to fill new dealer vacancies arising from staff turnover. Before beginning my dealing internship in South Africa, I spent a few weeks in the school to brush up on my game. I joined a course with five other students: Solly, Nini, Phindi, Ace, and Suzanne. All are in their twenties and officially categorized as PDIs. As we chat during our break on my first day, I learn that they, like my former fellow trainees in Nevada, are here not because of any long-standing fascination with the glamorous world of the casino, but to simply "make a living." Though all report being currently able to support themselves financially (through various informal sector earnings and intermittent employment in the formal economy), they actively sought work in the gambling industry as, in Phindi's words, a "step up in life." With a steady pay of twenty rand (about two dollars) per hour, dealing work will improve their quality of life—Solly, for example, plans to rent a modern apartment outside of the townships, while Suzanne wants to purchase new school clothes for her child. Furthermore, all view dealing as a first step onto a solid career ladder; from here they aspire to move into casino management or build a résumé with which to apply for jobs in the finance or retail sector.

Phumzile, a black woman in her early forties, is the instructor. She is a relative veteran in the industry, having commenced her career in the early 1990s as one of the few black dealers hired in the casinos of the former homeland of Bophuthatswana. As an experienced "Bop" employee, she proudly distinguishes herself from the new breed of "township" dealers (here again, we see how a simple black-white dichotomy obscures much about the South African social structure). As Phumzile goes over with me the dealing "procedure" here at Gold City Casino, I am right away struck by how dissimilar it is to that which I'd learned from Paula and the other instructors back in Nevada. Three variations are particularly noteworthy. First, there is no hand dealing at Gold City Casino—shufflers are used on all tables. Second, surveillance is much more invasive; not only cameras but also flat-screen computers and microphones monitor each table. Third, dealers may accept but not keep tips; any gratuities given to or played for us go directly into the "drop box" (i.e., to the casino's coffers).

Through informal conversation with Phumzile and other veteran casino staff (both black and white), I discover that these draconian elements of procedure are strange not just to me, as one socialized in the Nevada casino, but to them as well. They in fact represent a relatively recent—and radical—rupture with the way casino work had been organized during apartheid (that is, up until the mid-1990s). In the homeland casinos, dealers had shuffled cards by hand and were permitted to accept (and even hustle) tips, as Nevada dealers do today. Part II will examine in detail the historical process by which managers came to reconfigure dealing procedure in South Africa. The remainder of Part I draws upon my ethnographic experiences to illuminate how these changes have affected the informal culture of the workgroup and the experience of service labor.

GOLD CITY CASINO WORKERS:
SECURE THOUGH DISENGAGED

The tone and tenor of informal interactions among Gold City Casino dealers—as they take place not only in the employee cafeteria but also in various "off-site" spaces—contrast sharply with those I witnessed in the United States. Shop talk among Las Vegas dealers was characterized by concern over our job insecurity (hence the constant gossip about other job opportunities) and an active engagement with the labor process (especially the continual refinement of our tip-making tactics). But South African dealers, though they feel secure in their jobs, seem disengaged from the task of dealing.

South African dealers' job security derives from two main sources: the country's 1995 Labour Relations Act and the collective bargaining agreement in place between the casino and the dealers' union.[2] Both specify that workers may not be dismissed "without cause." Furthermore, the only two legitimate causes for dismissal are "serious misconduct" and "changes in operational requirements" (i.e., a severe business slowdown). In the event that the firm does invoke one of these causes to dismiss a dealer, additional policies regulate the process. Employees charged with misconduct, for example, must progress through "graduated disciplinary measures such as counseling and warnings"[3] of which dismissal is a step of last resort. And if a worker is laid off because of a business downturn, procedures are in place to preserve his or her employment with the company (such as transfer to another unit until business improves).

Despite such job security, Gold City Casino dealers evince no commitment to the company. In fact, their occupational culture is characterized by a cynical and often angry stance toward management. I watch, for example, as Solly, Phindi, and the other new dealers meet their coworkers. They are told in no uncertain terms that the twenty rand per hour they now earn is not as good as it first appears. First off, it is less than they deserve, since they must hand over to the casino any tips personally given them by gamblers. The company's policy of confiscating tips, in short, is collectively framed as a theft of what rightfully belongs to workers. In addition, new workers are encouraged to compare their nightly wages not to those of unemployed acquaintances outside the workplace, but to the vast sums of money exchanged nightly before their eyes. Consider my own exchange with the dealer Vely on a night when I was working with him on a roulette table:

> After paying out a large win, Vely spins the ball, and we wait while players place their bets. He says softly to me, "Do you see this man?" and nods toward a gambler at the end of the table. "I just gave him a 'pink' [a 1,000-rand chip]. For him it is nothing, but all I think is that it will take me two weeks of working like this to make just that one chip."
> "How does that make you feel?" I ask.
> "Crazy, man, like it's all just unfair."

Not only players' winnings but also the casino's are interpreted as evidence that dealers' wages are too low, as I recorded in my field notes:

> While dealing tonight, I notice that Tennyson on the table next to me has several players who are losing large sums. When our break comes, we walk back to the cafeteria together. Tennyson shakes his head and says, "Man, if I worked for a commission." I ask what he thinks about as he is collecting players' losing bets. He replies, "I can't stand it. I like paying out."
> "Why is that?" I ask.
> "Cuz if I take in fifty grand in a night, all I can think about is that is my whole year's salary I bring in for this company in a night, and I get none of it!"

"Backstage" facilities at Gold City Casino also compare unfavorably with the elegant amenities provided clients in the casino's "frontstage." While gamblers are provided free food and drink, the number of calories consumed by croupiers is closely monitored. All beverage dispensers and vending machines in the break room are equipped with scanners through which one's employee ID card must be swiped. In addition to a single meal, each employee is rationed but three additional food servings (such as a 6-ounce beverage or a candy bar) per 24 hours. Used to the limitless bounty of buffet food at Silver State Casino, I, too, expressed shock at this system. There is nothing worse than being exhausted at 5 A.M. on a graveyard shift only to discover that you have already exceeded your quota of dispensations from the coffee machine.[4]

The quality of the backstage amenities also felt unjust. While gamblers nibbled on toasted roast beef sandwiches, we scurried back to the cafeteria for an unappetizing daily meal. During my first lunch with my coworkers, I notice that I am the only one to help myself to the green salad. As I sit down, Bongiwe grabs my arm. "No, you mustn't eat the salad," she explains. "They are always finding worms in it. Best to stick to the meat. At least it is cooked." "Yeah," someone else chimes in. "Do you ever see [a manager] here eating with us? They order their meals from the restaurants rather than eat this slop." Our break room, meanwhile, is in a terrible state. Because we handle money constantly, our hands get quite grimy. After I dump my salad in the trash, I venture into the restroom to wash my hands, only to find the soap dispenser empty. During my nine months in the pit, it is not once refilled. The old Nescafe machine leaks constantly, sending a stream of milky coffee across the break room floor. This tends to attract cockroaches and other vermin. Workers complain about these conditions to the tables department head, who pledges to fix the coffee machine and upgrade the cafeteria food. During my fieldwork, however, no such improvements are made.

The end result of these numerous slights is a subdued, often acerbic, atmosphere behind the scenes at Gold City Casino. This was striking to me, having just arrived from Nevada, where employee break rooms are interactive spaces saturated with tip-talk—stories about your nightly toke intake as well as dreams of finding that "buck-seventy-five job." As a consequence, their low wages and job insecurity are pushed out of their immediate mental horizon. In contrast with such hubbub, the Gold City Casino break room feels eerily silent. Male dealers sit silently in a back corner, playing chess or catching a quick nap, while female dealers sit at a long table in the front, composing text messages on their cell phones or reapplying their makeup. Secure though disengaged, they experience relief breaks as but brief respites from onerous and unsatisfying work conditions.

THE CASINO AS PANOPTICON

Silver State Casino is characterized by decentralized control. Pit bosses, not video cameras, monitor the bulk of the action. Surveillance at Gold City Casino operates in the exact opposite manner, insofar as control is highly centralized. The work of floor managers is deskilled, while the camera crew does the majority of the monitoring. In short, the panoptic potential of the casino is fully embraced in South Africa.

Floor Managers: Deskilled "Tokens"

As my first week in the pits passes, I discover a striking difference between Silver State Casino and Gold City Casino regarding the demographics, duties, and demeanors of floor managers. In Nevada, this stratum of management remains mainly white and male; at Gold City Casino, the demographics of pit bosses mirror those of dealers, as eighty percent are PDIs (though many are veteran black employees from the homelands, not new black workers from the townships). While Nevada pit bosses spend most of their time watching dealers, South African pit bosses mainly do data entry work. And while, in the final instance, Nevada pit bosses identify with the casino (e.g., by sweating the play of a high roller), at Gold City Casino they consistently voice feelings of distrust and even anger toward the firm.

I spent one week shadowing three different Gold City Casino pit bosses, and another week working as one myself. These managers, I found, do little monitoring of dealers' physical or interactive job performance. Instead, they spend the majority of their time "tracking" gamblers' wins and losses. Alongside each table sits a touch-screen computer that feeds into a central database known as "PitTrak." These screens are the main interface with which floor managers interact. The left side of each screen is divided into seven rectangles, corresponding to seats on a blackjack table. All gamblers at Gold City Casino are given a "guest identification card," and when a player sits down at a table, the inspector swipes this card through a scanner. At this point, the player's name and gambling history for the day appear in the corresponding rectangle.

Pit inspectors are now responsible for "capturing" four types of data. First, they record what the gambler "buys in for"—that is, the amount of cash initially exchanged for chips. Second, when a player's card is swiped, a timer on PitTrak begins recording the amount of time he or she spends gambling. The inspector must pause this timer if the player takes a bathroom break. Third, the inspector must record the first three bets placed by each gambler so that PitTrak can calculate his or her average wager. And fourth, when a player finishes gambling, the inspector must record the amount of money, if any, he or she takes from the table. If the player has won a particularly large amount of money, the inspector will "make him a story"—that is, move his record to a sub-screen, where it is temporarily stored for senior management to inspect. The player is now "closed out."

The PitTrak system was designed to ensure security on the casino floor by maximizing the amount of information available to corporate management on the wins and losses of particular tables, players, and dealers. Inspectors, however, experience PitTrak as an affront to their understanding of the purpose of their work: that of monitoring dealers to ensure adherence to the standards of the craft. Indeed, I tracked over the course of two evenings the amount of time inspectors spent recording player data versus supervising dealers and found the ratio to be approximately 85 to 15.

Inspectors express cynicism over the company's vast investments in this technology. The automation of supervisory work, they claim, has rendered them redundant. Consider a lament shared with me by Michael, an inspector at Gold City Casino:

> The company doesn't care about us. Their philosophy is, "If you are not happy, then go on and leave, we'll replace you." ["Why is it like this?"] The machines. Things are so technology-dependent now. They don't need us. This place could run itself.

The PitTrak system serves also as a source of satire, with floor managers joking at the start of each shift that it is now time to "turn the tables on."

The tables department manager—a white British expatriate—concurs privately that the inspectors' assessment of the situation is correct: he could run the department with about half of his current managerial staff. It is only the government's quotas regarding the number of managers that must be employed that keeps staffing at its current level. In fact, he (and other senior managers) regularly referred to both the overstaffing problem and the extensive use of technology in the pits as "an empowerment thing" or "a PDI thing" (typically said with a sigh and a shake of the head).

PDI inspectors, however, do not interpret the deskilling of their duties as a natural and inevitable response to new labor regulations. They experience it as an attempt by top casino managers—80 percent of whom are white[5]—to diminish their authority and autonomy. The placement of PDIs into floor management positions is labeled by all as a form of shadow play, a public presentation to the state of black empowerment that contradicts the lived experiences of inspectors. I even hear black floor managers refer to themselves as "tokens" on three separate occasions.

Perceived token status translates into a sense of estrangement from one's employer. Consider the following narrative offered me by a pit boss concerning the process whereby control of the casino was centralized:

> When this casino first opened, it was supposed to be so different for us [blacks]. There was to be true development. We listened to the speeches and the talk about empowerment, and we did believe. But when things got running, we ran up against the old guard, the old boys' network. It is the same clique of people in charge, and they view these black managers as a threat. They do not want us to have any freedom, to take any risks. It is a slave-master mentality. If you are to raise questions or think independent, they will talk about you, blacklist you.

Another telling incident takes place one evening while I am working as an inspector. I am entering data into a PitTrak machine when I am joined by Lucy, a black pit boss who has worked at Gold City Casino since its opening. Suddenly, the phone on the podium at the other side of the pit rings, and Lucy hurries over to answer it. I cannot hear what she says from where I am standing, but I see that she quickly hangs up before walking back over with a scowl on her face. "That is the third time tonight this has happened," she says. "When I am on the other side of the pit, the phone rings, but then they hang up when I answer. I know it is surveillance. They watch me on the camera and do that just to punish me. For what, I don't know!"

Even though PDI floor managers are secure in their jobs, they nonetheless feel powerless to effect meaningful change in the way their work is structured. They express their resignation by neither working too hard nor taking their duties too seriously. Nearly all claim to prefer dealing over inspecting because of the extreme boredom associated with the latter task; the fact that inspectors earns three times what dealers make is the main factor keeping them in their current spots. I was particularly impressed by how the inspectors I shadowed have mastered a variety of shortcuts for doing data entry. These tactics free them—somewhat— from the hated PitTrak screens:

> "Inspecting is easy, man," an inspector tells me. "You don't have to enter everything right away, just fudge it at the end of the hour.
> "So what do you do then?" I ask.
> "Whatever you want—look around, chat to the pit boss. Mainly relax."

The Camera Crew

If floor managers at Gold City Casino don't keep an eye on dealers, who does? The answer is the video surveillance department, whose cameras and microphones constitute the main instruments of discipline in the pits. The contrast with Silver State Casino could not be more stark: here surveillance is centralized, focusing on workers rather than clients.

It is a truism that all organizations must tolerate some amount of "slippage" between official job requirements and the actual performance of work tasks—or so I thought before starting work at Gold City Casino, where I am immediately overwhelmed by how intent management seems upon ensuring strict adherence to procedure. In particular, I have a difficult time adjusting to the casino's "clean hands" policy. A Nevada dealer shows clean hands (claps and displays them palms-up) upon entering and leaving the pit (to prove they are transferring nothing onto or off of the table). At Gold City Casino, however, croupiers must show clean hands before and after they touch a chip, card, or themselves each and every time. To deal a single round of blackjack entails clapping one's hands five, ten, fifteen, or more times! Naturally, this slows the game down considerably; even though an experienced dealer can show clean hands in around a quarter of a second, the process still adds two to six seconds to each hand.

Like the no-tipping policy, the clean-hands rule is of recent origin. In the homeland casinos during apartheid, the more lax Nevada standards were the norm. But when drafting procedures for the new Gold City Casino, Empowerment Inc. executives made the conscious decision to tighten control. This involved not only more stringent rules, but also an intensification and centralization of the powers of surveillance. For instance, the number of surveillance cameras per table was doubled, and microphones were installed on each table so that dealers could be both seen and heard. Upon learning of these changes, it became clear to me that to understand the Gold City Casino as a service regime would necessitate gaining entrée to the camera room. I would have to observe the observers at work.

At first, the Gold City Casino general manager was reluctant to let me go this far backstage. After several weeks of pestering, however, I manage to persuade him to let me interview Andre, the head of surveillance. A white Afrikaner who spent twelve years with the South African Police Service before joining Gold City Casino, Andre is a serious-looking man. After a few minutes of conversation, though, he warms up and offers to give me a tour of his department. He escorts me through a set of metal doors, up a flight of stairs, and into the "camera room," where dozens of surveillance officers each watch six monitors simultaneously. As Andre explains what exactly his "men" (as he calls them, though about a quarter are women) do, I see even more clearly now how important security is to the house.

Surveillance officers' nightly routine consists of three general tasks. First, they constantly scan their monitors in search of a "live detection": a real-time observation of a croupier breaking procedure. In practice, the only procedure breaches that get noted are those related to security; never would an officer "detect" a worker dealing too slowly or not providing service to players. To motivate his "cameramen," Andre organizes for them what he calls a "game." Points are scored for each live detection and weighted by the severity of the sanction the offending worker receives. (A croupier who forgets to show clean hands but receives no punishment would generate one point; a croupier who incorrectly pays a losing bet and is fired would produce the highest possible score.) Andre rewards the weekly high scorer with a free dinner at one of the casino's restaurants. Besides keeping his cameramen vigilant, the game forces them to, in Andre's words, "watch each other like hawks."[6]

Surveillance officers also perform "audits" of workers who have attracted the suspicion of upper management. It may be the case that a dealer breaks procedure only irregularly. ("A croupier who repeatedly makes the same mistake may just be improperly trained," Andre explains, "but if they break procedure only at some times but not others, why is that? What's going on there?") Management may suspect an improper relationship between a dealer and player (as, for instance, when a gambler ceases playing when the dealer goes on break but begins again when the dealer returns). Or a particular dealer may have simply invoked a "bad feeling" in the gut of a supervisor. A surveillance officer will be assigned to watch the dealer's every move for the night. "Given enough rope," Andre reasons, "a crooked worker will always hang themselves."

The final duty of surveillance officers is the completion of "target reports." In this task, an officer monitors a randomly chosen dealer for a full hour. During this time, the officer fills out a form listing twenty different aspects of procedure. Next to each of these evaluation points are boxes marked satisfactory or unsatisfactory, as well as a space for written comments. Two of the evaluations deal with service (e.g., "Was the dealer courteous to players?"), but the remaining eighteen all focus on security-related aspects of procedure (e.g., "Did the dealer show clean hands at all appropriate times?" "Did the dealer announce all large payouts to the supervisor?").

In sum, at Gold City Casino responsibility for surveilling dealers (most of whom are black/PDI) resides with the (primarily white) surveillance team, not (black/PDI) floor inspectors. And while electronic surveillance in Nevada follows a consumer-focused logic (i.e., the intensity of monitoring is a function of the size of a gambler's wager), at Gold City Casino it is worker-focused. Surveillance officers constantly scan and randomly check dealers' routine job performance, regardless of the size of the action on the table. Despite their distance from the pits, these surveillance officers are the real floor managers, themselves trained and disciplined to maximize security.

A Note on Work and Authority

The centralization and intensification of casino control betray a concern—indeed, an obsession—on the part of executives with maximizing security at the expense of speed and service. Dealing, now deskilled, becomes a purely physical task, workers replaceable parts monitored mainly for evidence of larceny. Off the casino floor, in various venues, workers and floor managers refute this definition of their labor. The success of the business, they argue, should depend upon their service skills and professional acumen. As a young dealer informed the tables department manager at a staff feedback meeting I attended, "We are treated as second-class people." While such sentiments demonstrate that workers do not accept the legitimacy of managerial authority, in the pits themselves, its efficacy is beyond doubt.

The casino's camera crew cannot, of course, monitor every croupier constantly. The house nonetheless employs extreme means to convince workers that it can. Consider the nightly ritual by which the above-discussed target reports were delivered to dealers. At the end of each shift, a runner drops off in the main pit a stack of about fifteen reports. Pit bosses then announce which workers had been targeted that evening and hand them their reports (copies have already been placed in workers' permanent files). The seriousness with which the reports are received cannot be overstated. As they leave their tables, dealers congregate at the podium and shuffle through the reports, those in back calling out "Let me see!" "Am I in there?" Accustomed as I was to Silver State Casino's benign neglect of grind play, I asked one evening, "What's the big deal? They can't really be watching us all the time." Shocked at my ignorance, a fellow dealer retorted, "No, man. The cameras are there and they do watch us. I just last night got a target report, you see?"

Once I did the math, I realized my coworkers were not being overly paranoid. Each month, approximately 1,200 target reports are completed at Gold City Casino—about forty per day, or fourteen per shift. The 100 or so dealers working each shift thus have about a one in seven chance of receiving a target report on any given day.

Both the extent of routine surveillance—as illustrated by the sheer number of target reports—and the consequentiality of procedure infractions serve to crystallize the casino's panoptic power. As a croupier, I am included in the employee database from which names are selected for target reports. Mine are generally awful. My facility at handling chips receives low marks, as does my general "game security." And even after several months of work, I still forget to show clean hands as often as is required! Now I—a visiting student intern—am considered trustworthy by top casino managers, so my "failing" reports precipitate laughter rather than reprimands. Gold City Casino's croupiers, however, labor under a zero-tolerance security policy. Though punishments vary according to the circumstances of the offense (a new dealer who forgets to show clean hands will likely receive a verbal warning), the company reserves the right to initiate termination proceedings for any infraction that results in a financial loss (e.g., an accidental mispayment of a losing bet). Typical of workers' orientation to this regime of security is a fellow dealer's advice to me:

> Matlhora and I have been playing a game of chess during our breaks. As I wait for him to make a move, I complain about the poor marks I have been receiving on my target reports.
>
> "The key to being a good dealer," he tells me, "is following procedure."
>
> "What do you mean by that?" I press him. "To follow procedure?"
>
> "Making sure all your payouts are correct, that you show clean hands all the time."
>
> "Well, don't they ever get on us to go faster? To speed up?"

"Nah," Matlhora responds, shaking his head, "not really. Just worry about your procedure, that's all."

At Silver State Casino, my "game" had been acknowledged to be among the best in the house. This had been a great source of pride to me. At the time, I even imagined myself to possess some innate ability, a natural dexterity well suited to the craft. At Gold City Casino, however, my ego is laid low. Though I practice constantly, I am unable to meet my new employer's expectations—or match the skill level of my coworkers. Here, on the dusty outskirts of Johannesburg, in a garish gambling palace surrounded by impoverished townships, are dealers whose technical mastery of their craft matches—if not exceeds—that of those on the famed Las Vegas Strip.

As one final illustration of both the casino's quest for security and the reactions it engenders, we can compare two common types of worker infractions: procedure breaches versus unexcused absences from work. At Silver State Casino, there is no question that the former were more common. Nevada croupiers regularly bend the house rules to make tips, but it is rare that one would miss or show up late for a shift. In South Africa, the opposite is true. In fact, Gold City Casino management officially labeled every worker infraction as either an issue of "poor work attendance" (PWA) or of "poor work performance" (PWP). The former captured unexcused tardiness or absence from work, the latter a breach of dealing procedure. According to the shift manager in charge of maintaining the file on dealer "disciplinaries," PWAs outnumber PWPs at Gold City Casino by a ratio of nine to one. Estrangement from work, in sum, is expressed by not showing up on time, if at all; once on the floor, dealers display near total adherence to procedure, especially as it relates to security.

But what about speed and service? How are they performed? More generally, how do dealers manage the action and interactions on the tables? What sort of games do they play? To answer these questions, we delve even deeper into my participant observation fieldwork.

FOUR Gold City Casino

Employees of the Gold City Casino in Johannesburg experience despotic control over their service labor. Management maximizes surveillance, deskills dealing, and prohibits tipping, all in an effort to maximize security. Such policies in turn eliminate all incentives for workers to maximize their speed or provide service—or indeed, to appear agentive in any way. Why provide "emotional capital" or give strategy advice when such offerings can only invoke suspicion from management and anger from gamblers? As a consequence, the experience of dealing in South Africa is not an entrepreneurial game of making tips, but an effacement game of erasing the self.

SPEED AND SERVICE

Nevada croupiers deal quickly to maximize tipping opportunities. Because South African dealers earn only a flat hourly wage, they express no interest in systematically increasing their speed. Nor does the house pressure them to increase the pace at which they work. (On the contrary, managers worry that their investments in technology have so sped up the games that gamblers lose their money too quickly and leave the casino believing they have been cheated!) Target reports, as I explained in the previous chapter, focus on security, not speed. Floor managers, meanwhile, allow workers to set their own pace. They even assist dealers in disciplining overly enthusiastic greenhorns, as my early dealing experience attests:

> I report at 11 P.M. for my first graveyard shift and am sent to deal on a roulette table. The action is heavy, and I start off at full speed, picking up and stacking chips as quickly as I can. The dealer at the next table turns and says, "Hey, man, slow down, this is the graveyard." I start to laugh, but then realize the inspector is standing right behind us, and worry that he will not be pleased with my colleague's attempt to correct my overzealous attitude. The inspector merely chuckles, however, and shakes his head in my direction, essentially affirming the dealer's acknowledgement of my faux pas.

Gamblers, in contrast, do sometimes instruct dealers to speed up play. "C'mon, what are you waiting for? Deal, man," a player would call out to a croupier who had ceased dealing to chat with the inspector. Such requests are typically honored for a hand or two, but the ability of gamblers to discipline workers regarding speed is, for the most part, limited.

The moderate pace at which workers deal comes into high relief at the end of each shift. "Last five hands," the inspector announces to each table, after which the table is temporarily closed and the dealers sent to "see the man" (i.e., see the manager in charge of logging the dealers off shift). The croupiers' comportment now changes completely, for the quicker these final five hands are dealt, the sooner they can go home. Cards fly from their hands, while chips are cut out and collected in the blink of an eye. And when the final hand is finished, players are unceremoniously informed that "this table is closed," while requests for "one more game" are ignored. All that remains is to "sort the cards," that is, take the five jumbled decks out of the shuffling machine and sort them into their original five decks. (Even the order in which the suits in each deck are to be reassembled is preordained: hearts, clubs, diamonds, spades—remembered with the bittersweet acronym "happy croupiers don't swear.") The sorted decks are then fanned out on the table to "prove" to the cameras that no cards have been taken from or added to the table. After six months of doing this task I was still painfully slow at sorting the cards, relative to my fellow dealers. The inspector, who all night long had allowed me to deal at my own pace, would breathe down my neck: "Any day now. What's wrong with you from the U.S.A.? C'mon, c'mon, I need to go home." (Thankfully, other dealers would take pity and help me with the sorting and spreading of the cards.)

While Gold City Casino croupiers are not forced to work at a break-neck pace, they nevertheless deal at a speed that is by no means dilatory. Unafraid that management will interpret speedy dealing as evidence that they are capable of permanently intensifying their effort, South African croupiers deal relatively quickly, if only because to work any slower causes time to drag. When faced with gamblers who "know what they are doing" (i.e., not taking too long with their decisions), time "flies by" and the next break arrives before they know it. "It is better to be busy and go a little fast," a fellow dealer tells me. "You have more action and thinking. Not so boring." The opposite case is the dreaded "dead table," on which no one is playing and the dealer stands alone, staring off into space, with nothing to occupy or distract him or her. And because dealers are most likely to find themselves on a dead table during the graveyard shift, the excruciating boredom is only exacerbated by intense fatigue. Peter, a croupier at Gold City Casino, describes how to make it through such an ordeal:

> You just stand there and lean against the table and try not to go to sleep. But it's hard because all you can do is stare at the wall. You feel like you are going crazy.

As a research strategy and a means of initiating conversation, I often ask my fellow dealers whom they root for—players or the casino—when on the tables. While responses vary, many suggest a logic oriented toward a desire to maintain a "good flow" of work. For instance, Nontozi, a twenty-six-year-old croupier with four years of experience, informed me:

> This place is full of people who bother you. I want my game to go smooth, but they wait till you have just started the deal and then throw down a 100-rand chip. So you have to stop and call the inspector over and just stand there. Oh, these people, it is good to take their money, just to see the look on their faces.

Casino management, so focused upon security, also neglects to systematically monitor customer service. Corporate rhetoric refers to gamblers as the casino's "guests," yet management enforces no directives to provide them emotional labor. Croupiers in turn exert scarcely any effort to chat or converse with gamblers. Vikki, a twenty-four-year-old woman from a nearby township who has worked at the casino for three years, explains why she prefers dealing roulette over blackjack:

> I hate blackjack, because you just stand there with the gamblers all around you, and they can see you and talk to you. Roulette is better. If they try to talk to you, you can just turn around and move over to the chips and act like you are busy and can't hear them.

The larger workspace on the roulette table renders it preferable for Vikki because it provides her some degree of movement to carve out a space of noninteraction with clients, albeit brief.

The casino's non-tipping policy further eliminates any incentive to socialize with gamblers. As with the intensification of electronic surveillance, the decision by Empowerment Inc. executives to confiscate tips broke with what had been standard practice in the homeland casinos. Many longtime South African gamblers are in fact unaware of the policy, believing that their tips still go to the dealers. South African croupiers thus discourage gamblers from offering them. They emphasize that gratuities are not unappreciated, but that such interpersonal gifts should not go into the company's coffers:

> During a break, Cecelia (a young Afrikaans woman) asks me about what it is like to deal in a Nevada casino. I tell her about the tipping system, and how dealers are always trying to hustle tips from

players. She thinks for a few seconds, then says, "Here, that is the worst, when they try to tip you. I just tell them straight off to keep it. Go and buy your wife some chocolates. Cuz if you give it to me, it is just a waste for both of us."

Workers' efforts to educate gamblers concerning the true fate of tips seem to have succeeded. While tips collected by dealers in South Africa's homeland casinos represented about 5 percent of the overall casino win, at Gold City Casino, the figure is about one-twentieth of that amount, with tips equal to just 0.23 percent of the casino win. Wise gamblers, furthermore, stop novice players from tipping, in the process expressing solidarity with workers over the inequity of the new tipping policy. Nor was it uncommon for a player to tell a dealer: "If I win the big jackpot tonight, don't worry. I'll meet you down the street at the petrol [gas] station." The implication is that the worker would be handed a tip after work, in a place where management could not reclaim it. Many of my coworkers in fact claimed to have taken part in at least one such furtive rendezvous.

TACTICS OF AN EFFACEMENT GAME

While not required to perform service on the tables, croupiers must and do interact with players during the course of the games. Provided such communication is not perceived to be a form of collaborative cheating, this interactive space is an autonomous one. Drawing upon my six months of dealing, as well as video and audio recordings of approximately 100 games dealt by other workers that I was granted permission to view and transcribe, I describe the tactics deployed by Gold City Casino dealers to manage interactions with gamblers.

At Nevada's Silver State Casino, dealers play a work game oriented to the formal goal of making "tokes." They influence and claim credit for game outcomes, thereby inducing a sense of indebtedness in players, even at the risk of provoking anger when players lose their bets. They are, in short, active game participants. My socialization into this occupational subculture left me ill-prepared for dealing at Gold City Casino.

Strategies for claiming agency that had worked so well in Nevada were now entirely inappropriate. My own experience of relearning my craft in South Africa—of suppressing my entrepreneurial "instincts" and learning new strategies of impression management—though frequently funny and sometimes stressful, represents a unique opportunity to highlight cross-national differences in how service work is organized.

Service work games are played in relation to clients, so it is important to consider differences in the beliefs and abilities of gamblers in the United States versus South Africa. In Nevada, "the book" (basic strategy) occupies a central, even sacred, place in the culture of the casino. Of course, there are exceptions; when in the midst of a prolonged losing streak, even the most rational of gamblers may appeal to (or curse out) their deity of choice. In general, though, "the book" functions as the final mediator of decisions and disputes on the table. The typical South African blackjack player, in contrast, exhibits neither knowledge of nor faith in basic strategy.[1] The gambler does not treat the game as a personal contest with the dealer, in which the odds can be maximized through the mastery of statistically proven decision rules, but rather acts as if the table were a unitary entity and gambling a collective enterprise. Players behave, in short, as though all gamblers can win every time, provided they make the correct combination of decisions during the determinative phase of the game.[2]

To illustrate, I will discuss two striking manifestations of this belief. The first involves the need to retrace game outcomes. After the conclusion of each hand, players watch closely the first few cards to come out of the shuffling machine at the start of the next; they do so to discern what would have happened had certain players made different decisions during the previous hand. While this is a classic gambler's fallacy, at Gold City Casino it could disconfirm or, as in the example below, confirm the correctness of a player's decision:

> Four men are playing blackjack. The dealer has a jack showing. The first three players have eighteen or higher and do not take any cards. The last player to go (commonly referred to as "third base") holds a sixteen and is unsure what to do. "Should I hit this or surrender?" he asks aloud, but before anyone can respond, he gives the signal to surrender.

The dealer then draws a three and a four, arriving at seventeen, so that the three remaining players win.

"You see?" third base says, "I'm glad I surrendered. It's better."

But another player disagrees. He says, "Let's see." All then watch as the dealer deals out the first card of the next hand. It is a six (which, if third base had not surrendered and instead taken the dealer's three to give himself a nineteen and the dealer then an initial fourteen, would have given the dealer a final tally of twenty instead of seventeen).

Third base is now doubly excited: "Twenty! I'm glad I surrendered." The other players now nod in agreement.

Mastering this art of retracing post hoc the outcomes of decisions not made is one of the biggest transitions I had to make while relearning to deal.

Second, it is believed that the collective fate of the table is linked to the number of open "boxes" on the game (i.e., the number of playing spaces occupied by bets). When a table is "hot" (players are winning), the number of open boxes must remain constant. Conversely, players must open or close boxes to fix a cold table. I discover this custom the first time I play blackjack in South Africa:

Sitting down at a blackjack table with only one other player—a white man in his forties—I set down a 50-rand chip on an empty box and await my cards. The man looks at me with a strange expression on his face, something between bewilderment and disgust. "Can't you see there's only one box open?" he says, obviously irritated.

Having no clue what he means, I shrug and grin apologetically, then turn back to the dealer, an African woman who is smirking at my ignorance—feigned or real, she cannot seem to tell. The man plays his bet in a huff and stares at me angrily as I play my hand. After winning my first wager, I lose three in a row and get up to leave.

"You see? You see?" he shouts with satisfaction as I walk off.

This man had expected me to "play behind him," the norm when first sitting down at a blackjack table in South Africa. This entails placing your bet in a current player's betting box, preserving the number of open boxes but ceding to a stranger all decisions concerning your wager! As one accustomed to the "individualistic" Nevada scene, I found this bewildering.[3]

For the croupier, retracing alternate game outcomes and preserving the number of open boxes are not simply superstitions; they are conditions under which interactive currencies of blame and credit are created. Most important is the implication that the standards for evaluating individual decisions are fuzzy and unsystematic (the antithesis, that is, of "the book"). For instance, when a player holds a twelve and the dealer's up-card is a seven, basic strategy dictates to hit the hand. In Nevada, if a player does so, receives a ten, and busts, other players typically offer condolence ("Good play, you had to do it," or "That's why they call it gambling"). They then continue with their own hands, the loser's play forgotten. At Gold City Casino, the first time I compliment a player on making the correct decision despite having busted, he responds: "What are you talking about? Can't you see I lost?" Here the correctness of a play becomes apparent only *after* the hand is finished. If, in the situation just described, the dealer should subsequently draw a four and a nine (for a total of twenty instead of the seventeen the dealer would have tallied had the player in question not hit his twelve), another player who was dealt an eighteen may say, "What is wrong with you? The last player to go must always stay put when the dealer has a seven!" "No, no," the offending player may counter, "The dealer will always draw a queen after hitting a ten. Something is wrong with [the dealer]." (This example is drawn verbatim from my fieldnotes.)

The principles governing gamblers' decision making at Gold City Casino are unsystematic and inconsistent. As a result, a space of struggle opens naturally during the course of a hand over the assignment of blame and credit. In Nevada, such indeterminacy would have been a valuable asset to dealers, an opportunity to present themselves as active agents on the tables. In contrast, in South Africa, a dealer's interests in allocating responsibility derive from diametrically opposed incentives, resources, and constraints (i.e., no tips, diminished skills, and intense surveillance). Dealers must and do manage interactions so as to above all else absolve themselves of responsibility for outcomes good or bad; such "self-erasure" is the primary interactive strategy utilized by croupiers, the component tactics of which I will now describe.

A HOT TABLE: DENYING CREDIT

When a Nevada blackjack table is hot, it is in a dealer's interests to take credit for players' wins. In South Africa, dealers do the opposite: they deny—and often actively deconstruct—their own agency, seeking to become invisible to both players and the house. This is not surprising, given that assisting players offers no material rewards (tips), draws unwanted attention from the surveillance cameras, and risks raising players' ire if assistance goes awry. Nonetheless, I had to experience firsthand the combined effects of these "agentive disincentives" before I could snap out of the entrepreneurial mind-set I had honed in the pits of Silver State Casino:

> During my first few nights behind the tables, I find that I am constantly tempted not only to advise players on strategy, but also to falsely take credit for positive outcomes. Unable to resist, I soon learn the pitfalls of this approach when two Afrikaner men sit down at my table and pick up on my accent.
>
> "Uh-oh, he is from Las Vegas and knows all the secrets. We are screwed now," one says.
>
> I play along, moving easily into a soft hustle, "Oh yes, I know all the tricks, but don't worry, I'll take care of you gentlemen." After a couple of uneventful hands, I deal each of them a fifteen and myself a queen as the up-card.
>
> While the smart gambler here surrenders, both men are adamant that to do so would be "sissy"; they will play it out. "Well, then," I say, drawing upon my knowledge of basic strategy, "you'd better hit the fifteens, cuz they won't hold up against this queen." But the players are suspicious, because, they tell me, I have just dealt myself a queen, and "pictures always follow each other." But they give in and call for hits. Both cards are fives, giving them each a score of twenty.
>
> I play this up—"See what I can do for you?"—while they nod their heads in agreement, amazed at the American croupier who can seemingly work magic. Their astonishment is short-lived, however, as I proceed, much to my own dismay, to pull an ace for myself. In combination with my queen, I now have twenty-one.
>
> As I hurriedly collect their bets, the men are furious. They storm off, but not before informing me: "You are disgusting. I can't even look at you."

In Nevada, such a display of anger on the part of gamblers would have been experienced as unpleasant, but it would have been quickly rekeyed. An intense emotional display, even an angry one, is good for a Nevada dealer; it symbolizes your agency and testifies to your capacity to win a few hands for a George, thereby invoking blame's opposite: gratitude. But at Gold City Casino, what's the point of claiming agency? Even if these two players had won their hands and offered me a tip, I would not have been permitted to keep it. I discuss this episode after work with Phumzile, who wholeheartedly agrees with my assessment. She then offers the following meta-advice concerning the pitfalls of aiding players:

> Never tell the gambler what to do! Even if it is a beautiful woman and she wants to hit a nineteen, and you want to say to her, "No, you must stand!" ["Why?"] What if she stands and the next card to come out is a two? Now her boyfriend is coming to the table, and he is angry and blaming you for giving her the bad advice, and they are calling the pit boss over and saying they wanted the two! It's not worth it.

Claiming credit for players' wins, in short, offers no benefit; it only increases the chances that your actions will invoke displays of anger from players.

To become a croupier in South Africa is to master a series of self-presentational skills that deny your own agency. Most fundamentally, it entails mustering the willpower to refuse any invitations to take credit for gamblers' wins. If a player asks you for advice on whether or not to take another card, a fellow dealer explained to me, it is best to "tell them to ask the table [i.e., other gamblers] what to do. Then you cover yourself from taking the heat." Occasionally, instead of simply saying, "Hit me," a player will ask the dealer directly for the exact card needed. A player with fifteen will shout: "Give me that six!" Or, concerned about seeming too greedy, the player may ask for slightly less than he or she needs: "Just a four or five, that's all." Some even utilize reverse psychology by demanding a bust card—now the player with fifteen yells: "Make it a ten!" Though the dealer may smile at the player's humor, he or she must give no indication of having attempted to act upon such requests.

Denying credit is difficult, however, when you do deliver the requested card and the player thanks you personally. You must now somehow convey that gratitude is unwarranted because the outcome, however positive, was beyond your control:

> Suzanne is dealing to a table full of gamblers. Her up-card is an
> eight, while everyone on the table has at least an eighteen. She pulls
> a nine, giving herself seventeen, and everyone wins. A gambler
> exclaims: "That was a brilliant result! Thank you, Suzanne."
> Suzanne says nothing, however. She merely chuckles and shakes
> her head as she cuts out players' winnings.

Unlike her foolish American colleague in the previous anecdote, Suzanne declines the invitation to appear agentive. In response to a player's offering of gratitude, she shakes her head and laughs, not only refusing credit but emphasizing the absurdity of the idea that she could be responsible for the game's outcome.

The dealer must not only deny his or her own agency but also allow players to take credit for wins. This can entail simply endorsing a player's own endorsement of his or her decision:

> The gambler on third base has just opted not to hit his sixteen against
> the dealer's nine (a bad move according to the decision rules of basic
> strategy). The dealer draws a seven and a ten, busting.
> "You see? I saved the table," says the gambler.
> "Yeah. Sure. Well done," replies the dealer.

When the table is hot—with the dealer busting and delivering black-jacks—struggles often ensue among players to claim credit. While often entertaining, these struggles are irrelevant to the South African croupier, as long as they deflect attention away from the dealer. Alternately, a hot table may induce among players a feeling of bonhomie, a sense that they are collectively making the correct combination of decisions. After each hand, gamblers compliment one another's play and exclaim, "We got it that time!" For the dealer, such situations are ideal.

By resisting invitations to take credit for a hot table, dealers preemptively strike down any suspicions that they are influencing game outcomes. Actively denying one's agency is equally important when dealing at the opposite, and much more common, table "temperature."

A COLD TABLE: DISPLACING BLAME

Nevada dealers use a classificatory schema to divide the otherwise amorphous mass of casino patrons into two groups: Georges and stiffs. At Gold City Casino, the relevant principle of classification is not between types of players but between types of tables. The first thing a dealer must discern upon stepping up to a table is whether it is hot or not. A hot table, as we just witnessed, is fine as far as gamblers are concerned (though the problem arises that managers may be suspicious that the dealer is assisting players). On a cold table, croupiers are fine in the eyes of management, though they are now easy targets for abusive outbursts from losing gamblers. And while Nevada dealers' game of making tips provides them a cognitive frame through which to reinterpret anger—forcing an "asshole stiff" off your table becomes a personal challenge and a badge of honor in the break room—at Gold City Casino, an irate gambler represents merely an occupational hazard to be assiduously avoided or, failing that, simply endured.

When a table goes cold—for example, the dealer repeatedly draws twenties and twenty-ones while players seem to repeatedly bust—something has gone awry, and blame must be assigned. While croupiers are an obvious target, they may not be held culpable initially. Should the dealer pull a blackjack after a string of players' wins, the table may view it as a temporary aberration, and players' spirits will remain high. And if a hand involves a highly contentious decision, blame may be assigned to the gambler who made it. Consider the following example:

> There are five players on the table. The dealer's up-card is an eight.
> A gambler who goes by the name of Jay has a four and a two, for an
> initial total of six. He hits, asking, "A three, please." He receives a
> seven, giving him thirteen. "Another three, please." Down comes a ten,
> busting Jay.
>
> Another player is very angry and points at Jay's hand. "See! Bust!"
> [If Jay had stayed on his nine, that is, the dealer would have gone eight,
> seven, ten, busting herself.]
>
> While it is ludicrous to imply that he or any player should ever stay
> on a six, Jay nonetheless accepts the blame. "Sorry! I had to do that," he
> says.

As players' losses mount, however, and the table temperature shifts from hot or lukewarm to downright frigid, tensions mount and players become less willing to accept blame. They themselves now put into play strategies to ensure they are not held responsible for bad outcomes. For instance, when confronting a tough decision, a player may ask the table at large for guidance:

> The dealer's up-card is a three. The first player to go holds a twelve. He announces to the other players: "I don't know what to do. Talk to me."
> "Up to you," another player responds.
> But the original player persists, "Well, do you think there's a little one coming?"
> "Hard to say, do whatever you think."

By requesting assistance from fellow players not once but twice, he obtains permission to make the choice as he sees fit. This act can be seen as writing an insurance policy in case his choice turns out incorrect. It is known in the lingo of Gold City Casino as "covering your ass."

A player may also blame other gamblers for their poor decisions:

> The dealer's up-card is a four. Every player on the table has been dealt a hand totaling somewhere between fourteen and seventeen. No one takes an additional card. The dealer now draws a six and a ten, giving herself twenty. An old man at third base who had been dealt a seventeen is very angry at the table, for he believes that "someone must always draw somewhere" [i.e., at least one player on the table must take a hit, otherwise the dealer will draw a good hand]. He elaborates, pointing at each player's hand one by one, "Sixteen! Fourteen! Fifteen! Plenty of places to draw!"

From the croupier's point of view, such hands are unproblematic insofar as they entail a circulation of blame among gamblers. Yet sooner or later, the moment arrives when croupiers themselves are pulled into the attribution contests. When this occurs, dealers deploy several strategies for parrying players' attempts to blame them for their losses. These tactics form the backbone of South African croupiers' work game, and though they require great skill, they succeed only insofar as they symbolically erase the croupier's own agency on the tables.

A common defense against a player's accusation that you have affected a game outcome is to displace blame onto the shuffling machines. Gareth, a twenty-five-year-old Afrikaans dealer, explains why and how he does so:

> You see, Jeff, dealing is a lose-lose situation. When a gambler wins, he takes the credit for it. He made a brilliant play. But when they lose, it's your fault. Give me a picture [i.e., a ten-valued card], they say. You give them a six, and they get pissed. Look, I say. Here's the [shuffling] machine. Here's the card, here's my hand. I simply bring the card out of the machine and to you. What can I do, man?

If the stakes are not high, and the player's losing streak is not an extended one, blaming the shuffler is an excellent tactic. It is not uncommon for a player to collude in attributing responsibility to them, even:

> Mr. Fan, an elderly Chinese gentleman and a casino regular, has lost several hands in a row at blackjack. He points and yells at the shuffling machine, "Come on you, give a blackjack!" The dealer, Byron, plays along. "Yeah, yeah, you tell it!" The inspector, too, gets into the act, pushing to the point of anthropomorphization the attribution of agency to the shuffler: "It knows you Mr. Fan, and it's out to get you!" Mr. Fan now grabs a small sign on the table and places it between him and the shuffler. Scrunching down in his chair, he exclaims, "Maybe now it can't see me!"

I quickly learn the value of the shuffler to croupiers. Even the fact that they frequently malfunction can be used to deflect attribution attempts:

> I am dealing on a high-stakes blackjack table. There is only one player, a middle-aged man in an expensive Italian suit, with his fancily clad girlfriend sitting beside him. He is a terrible player, surrendering when he should hit, hitting when he should surrender, and he blows through 10,000 rand in about twenty minutes. He does not say a word and neither do I, because I can sense his anger building, and I am nervous he will blow up and lash out at me. To make things worse, the shuffling machine jams after practically every hand. As a small red light blinks on the top of the machine, I must call over the inspector to assist with opening and unjamming it. He

whispers to me: "This one is fucked. They keep telling us they'll replace it. Just do your best with it."

Upon turning back to the gambler, I say, "I'm sorry sir, this machine seems to be acting up. We're working on a replacement."

To my immense relief, he responds, "Well, now we know why I'm losing."

I naturally nod my head in agreement and cast the shuffler a disdainful glance. It, and not his terrible strategy or my actions, is the true culprit.

Responsibility may also be redirected back onto players. For instance, the croupier can draw attention to a problematic decision made by one of them during the course of the game. Consider my attempt to inoculate myself from blame:

I am dealing to a table packed full of players. The player at third base decides to stay on his "soft seventeen" when I have a seven showing [a soft hand is one composed of an ace and a number—because an ace counts as either eleven or one, it is often a good idea to hit a soft hand; this is one such situation]. The table utters a collective groan, dismayed that this player is not going to draw another card. Before moving on to my own hand, I double-check with this gambler: "No card, sir, are you sure?" He repeats his request to stay, and I proceed to hit my own hand with a four and then a ten. Twenty-one for me. As I collect the bets, I shake my head and roll my eyes at third base. The other players collude with my assessment, casting him evil glances and muttering obscenities his way.

Blame preemption is also accomplished by playing upon gamblers' superstition concerning the optimal number of open boxes. If the dealer wins several hands in a row, he or she may ask the table before initiating the next game, "Leaving three boxes open? You sure?" If players respond in the affirmative, they implicitly agree to accept at least some responsibility for the outcome of the upcoming hand.

Essential to the ability to deflect blame is the capacity to quickly calculate at the conclusion of a hand "what would've happened" had different decisions been made. This allows the dealer to take the initiative in assigning fault for players' losses:

The dealer's up-card is a two. The first three gamblers stay put with twenties. The player at third base has a thirteen. He hits and takes a three. "No more!" he says.

The dealer then hits her two with ten, four, five. "Twenty-one."

"Aayyyy," several players moan.

The dealer now points to the hand that hit and says simply, "nineteen" [i.e., if the player hadn't hit the thirteen, the dealer would have gone two, three, ten, four, for a total of nineteen, not twenty-one].

One of the players who had twenty exclaims, "Nineteen! I would've won!"

The guy who drew a card realizes his mistake and apologizes, "Oh, man, everybody was winning. Sorry."

Such skill at calculating alternate outcomes comes with practice, and it constitutes a decisive edge for dealers in controlling the distribution of blame and credit.

A time invariably arrives, however, when blame can no longer be deferred or deflected and dealers must, in their own words, "take the shit." These are moments of intense player anger. If the lone player on your table bets his entire bankroll on one hand of cards, only to lose by a point, he is unlikely to accept blame. If a player feels elated after hitting a thirteen with a seven to make twenty, only to see the dealer hit his sixteen with a five to make twenty-one, she may exclaim, "That shouldn't have happened!" And if, despite repeated attempts at opening and closing boxes, a table goes cold, the dealer becomes an increasingly attractive object of reproach. At such moments, croupiers are completely conspicuous on the table, targets of player anger and abuse. I was told one October night by a large and intoxicated gentleman that, having lost his whole week's salary due to my devious dealing, he would "be waiting for me" in the parking lot after my shift. (Although his threat turned out to be idle, I nevertheless rode home that night with two former rugby players employed as security officers.)

To give a sense of how such extreme emotions emerge during the course of the games, I present a transcription of four blackjack games as they occurred in sequence in early December 2002. The dealer is Grace. Two gamblers—Alex and Jimmy—are wagering large sums; as their losses build, their anger grows, culminating in physical threats toward her.

Hand 1: Grace's up-card is a king. The first three players bust. Alex is on third base. He has been dealt a two and a three. He asks for "a five and a picture, please." Instead, he receives a ten and a king, busting. "What's going on here? We're getting nailed to the floor, ceiling, walls, everywhere."

Hand 2: Grace's up-card is an ace. Says Jimmy, "Lovely, fantastic. Why are you doing this to us? This is the worst table I've ever seen in my life." Grace is silent, saying nothing in response and avoiding eye contact. Jimmy and Alex both draw until they reach seventeen and eighteen, respectively. Grace now draws a two, two, four, giving herself nineteen. Alex says nothing, but whistles and shakes his head. A woman walks up to the table with chips in her hand and asks how things are going. "It's not going. Believe me, I know; I've lost 2,000 bucks," responds Jimmy.

Hand 3: Before the hand begins, Alex attempts to "bribe the dealer" by offering her a 12.50 chip: "I give you a present." "What? Do you think this will make her change?" Jimmy retorts. Alex busts, but Grace pulls only a seventeen this time, for a tie with Jimmy. Visibly flustered, Grace accidentally picks up Jimmy's bet before realizing it had been a tie, and puts it back.
> Jimmy: "Have you got a problem with your hands?"
> Grace: "No, it was a standoff"
> Jimmy: "You're used to taking. That's a bad problem."
> Grace: "I am gonna pay. Pay all the time, not take."

Hand 4: Grace's up-card is a queen. All the players hit their hands until they have tallied seventeen or better. Things go from bad to worse for Grace, who draws a six and then a five. Jimmy is livid: "She has sixteen and doesn't break. That cannot happen. I'm gonna have to break her fucking legs."

This series of hands illustrates several themes of this chapter: the temporal flow of the gambling session, whereby players' anger accumulates concurrently with their losses; the problematic nature of tips insofar as they imply some degree of croupier control over outcomes (hand 3); and dealers' inability to deflect blame as players' losses mount.

How do dealers manage these moments when attempts to establish invisibility on the tables fail? One tactic, illustrated by Grace, is to adopt

a conciliatory pose. Having been rendered a conspicuous game participant against her will, she attempts at the end of hand 3 to make amends
for her failings: "I am gonna pay. Pay all the time, not take." A second
defense is to stage a counter-attack. The dealer can, with varying degrees
of subtlety, strike back at gamblers. Consider the following pieces of
advice offered me by coworkers: "Just say, 'My sister sleeps with who? I
didn't know that, sir, but thanks for the information.'" "Kill them with
kindness, smile when they lose. It'll drive them crazy." This tactic was,
of course, dangerous in that it risked escalating the conflicts, and it was
unclear what dealers had to gain from escalation. The third and most
common defense mechanism was to fortify one's emotional core against
interactive assaults. Veteran dealers would simply advise neophytes to
develop a thick skin: "Try to ignore them." "When they get mad at you,
just remember that you didn't hold a gun to their head and force them
to come in here."

A NOTE ON RACE AND GAMES AT GOLD CITY CASINO

The workers' game of self-erasure is remarkable for the extent to which it
entails a "de-racing" of participants' selves. Race permeates all aspects of
life in contemporary South Africa. It is possible, however, to distinguish
analytically the racial origins of Gold City Casino's despotic service
regime from the ongoing dynamics of the games now played inside of it.[4]
Managerial decisions concerning surveillance, technology, and tipping
were made by entrenched executives at the twilight of apartheid, as I
will show in Part II. These decisions represented a direct response to the
political revolution and its new black empowerment policies. And on the
casino floor, the decisions constitute concrete rules and incentives, transforming service work into an onerous existence inside a panopticon.

But to survive a panopticon once it is established requires common
strategies from all inhabitants, regardless of their ascriptive characteristics. For example, the target report policy described in the previous
chapter was implemented by managers out of a concern that new "PDI

workers" would pilfer chips. The algorithm selecting tables for target reports, however, does not take into account the race of the worker. As a result, white croupiers (myself included) play the same effacement game as their black coworkers (seeking to avoid suspicion from management and anger from players), not the entrepreneurial game that structures work in Nevada.

This is not to imply that worker-client interactions at Gold City Casino are never experienced in terms of dominant racial schemas. During my six months behind the tables, I observed four attempts by black croupiers to recast disputes with gamblers in racial terms. For instance, one night I heard a white gambler collecting his winnings say sarcastically to the dealer, Matlhora: "Good boy."[5] Matlhora froze. "Man. I am a man," he asserted, and he refused to deal again for several minutes. Upon being relieved for his break, Matlhora confronted Helen (the pit boss), and an argument broke out. Though I was too far away to hear the exchange, I later asked Matlhora what had been said. He told me that he was upset that Helen did not intervene in the dispute: "It is not right that the casino lets the gamblers treat us with disrespect, call us anything they want. If a gambler loses and wants to swear, that is fine, but it does not have to be personal against me. It is not right, and especially when it is a white man saying it to a black man."

When the audience for workers' attempts to racialize gambler's out-bursts comprised casino managers, they were doomed to fail. I later asked Helen for her perspective on Matlhora's complaint. Helen was one of the first black dealers hired in South Africa's homeland casinos during the early 1990s. Laughing, she explained to me why she took no action to intervene: "Oh, these gamblers are nothing compared with what we used to put up with in the old days. The problem is with these new dealers [the township PDIs], they are too sensitive. They are from the townships and different from the Bop [Bophuthatswana] people who worked in the old casinos." As a compromise, Helen had sent Matlhora to a different table when he returned from break. In the coming chapters we will explore further Helen's career in the casino industry, for it illuminates the history and evolution of management strategies in South Africa.

RECAP OF PART ONE

A comparative ethnography of casino dealing in South Africa and the United States reveals radically different managerial strategies for organizing service labor. Gold City Casino is best characterized as a despotic service regime. Corporate executives centralize surveillance, deskill dealing, and outlaw tipping, all in an effort to maximize security. These methods contrast with those found at Silver State Casino, where control is decentralized to floor managers who allow workers to shuffle by hand and hustle tips. In granting workers autonomy to operate outside of official rules, Nevada managers create a hegemonic service regime. These two regimes in turn generate two different sets of strategies for making a living behind the tables. The work game at Silver State Casino involves acting as an entrepreneur; to make tips is to control the allocation of blame and credit. The work game at Gold City Casino demands strategies of effacement; to avoid the ire of managers and gamblers, a croupier produces the impression that he or she lacks agency.

The games of entrepreneurialism and effacement converge in terms of their effects upon worker commitment. In neither country do workers evince loyalty to their employer. They neither systematically identify with the house during the games nor espouse any loyalty to the firm generally. Yet the two games do produce divergent patterns of conflict. In the United States, participation in the entrepreneurial game diffuses overt conflict between managers and workers. Dealers blame stiffs for their low wages, while potential anger over their lack of job security is mitigated by their frequent lateral movement across firms (as workers "chase tips"). In South Africa, workers also feel undervalued and underpaid, but they blame top management for their plight. Memories circulate of a time before the shuffling machines and the no-tipping policy, before workers were treated as mere "tokens" to satisfy state quotas.

This is how the two service regimes function today. But why are they so different in the first place? How are we to explain contrasting patterns of control and consent in the United States and South Africa? Why does management make radically different decisions for organizing service labor in the two countries? To answer such questions is the task of Part

II. It will require that we leave the pits and venture out into the larger worlds in which the casinos are embedded. For it is only by considering the social, economic, and especially political forces impinging upon the workplace that we can make sense of a particular labor regime, service or otherwise.

PART TWO Beyond the Scenes

FIVE The Politics of Producing Service

Imagine that you are a casino manager charged with monitoring the action in a large and busy casino pit. There are twelve games going on simultaneously—twelve tables chock-full of gamblers laughing, howling, and smoking. Hundreds of transactions take place every minute, far more than you can personally verify—more transactions, in fact, than can be captured by the surveillance cameras perched above the pit. A "sharp dealer" may be pinching chips, but you also worry that a savvy gambler may bilk one of your greenhorn staff. Those "bean-counters" at corporate have been breathing down your neck all month, while officials from the gambling board keep poking their noses around. (And to top things off, you're battling a nasty hangover tonight that makes it hard to concentrate on anything at all.) What sort of strategies and shortcuts do you devise to keep a handle on the action?

Part I documented divergent solutions to the dilemma of crafting casino control. It revealed that managers in the United States and South Africa make different decisions regarding the use of technology to routinize dealing, tipping to remunerate workers, and surveillance to monitor the tables. Silver State Casino represents a hegemonic service regime in which dealing is organized as a craft, workers are permitted to accept tips, and floor managers patrol the pits. As a consequence, Nevada croupiers experience work as an entrepreneurial "game of making tips." Gold City Casino, in contrast, is a despotic service regime in which the panoptic potential of the casino is embraced. Managers deskill dealing, forbid tipping, and centralize control; croupiers, as a result, play an effacement game in which they must dissimulate their own agency on the tables.

But if Part I synthesized the symbolic interactionist theory of Erving Goffman with the materialist approach of Michael Burawoy to illuminate the experience of working within these two service regimes, Part II extends beyond the casino floor to uncover why casino managers in the two countries structure labor and leisure so differently. Drawing on the work of Pierre Bourdieu—particularly his ideas of field, capital, and habitus—the analysis moves "up" in institutional space, considering the interests of corporate managers and state regulators, and back in time to see how these interests (and the strategies they engender) have evolved over time. The overall argument is that mainstream theories of managerial decision making are too economistic and individualistic. They fail to see that worlds of work are embedded within and influenced by larger worlds of politics and culture. In fact, labor regimes in the United States and South Africa differ because of the divergent symbolic logics of the fields into which they have been inserted. Neoliberal and postcolonial capitalisms generate unique industry rules, which in turn shape the experience of service work via the intermediary of a managerial habitus of control.

This chapter crafts the analytical tools needed to extend from interpersonal interactions on the blackjack tables to institutional dynamics in the political field. First, I evaluate existing theories of management and control; next, I explain how the comparative design of this study permits us to isolate the importance of the state for shaping service labor. Finally, I elaborate upon the idea of a managerial habitus as the key to solving the puzzle of divergent service regimes.

EVALUATING THEORIES OF WORK AND AUTHORITY

Why would two firms selling an identical service organize the same production process differently? The structuralist tradition within industrial sociology emphasizes the influence of external economic structures upon internal managerial control strategies. Canonical studies of manufacturing firms, for instance, pointed to the degree of competition and concentration within an industry, leading to Harry Braverman's famous argument that large, monopolistic firms will deskill work to lower labor costs and maximize control over workers (the shuffling machines ubiquitous throughout Gold City Casino would at first glance seem a perfect illustration of the Braverman thesis).[1] However, a strictly structuralist paradigm cannot explain the differences between our two cases. It is not that its arguments are inherently flawed; in fact, they have explained regimes of control in a variety of empirical studies. But the main variables considered by structural theories are here controlled for, in that the two firms I studied, Upstanding Inc. and Empowerment Inc., are both large, publicly traded corporations operating in competitive urban markets. Furthermore, both Silver State Casino and Gold City Casino draw their front-line service staff from local secondary labor markets (immigrant enclaves in Nevada, black townships in South Africa).

Marxist theorists argue that regimes of labor control must be situated within the larger balance of class power in society.[2] Erik Olin Wright, for instance, maintains that workers may check despotic control strategies by engaging in strikes and other work stoppages.[3] Such workplace power is undoubtedly important, but here, too, it is controlled for: dealers in the United States and South Africa occupy identical positions in the casino production process, and table game revenues constitute about the same proportion of revenues at both casinos. But workers may also derive power from their capacity to organize unions and collectively bargain with employers. Such associational power does differ across our two cases, but in the opposite manner predicted by theory. Employees at Gold City Casino face a despotic work regime despite being represented by the service union COSATU, whereas Silver State Casino workers are granted autonomy even though they have no union representation at the major casinos.

Labor economists would in turn explain work regimes through reference to workers' market power—that is, the relative supply of appropriately skilled employees in the local labor market. If managers face a labor shortage and employees have other means of survival available to them (such as unemployment benefits or better job options), the firm should utilize hegemonic control. Conversely, despotic labor regimes should be found where a loose labor market permits managers to easily replace uncooperative workers. At first glance, the labor market for casino employees in Nevada and Gauteng do look quite different. The vibrant (and famously "recession-proof") Nevada economy keeps the state's unemployment rate at about 5 percent; in Gauteng, though it is the most economically active province in South Africa, the figure hovers around 20 percent.[4] (And we should not forget that unemployment may have dire consequences for marginal populations in underdeveloped countries such as South Africa.)

But my fieldwork revealed that managers' perceptions of labor supply did not correspond at all with overall unemployment rates. Silver State Casino pit bosses report that finding suitable staff is rarely a problem— openings are easily filled with experienced workers seeking to move up from smaller casinos, while dealing schools produce scores of new workers monthly. In contrast, in South Africa, managers consistently complain of a dearth of competent workers in the local labor pool. They do not have at their disposal labor market intermediaries (such as small firms or training schools); instead, they train all new workers from scratch, increasing the cost of labor turnover. Furthermore, my coworkers at both Silver State Casino and Gold City Casino considered casino employment essential to their life chances. Possessing industry-specific skills and lacking education credentials, they expressed concern over their alternative employment prospects. And in neither country were workers willing to put up indefinitely with working conditions they considered unacceptable. Upon comparing the annual voluntary turnover rate at the two casinos, I found that despite the high unemployment rate in South Africa, workers at Gold City Casino quit their jobs at about the same rate as those at Silver State Casino.

Structural, Marxist, and economic theories fail to explain divergent worlds of casino labor. What about the "new sociology of service work"? Scholars in this field argue that power dynamics within service firms are unique because of the immediate presence of clients at the point of production. Interactions between workers and clients, for instance, may be colored by long-standing, durable status hierarchies in society (such as those based on race or ethnicity). According to this line of thought, we would find contentious service interactions in South Africa because of the recent, dramatic upheaval in the status hierarchy. White gamblers would take out their frustration on black dealers, who in turn would adopt the submissive interpersonal displays that were essential for survival under apartheid. In the United States, in contrast, because official segregation ended decades ago, we would find more equal and harmonious relationships between white clients and workers of color.[5]

However, had racial or ethnic tensions between players and dealers been the driving force behind workers' games, I should have observed variance in how different groups played them. I did not. All dealers, regardless of their race, ethnic, or gender[6] identity, played an entrepreneurial game in Nevada and an effacement one in Gauteng. The intense organization of dealing work, in other words, exerted a leveling effect upon pre-existing status differentials. My own experiences were a key test case. In South Africa, I, a white male from the United States, should have been able to carve out agency and establish leverage over gamblers. Yet the structure of the work process (a dearth of positive incentives plus a desire to avoid negative censure in my target reports) quickly transformed me from a "hustling" dealer into a quiescent croupier.

If not ingrained status tensions, perhaps differences between

American and South African consumers affected the service encounters. Arlie Hochschild, for instance, argues that despotic control in service industries will be tempered to the extent that clients expect "emotional labor" from workers.[7] In a similar vein, Robin Leidner argues that there are "limits to the routinization of service work": if managers view clients as unpredictable or untrustworthy, they will empower workers to control them.[8] The point is that managers' perceptions of consumers can influence strategies for controlling workers. But here, too, these factors are essentially controlled for. At both Silver State Casino and Gold City Casino, managers regarded gamblers with suspicion and odium, seeing them as demanding and troublesome. Routinizing technologies were furthermore often adopted or discarded in contradistinction to clients' capacities and desires. For instance, although Silver State Casino managers voice concern over card counters, they refuse to systematically automate dealing with shuffling machines, even though the devices completely eliminate the threat of counting. And although card counting is not considered a major problem in South Africa, shufflers are ubiquitous throughout the country's casinos. In fact, managers at Gold City Casino acknowledge that shufflers alienate clients by speeding up play too much (leading players to quickly lose their money and leave believing they have been cheated). Though they constantly brainstorm ways to slow down the games (e.g., by requiring dealers to pause for several seconds after each hand), the managers never consider a return to hand-shuffling.

Managerial perceptions of clients' preferences—and, indeed, the labeling of casino labor as "service work" in the first place—are less independent variables affecting control strategies than outcomes of larger political struggles. The various theories considered thus far, though they often offer powerful explanatory leverage, are synchronic in nature—they restrict their purview to present conditions (the degree of competition within an industry, the desires of consumers, etc.). The comparative design of this study, however, allows us to look into the past in order to discern the true explanation for divergent worlds of service work: the emergence of state regulations for governing the industry and its key markets.

FROM DIFFERENT TO DIVERGENT SERVICE REGIMES

Casinos in the United States and South Africa were not always organized so differently. In fact, they were initially identical! Consider the histories of Upstanding Inc. and Empowerment Inc. Both were founded by eccentric (if disreputable) businessmen in monopolistic, unregulated environments (early Nevada and the apartheid-era homelands). Managers throughout both firms routinely discriminated against workers of color, resulting in an ethnically homogenous (white) dealing workforce. And in both cases, casinos granted these workers autonomy to make tips, with floor managers responsible for regulating the resulting entrepreneurial "hustling games." Had Erving Goffman traveled to South Africa in the 1970s, he would have found a culture of table-top interactions identical to that which he documented in Nevada at midcentury. In other words, he would have found parallel hegemonic service regimes.

Yet while this regime has remained unchanged in Nevada through the present day, in South Africa there occurred a radical redesign of service labor in the mid-1990s. At this time, Empowerment Inc. managers centralized and maximized control, in essence imposing despotic control. The puzzle is thus not simply one of synchronic differences in the organization of service labor, but one of divergent trajectories of change (in South Africa) versus continuity (in the United States). Rather than bringing complexity to the issue, however, the introduction of time to the analysis points to a solution. Consider the timing of the divergence. Service labor in South Africa was transformed from a hegemonic to a despotic regime during the transition from apartheid to democracy. Does this not suggest that even casinos—the paradigmatic leisure industry—must be situated in their larger political environment? The following chapters will demonstrate that the ultimate cause of divergence in the structuring of service work in the United States and South Africa is the system of industrial governance in each country.

That states can influence the way work is organized is by no means a controversial statement. There is far from a consensus, however, as to how specific policies and regulations come into being, and how they subsequently affect managerial decision making. For the present cases, we would have to ask the following: How were gambling regulations (and economic policies generally) crafted during the transition from apartheid to democracy in South Africa? What about these new rules precipitated the imposition of a despotic service regime? And why has a hegemonic service regime persisted in Nevada despite the many social and economic changes that have taken place in the United States over the past fifty years?

Perhaps the most common answer to such questions is to simply associate less regulation with more despotism. The extreme case would be an unregulated, "anarchic" market in which managers are free to abuse and drive workers. This is the framework typically invoked to imagine labor regimes in the global South, where governments attempt to attract outside investment by engaging in a "race to the bottom"—a process epitomized by "free-enterprise zones" in which business regulations and worker protections are curtailed or eliminated.[9]

The "race to the bottom" paradigm obscures more than it illuminates, however, insofar as it assumes a simple binary of "advanced" versus "underdeveloped" states. The former are assumed to have strong governments that pass substantive laws to protect workers; the latter, weak states that fail to develop protective legislation. But consider the case of South Africa. The ruling African National Congress party actively intervenes in the economy to formally guarantee the rights of workers— especially those of the previously disenfranchised black citizenry. And like their United States counterparts, gambling industry regulators in South Africa monitor casinos closely, exercising leverage over firms in line with a "privilege theory" of licensing. Interested as they are in using casinos as a source of tax revenue, governments in both countries make sure that consumer markets are "free." But they also enforce regulations guaranteeing that the industry's capital markets remain "clean" (i.e., that nefarious elements do not control the industry) and that its labor markets operate "fairly" (free of discrimination). In sum, we cannot dismiss differences in the organization of service work in the United States and South Africa as due to a weak versus a strong state, or even first-world versus third-world governmentalities. In both countries, regulators claim authority over firms and their key markets.

FROM STATES TO FIELDS, RATIONALITY TO HABITUS

Regulations governing capital and labor markets do not shape service interactions simply and directly. What, then, are the mechanisms through which formal regulations produce nation-specific "games of work"? How are we to trace a path from a requirement issued by the Gauteng Gambling Board that 60 percent of the province's pit bosses be black to a Gold City Casino dealer's experience of labor in a panopticon? From the forced removal by regulators of Silver State Casino's initial owner to the entrepreneurialism exercised by workers there today? To see such pathways requires that we analyze the state as a dynamic field of action, and managers as active intermediaries between this field and the everyday lifeworld inside the firm.

One way to think of managers such as casino executives is as rational actors. Like idealized versions of scientists or engineers, they sit in quiet offices far from the chaotic environs of the casino floor, analyze objective data on wins and losses, and plan out the "one best way" (in the words of Frederick Taylor, pioneer of the theory of scientific management) to organize the action in the pits so as to maximize profits.[10] But do managers really act this way in practice—as atomized, perfectly rational decision makers? A large body of social scientific literature suggests that they do not. Organization scholars, sociologists, and anthropologists—as diverse as their theoretical projects may be—all argue that rational choice theories of management place too great an emphasis upon the cognitive and calculative, as opposed to the emotive and everyday, dimensions of decision making.[11] Managers, the argument goes, are each day inundated with information ranging from formal financial reports to informal departmental gossip. Much of it may be ambiguous or even inaccurate. To sort through and make sense of such "data," they rely on embodied forms of knowledge and taken-for-granted decision-making heuristics (in the vernacular, "gut feelings" and "the way things are done around here"). As a consequence, managers are not simple "transmission belts" that translate state policies into "shop-floor" regimes; they are active intermediaries whose biographies and personal identities will shape the way they organize work.[12]

To account for the practical and active dimension of managerial decision making at Silver State Casino and Gold City Casino, I put to use Pierre Bourdieu's idea of the habitus. At its most basic, the concept denotes a way of being in and acting upon the world; it is a "system of durable, transposable dispositions."[13] These dispositions are produced by one's early socialization experiences and subsequent trajectory through various social fields. And they in turn give rise to specific "position-takings"—in the case of managers, concrete choices for organizing firms along with the workers and consumers inside them. In short, the habitus, as both a product of the larger environment and the source of immediate decisions (as, in Bourdieu's words, a "structured and structuring structure") represents a powerful and parsimonious tool with which to link the "micro" and the "macro."[14]

Even in large bureaucratic firms, managers may be less constrained by a codified "one best way" than guided by a corporeal sense of "the right way" to do things. Habitus, "an informal and practical rather than a discursive or conscious form of knowledge," captures well this motor of action.[15] For instance, casino managers, though they work under general directives to maximize quarterly earnings, nightly encounter myriad "situations" in which the proper course of action is not clear.[16] They often "go with their gut," making decisions based upon an embodied sense of what is right and who can be trusted. Halfway through his shift, the tables manager may receive a call from the pit reporting that table seven has lost ten thousand dollars (or rand) in the past hour. Who's dealing? Jake? He's had suspicions that guy may be sneaking money off the table. Perhaps it's that team of card counters about which there have been rumors. Or maybe it's just a bad run of cards; it happens occasionally. Often there is no way to know for sure, even after the fact. Courses of action, meanwhile, must be decided upon quickly. Casino managers, in sum, act in line with a fuzzy logic or unscientific calculus, rather than as rational actors possessing perfect information.

The habitus concept also allows us to recast "micro-level," casino-specific decisions as more general strategies for managing resources within larger institutional fields. (Bourdieu frequently described the habitus as a tacit "feel for the game," and social action as analogous to that of players managing their bankrolls during a session of poker).[17] The essential point is that at any given point in time, social actors have at their avail a portfolio of capitals that may be preserved, exchanged, or even gambled away. Of course, casino managers deal mainly in the medium of money—the paradigmatic form of economic capital. Though hard currency is rarely seen on the casino floor, the ubiquitous gaming chips on the tables, the plastic markers that gamblers acquire on credit, and the metal tokens spat out by the slot machines all signify concrete monetary values. Furthermore, an extensive system of record-keeping tracks the flow of economic capital throughout the property. Each morning, the casino manager receives a report summarizing each pit's wins and losses during the previous night, and casino firms report their earnings to shareholders annually.

But economic capital is not the only relevant resource for managers. Other forms of value circulate within the world of the casino, and economic capital may at times be accumulated through or sacrificed for such currencies. For instance, although casino firms look like impersonal bureaucracies on paper, they in fact comprise vast webs of interpersonal relationships (many of which extend beyond the casino itself to other firms and into the local labor market). For managers, such ties (especially the number and strength thereof) constitute a resource—a form of social capital—that can be mobilized towards various ends. In addition, because the industry's very existence depends upon the granting by regulators of a "privilege license," casinos must stay in the good graces of the state. In other words, managers must maintain a critical amount of symbolic capital (legitimacy and positive recognition) within the larger political field, even if this at times entails sacrificing economic revenues. During World War II, for instance, Nevada casinos self-imposed curfews to counter criticisms from federal officials that soldiers were being debauched in the state's gambling houses. Economic capital, in sum, is both the default currency in the casino and a fungible form of value.[18]

How does one observe or operationalize a habitus? The most common method is to analyze it through its effects. As long as a social actor possesses a minimal amount of discretion,[19] he or she will express a habitus through the concrete choices made in daily practice. A particular disposition, we may say, generates particular position-takings. Managerial action is in this sense neither overdetermined (as rational choice theory would have it) nor entirely free. It is contextual, and may be situated along two dimensions: the actor's own personal biography (his or her trajectory through social space, so to speak) and the actor's current position within a larger field of action. The ideal research situation is thus one in which we may compare how two similarly constituted habitus operate in different fields. And this, it turns out, is precisely the situation we find before us.

The initial cohort of casino managers in the United States and South Africa came of age in essentially identical environments, and as a result they developed identical managerial *habitus* and adopted identical position-takings regarding the organization of service labor. Chapter 6 explores these convergent origins. It shows that casino proprietors initially plied their trade in primordial political fields with few formal rules to govern the industry. As a result, they developed a traditional habitus of control expressed through a constellation of practical schemas for organizing production, such as the use of particularistic hiring criteria and informal concessions offered to workers.[20]

Eventually, however, these primordial political fields solidified, and the long-standing "pariah" gambling industries moved from the margins of society to the center of national debates over how to advance the overall social good. This is the tale told in chapter 7. As casinos became objects of regulatory scrutiny for the first time, the practical strategies of the traditional managerial habitus now became stigmata. States subsequently passed laws to regulate the character of operators and their labor market practices.

But how did the traditional managerial habitus respond? Chapter 8 answers this question. It argues that while the general goals of casino regulation in the United States and South Africa look similar, in practice they possess quite different valences. In the neoliberal political field of the United States, symbolic capital is garnered through the successful presentation of oneself as a "clean" corporate citizen; in the postcolonial political field of South Africa, symbolic capital comes from reforming one's labor market practices so as to "empower" black workers. As casino managers encountered these new fields, the traditional habitus remained in place but began to generate very different position-takings. In the United States, it led to a preservation of long-standing hegemonic strategies of control; in South Africa, it produced a new, despotic service regime. Both cases illustrate the important mediating role play by the managerial habitus in transforming institutional field struggles into concrete games of work for croupiers.

SIX Cut from the Same Cloth

CONVERGENT HISTORICAL ORIGINS

In both the United States and South Africa, early political leaders sought to forge a "modern," "civilized" national identity by banning various vices, including gambling. Yet in both countries, there were important exceptions to this larger trend: jurisdictions of dubious political status— the homelands of apartheid South Africa, the U.S. state of Nevada—that opted to legalize gambling. The leaders of these states, politically secure but economically vulnerable, sought to use casinos to attract outside capital and generate tax revenues. They did not, however, invest significant resources in the regulation of their new gambling houses. As a consequence, early casino owners operated on the margins of society, for the most part free from regulatory oversight.

Analogous political origins produced identical practical strategies for managing the leisure firm. To finance their operations, early casino proprietors secretly drew upon ignominious capital sources (organized crime syndicates in Nevada, apartheid leisure firms in South Africa). And to guarantee the security of the transactions on the tables, they recruited "trusted" workers who fell in line with dominant racial stereotypes (thereby setting up casinos as segregated spaces).[1] Although the questionable composition of the industries' capital markets and labor markets would eventually draw unwanted attention from regulators, in the initial years of legal gambling, they allowed operators to accumulate great profits.

In this chapter, I first construct a comparative historical genealogy of gambling policy in the United States and South Africa, commencing from the initial moments of nation-state formation. Although the underlying assumptions and reasoning often differed, by the early twentieth century, the formal policy goals in the two countries converged upon the prohibition of casinos. Next, I describe the dynamic through which local political entrepreneurs subverted prohibition by legalizing casinos as part of their economic development plans. Finally, I reconstruct managers' initial strategies for organizing labor and leisure inside their casinos. Though separated by several decades and thousands of miles, the first casinos in both the United States and South Africa were governed by a *traditional habitus of control* that in turn generated hegemonic regimes of service work.

PROHIBITION, PURIFICATION, AND DEVELOPMENT

Wagering Puritans

We begin in the British colonies of North America that would eventually become the United States. Between the founding of the first colonial settlement in Virginia in 1607 and the 1776 Declaration of Independence from British rule, the proper regulation of gambling was a continual source of contention among colonists, and it remained so during the writing of the country's constitution. The issue of the wager, we may say, was inseparable from larger questions concerning the nature and future of the new nation.

Early colonists engaged in myriad forms of gambling, from private poker games to public horse races. This caused concern among Puritan leaders, intent as they were on maintaining moral rectitude in their "New World."[2] However, English common law, upon which much of early U.S. law was based, did not directly prohibit gambling; it merely made gambling debts legally unenforceable.[3] Nor does the Bible contain specific prohibitions against wagering; in fact, the casting of lots to discern God's will is a central device in many biblical stories.[4] The Puritans thus actively crafted prohibitive legislation, often using tortuous rationales. Gambling, for instance, was framed as evil insofar as it encouraged citizens to rely on chance rather than hard work[5]—a sure sign of damnation within the Calvinistic worldview.[6] And because small-scale wagering was easily concealed, tithingmen were employed to surreptitiously monitor games played behind closed doors.[7]

The colonial Calvinist heritage of complete prohibition did not, however, carry over as social policy for the new nation. Puritanical restrictions upon gambling were gradually relaxed during the seventeenth and eighteenth centuries, mainly through exemptions allowing public institutions to operate gambling provided they used profits for "good works." Much colonial development was financed in this manner, as churches, city governments, and even universities such as Harvard and Yale administered raffles and lotteries. Such was the context in which members of the Continental Congress of 1774 debated a gambling policy for the incipient nation. George Washington, an inveterate gambler himself, was among those who advocated explicit prohibition, for he believed gambling undermined troop morale during wartime.[8] But the federal government ended up staying silent on the issue. It placed gambling within the realm of state rights (via the Tenth Amendment), reserving for itself the right to police gambling only when it involved interstate commerce.

The late eighteenth and early nineteenth centuries witnessed a short-lived though consequential period of laissez faire gambling in the United States. Lotteries flourished as new professional management companies ran large national sweepstakes that displaced most small-scale, "non-profit" lotteries. It was also during these decades that there emerged precursors to the modern casino. Along the North American frontier—in the port cities of the Mississippi River and on the vessels that traveled among them—the country's first professional proprietors of casino-style games began plying their trade. To lure in frontiersmen, they frequently bundled their gambling games with various other vices inside a CBS (casino/bordello/saloon). Historians pinpoint 1827 as the year of the country's first stand-alone casino, in New Orleans.[9]

The United States' laissez faire era of gambling proved ephemeral. Lotteries were eradicated during the antebellum era after Jacksonian reformers charged several large operators with rigging contests.[10] Casinos, meanwhile, were a continuous object of contention along the ever-expanding frontier. As cities and towns were settled and stable institutions of government solidified, conflict would arise between "enlightened" newcomers and incumbent frontiersmen. The former, who represented constituencies such as homesteaders and religious groups, framed the "heathen" habits of the frontiersmen—especially their patronage of the CBS—as detrimental to the public good. Repeatedly, "the sodbusters . . . triumphed over the veteran frontiersmen by passing . . . comprehensive gambling law" (triumphs often symbolized by a public lynching of a handful of gambling operators).[11] The net result of this dynamic was an ongoing western migration of gambling operators seeking a safe haven to ply their trade in the liminal space of the frontier.

The final demise of frontier gambling came at the hands of the Progressive movement, which swept state governments around the turn of the twentieth century. As a political philosophy, Progressivism denounced corrupt business practices and advocated for the protection of consumers and citizens.[12] Along with alcohol, gambling was one of its favorite targets. But Progressives focused less upon protecting the moral character of the gambler (as the Puritans had done) than upon taming the profit motive of the proprietor. They typically banned gambling only when the operator acted as a "bank" (i.e., by directly betting against gamblers) rather than as a "host" (by charging a set fee for each round of gambling). The rationale was that only in banked games would proprietors have an interest to defraud players or persuade them to wager beyond their means. In practice, this distinction proscribed casino-style games, and by 1909, California, Nevada, Arizona, and other western states had all outlawed casinos.

Nevada Exceptionalism

Nevada was the only state to buck this early twentieth-century wave of prohibition when it relegalized casinos in 1931. The standard historical narrative points to the effect of the Great Depression upon the state's economy: casinos were perceived to be a way to stimulate economic activity during tough times. But if the Depression did not precipitate casino legalization in other states, what accounts for Nevada exceptionalism? The answer is found in the political process through which it became a state in the first place. Nevada's origins as a "fictitious state" created a political elite that was not only in need of new revenue sources but also relatively buffered from public concerns over legal gambling. (It possessed, we could say, an asymmetry of political and economic capitals.) To understand the subsequent trajectory of casino regulation in the United States requires that we know the early history of Nevada.

In order to admit Nevada into the union, normal criteria for statehood had been circumvented. The United States acquired the Utah Territory (including the land now constituting Nevada) in 1848 following its victory in the Mexican-American War. But white settlers soon fled the territory, following a call from Mormon leader Brigham Young to gather in Salt Lake City in preparation for the Utah War of 1857. The following four years, in which there existed no stable government in Nevada, is referred to as a period of political anarchy.[13] Nevertheless, in 1861 the area was declared an official territory, and in 1864 a state. The historical consensus is that Nevada did not meet the typical standards for statehood,[14] and was deemed such by President Abraham Lincoln only in order to "assure the passage by Congress of the Thirteenth Amendment, which would place the Emancipation Proclamation in the Constitution," banning slavery.[15]

Despite the noble ends for which its statehood was granted, its lack of an independent civil society and a stable government left Nevada vulnerable to control by outsiders. Following discoveries of valuable ore—especially the rich Comstock Lode of 1859—outside interests seized control of the Nevada government, effectively transforming the state into a mining colony.[16] These interests consisted primarily of a clique of financial speculators based out of San Francisco and known as "The Bank Crowd." They owned Nevada's main mining concern (the Ophir Company) as well as the railway system throughout the state (the Virginia & Truckee and Central Pacific Railroads). In turn, and "because of their economic power within the state, The Bank Crowd [was] able to generally have their way in the political arena."[17] Through systematic bribery and vote buying, they controlled the state senate and legislature, while the Crowd's head lawyer, William M. Stewart, served as Nevada senator in Congress for four decades.[18]

By the turn of the twentieth century, and following the depletion of the Comstock Lode, The Bank Crowd could no longer maintain their "Comstock Aristocracy."[19] Into the resulting political vacuum stepped Nevada's incipient Progressive movement, spearheaded by a small group of academics and administrators associated with the state university in Reno. They had long sought to cleanse the state of its desultory frontier image, and they eagerly latched onto the national anti-gambling cause. The Nevada Progressive Party's crowning achievement would in fact be the 1909 state act prohibiting gambling.[20] But the act, like the power of the cultural elites who championed it, proved short-lived. For even in the early twentieth century, Nevada remained very much a frontier society lacking the bases of support necessary to sustain a Progressive movement. Consider that in 1930, the year before gambling was decriminalized, the state's population density was one person per square mile, and the male to female ratio sixteen to one.[21]

Nevada's Progressives soon succumbed to a new political machine, this one native to the state. It was headed by one George Wingfield, a former card dealer who had been lucky enough to stumble upon Nevada's last great silver lode, around the town of Tonopah in 1900. He parlayed his finding into control of a major mining concern and, through it, the state's banking and real estate systems as well. Operating out of a small office in downtown Reno, Wingfield and his minions pandered, pressured, and otherwise influenced state officials. "His domination of the state was so complete," his biographer wrote, "that he was charged with running both of its political parties to suit his own purposes."[22]

It is in the context of the rise of the Wingfield machine that we must place the 1931 casino legalization bill. It represented the victory of a powerful (if corrupt) economic and political clique over a weak (if sincere) cultural elite. The interests of Wingfield and the politicians he controlled, furthermore, were economic at root. The gambling bill was in fact but one of several pieces of legislation passed by the Wingfield machine intended to stimulate economic activity through the creation of a comparative advantage in the realm of morality. Lax incorporation laws had been passed to attract entrepreneurs to the state, personal income taxes had been repealed to encourage westerners to relocate, and marriage and divorce laws had been carefully crafted to attract both aspiring newlyweds eager to marry and disgruntled spouses ready to be "Reno-vated." By 1931 there was no longer any reason to treat gambling differently, as a matter of personal morality or political legitimacy, rather than as a component of a larger economic stimulus plan.

Prohibition and the Apartheid Project

Nevada exceptionalism regarding gambling policy derived from its origins as a "fictitious state." A transient, gender-skewed population along with an unsound economic base created conditions in which a secure political "aristocracy" could afford to treat gambling law as strictly an economic issue. When we turn our attention from the United States to southern Africa, we find a strikingly similar story: gambling prohibition played a key part in the symbolic politics of nation-building, while largely fictitious states legalized casinos as a last-ditch development strategy.

Colonial authorities in early South Africa, like those in the American colonies, banned gambling. Wagering was by all accounts widespread among Dutch settlers in the Cape of Good Hope region after the first European settlement was established there in 1654. Bars and canteens along Table Bay offered a variety of card games, while settler organizations in Cape Town operated small-scale lotteries known as "art unions."

But the controlling authority—the Dutch East India Company—grew concerned over the effect of gambling upon the work ethic of colonists, and so passed a broad law forbidding gambling in the Cape in 1673.[23] As was the case in the United States, prohibition was more easily specified on paper than policed in fact. Authorities subsequently shored up prohibition by banning card games (in 1740) and nonprofit lotteries (in 1780).

The British seized control of the Cape colony from the Dutch in 1798, setting in motion a pattern of conflict between colonial powers that would last until well into the twentieth century. In response to perceived harassment from their new British rulers, descendants of the original Dutch colonists—known as the Boers, or Afrikaners—"trekked" east and north from the Cape during the nineteenth century. This inland expansion bore a number of similarities to that which took place in North America. In both cases, migrating colonists violently displaced (and sometimes systematically exterminated) native peoples. In addition, both migrations were legitimated by an ethnic and national ideology of manifest destiny.[24] And, perhaps most remarkably, on both frontiers ongoing disputes took place over the meaning and fate of gambling.

The best-documented example for South Africa is provided by Charles Van Onselen in his social history of Johannesburg's mining industry.[25] Following the discovery of diamonds in 1867 and gold during the 1880s along the rich reef of mineral deposits known as the Rand, a handful of mining companies established control over the region and recruited black African men to work the mines. To house this labor force of 25,000-plus, the companies constructed a system of on-site dormitories. And to prevent the workers from accumulating savings and leaving the mines, the companies illicitly supported a variety of vice industries in the compounds—gambling, prostitution, and breweries. British authorities, who fought the Afrikaners for control of the Rand during the late nineteenth century, outlawed gambling on the mines following their victory in the Boer War of 1899–1902. Nonetheless, various small-scale gambling industries continually sprouted up, even after the unification of British and Afrikaner territories in 1910. In all of the four provinces constituting the new Union of South Africa—the Transvaal, Orange Free

State, Cape Province, and Natal—local disputes over gambling were commonplace events.

Although Britain prevailed militarily in the Boer War, British settlers in South Africa were always outnumbered by Afrikaners. The latter eventually achieved political supremacy though a series of white-only elections, culminating with the 1948 victory of the arch-conservative National Party (NP). The NP, eventual architects of apartheid, advocated Afrikaner nationalism and propagated a vision of a morally and racially pure South Africa. Integral to this vision was the proscription of various "vices" among the white citizenry, ranging from miscegenation to pornography to gambling.

In 1965, the South African Minister of Justice (and future prime minister) John Vorster announced his intention to wipe out wagering in all its forms. He pushed through parliament a National Gambling Act, arguing in an impassioned speech: "We should combat the evil of gambling, [for it] undermines the morale of any nation."[26] Even penny wagers on pinball games, he believed, could have deleterious effects:

> I am going out of my way to get rid of every pin-table in every café
> as far as it lies within my power to do so. I have seen children
> standing in cafés for hours on end . . . wasting their time playing the
> "one-eyed bandit" [sic] and goodness knows what other games. . . .
> I do not think it is necessary that this kind of temptation should be
> placed in the way of children.[27]

The NP's rationale for prohibition here echoed less the Progressives' policing of proprietors than the Puritans' concern with citizens' character. South Africa's Gambling Act in fact banned only contests of *chance* rather than those requiring *skill*, since only the former—in which "man" relies on luck rather than effort—undermines the work ethic of the populace.[28]

As in the United States, various forms of illegal gambling thrived in South Africa despite official prohibition. Authorities often turned a blind eye to raffles operated by churches and charities, while illegal card rooms repeatedly surfaced in cities and suburbs.[29] Nor could the police eradicate various forms of gambling played by black and coloured (mixed race) South Africans. Just as urban African Americans operated an underground lottery known as "the numbers" for decades, black South Africans took part in an illicit urban lotto known as fahfee.[30] But only one form of gambling would receive official sanction to operate in apartheid South Africa: casinos placed in the desolate "native reserves." It is to the origins of these homelands and their gambling resorts that we now turn.

Cabana Republics

A morally pure white citizenry was but one-half of the apartheid project. The other entailed the sequestration of the black population onto a series of independent and self-sustaining homelands—13 percent of South Africa's land area to house 75 percent of its population. At first glance, these entities bear little resemblance to early Nevada. And while we must be careful not to overstate their similarities, in both cases there eventually emerged political aristocracies possessing an imbalance of political versus economic capital.

When NP leaders latched upon the homelands as, in the words of Prime Minister P.W. Botha, the "bottom line" of apartheid, they made a radical break with the existing system of segregation, in which some permanent black presence in South Africa had been tolerated.[31] Apartheid, meaning roughly "separate development," demanded the total and permanent fractionation of blacks and whites. Three key pieces of legislation, all passed in 1950, established the basis of this project. The Population Registration Act assigned all citizens a single racial/ethnic identity (for blacks, these were tribal affiliations), the Immorality Act froze these identities by prohibiting miscegenation, and the Group Areas Act consigned each black tribal group to their own homeland (the four largest homelands—the Transkei, Bophuthatswana, Venda, and the Ciskei—were referred to simply as the "TBVC states"). Between 1960 and 1983, three million black South Africans (one-sixth of the country's population) were relocated, often forcibly, in line with the apartheid plan.[32]

Despite National Party rhetoric, the homelands possessed few independent political institutions and certainly no robust civil society. Men left to seek work in South Africa's mines, creating a skewed gender balance and disrupting family structures.[33] The blueprint for homeland governments, meanwhile, was established by South Africa's Native Administration Act, which specified that each homeland was to be ruled by a traditional tribal chief under whom various regional chiefs would serve.[34] And while chiefs were granted an array of powers and rights—most notably official ownership of the land—NP officials in Pretoria exercised de facto control over homeland governments insofar as they appointed the chiefs and possessed ultimate authority to create, modify, and revoke homeland law.[35]

The homeland system was designed to benefit not only the Afrikaner state but also South Africa's mining industry. The former desired to prevent permanent urban black settlement in South Africa, where oppositional identities might foment.[36] Especially important in this regard was the chief system, intended to foster "tribalism" among blacks.[37] The South African Chamber of Mines, meanwhile, viewed the reserves as a source of cheap labor.[38] Workers commuted daily to the mines from the homelands, where a subsistence economy would, in theory, lower companies' wage payments.[39] The notorious Pass Law Act of 1952 regulated this movement of workers between the homelands and the mines.

The interests of the mining companies, however, were in constant tension with those of the South African state. Should the homelands prove to be economically self-sufficient, there would be no incentive for men to leave for work in the mines; should they become completely desolate, there would be a mass exodus to the cities.[40] By the late 1960s, this latter scenario was materializing. Years of overcrowding and poor land use had rendered agriculture impossible. Over 70 percent of homeland residents were unemployed, and homeland GDP per capita was only one-twentieth that of South Africa as a whole.[41] Massive squatter camps became permanent fixtures on the outskirts of South Africa's cities, with only 40 percent of blacks residing in their assigned homeland.[42] The apartheid system, in short, was in serious danger.

The National Party responded by radically overhauling South Africa's racial state. On one hand, it granted strategic concessions to black workers; for instance, in 1972 a committee headed by Afrikaner high judge Nicholas Wiehahn formally recognized black trade unions in South Africa.[43] On the other hand, the party redoubled its efforts to make the homelands appear politically and economically independent.[44] Apartheid planners crafted flags and anthems for these states from scratch (though no major nation ever recognized the homelands as sovereign entities).[45] And they put in place incentives to encourage private firms to relocate to the homelands.[46] Such is the context in which we must view the birth of homeland casinos.

In 1971, the South African Parliament passed the Self-Governing Territories Constitution Act, which allowed each homeland to set its own laws regarding gambling. During the next decade, tribal leaders of all four TBVC states legalized casinos (as well as other "vices" such as pornography and interracial romance).[47] Gambling liberalization did invoke protest from some local black communities, but such resistance did little to sway the tight-knit clique of tribal chiefs. Like their counterparts in early Nevada, they were well buffered from civil society and so could "afford" to treat gambling as a means of revenue generation.

ONE TALE OF TWO INDUSTRIES

The same conditions that led political leaders in Nevada and the homelands to legalize casinos—i.e., an asymmetry of political and economic capitals—shaped the organization of the industries in their early days. Unconcerned about public legitimacy and desirous of industry revenues, state officials granted operators considerable latitude to organize the pits as they saw fit. Free from oversight, casinos in turn formed illicit monopolies and took steps to segregate labor and consumer markets.

Nevada, the Early Years

During the first two decades of legal gambling in twentieth-century Nevada (approximately 1931–1949), the industry continued to look much as it had during its frontier days. The initial cohort of casino owners consisted of veteran "gamblers" whose roots lay in the nineteenth-century world of the riverboat and the CBS.[48] To obtain a license to operate a gambling house, all they had to do was pay the local sheriff a small set fee, of which 25 percent went to the state tax commission and the remainder to the county.[49] The sheriff would occasionally stop by to make sure the license was renewed, but in general, the state passed no major laws regulating casinos.[50]

Casino proponents had hoped that the 1931 gambling bill would stimulate tourism. Prior to the advent of mass air travel, however, the overland journey to Nevada remained an arduous one, and the casino industry initially grew only modestly.[51] Absent the desired influx of tourists, proprietors continued to run their casinos to cater to a traditional market of miners and manual laborers. This entailed nothing fancy in the way of décor. These were "sawdust houses"—a few tables in the back of a saloon otherwise lacking in amenities.[52] "Dirty . . . old cigar filled rooms," an owner from this era described them, "People just betting, playing twenty-one . . . it wasn't the most savory places in the world."[53]

The clientele of the early Nevada casino mirrored that of frontier society generally: working class men of European descent (see figure 4). But as the demographics of the state shifted over the succeeding decades, casino owners reacted with a mix of openness and obstinacy. On one hand, the growing female population showed an interest in gambling (especially on the new slot machines) and were by all accounts permitted (if somewhat grudgingly) into this previously all-male world. But the story was different for African Americans.[54] Though they made up less than 1 percent of the state's population in 1931, African Americans arrived in large numbers over the next two decades, seeking work on several major federal construction projects in the state.[55] But casino owners refused to admit these new Nevadans into their premises.[56] In northern Nevada, African Americans could gamble only in Reno's Chinatown, while a Las Vegas ordinance specified that "Ethiopians" may gamble only at clubs that "cater to others of that race."[57]

The decades following World War II represented a second period of legal gambling in Nevada, one characterized by continuity in some

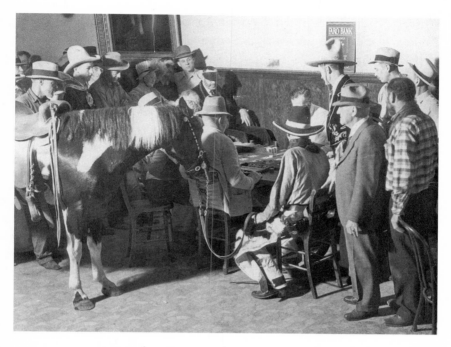

Figure 4. An early Nevada casino. Courtesy of UNLV Libraries, Special Collections.

areas but abrupt change in others. Consider the transforming consumer market. The rapid growth of urban southern California, coupled with improved transportation routes to Nevada, led to dramatic industry growth during these years. To appeal to this new tourist market, proprietors added various amenities to their casinos, transforming them from sawdust houses to "carpet joints."[58] Gambling was now packaged with restaurants, hotels, and entertainment—all "themed" in line with exotic motifs intended to produce for patrons a unified world of leisure.[59] Casino operators, in stylizing their resorts, were mimicking emergent staples of middle-class American culture such as the suburb and the shopping mall.[60] Yet Las Vegas and Reno still provided various other "vices," as evidenced by the sex industries that grew alongside (and often within) the casinos.[61] And although casinos made a concerted effort to expand their market along class lines, Nevada's burgeoning

African American population suffered continued exclusion as clients. Famous black performers such as Sammy Davis Jr. would be contracted to perform in casino showrooms but would have to dine and sleep in bunkhouses on Las Vegas's segregated West Side.

Another important transformation during this period involved casino ownership, as the initial cohort of frontier proprietors was displaced by organized crime syndicates based out of southern California and the eastern United States.[62] Many of these syndicates had already been operating illegal casinos in other states, and Nevada represented a safe site for expansion. But the state offered syndicates something more: an opportunity to both launder money (i.e., to falsely account for profits accrued in illegal enterprises elsewhere) and skim revenues (to undercount casino cash flows and pocket the remainder tax-free). By the early 1950s, these two practices were institutionalized throughout the state's casinos.[63]

The general organizational structure of the syndicate casino has been described as onion-like.[64] At its center were syndicate leaders, who supplied investment capital and were the ultimate beneficiaries of the skims, but whose influence remained mostly hidden. Syndicate bosses in turn recruited confederates with no criminal records to serve as figurehead owners and executives; their names, not those of the true financiers, appeared on official licensing documents. Because known crime figures could not openly work on the casino floor, syndicates had to trust their floor managers to oversee daily operations. It was a system that worked well as long as profits and revenues flowed in. And this they did, as statewide casino revenues (at least those that were officially reported) grew from 22 million dollars in 1945 to 194 million dollars in 1960. During this time, there also occurred a consolidation in ownership, such that by the beginning of the 1960s the majority of the state's casinos belonged to a handful of syndicates.[65]

As deceptive as the structure of the syndicate casino may have been, it did not escape the notice of the public, the press, and—eventually— federal law enforcement agencies that something was amiss in the Silver State. But how were crime syndicates able to take over the casino industry in the first place? To answer this question, we must consider the perfunctory system of regulation that characterized Nevada at mid-century.

A Policy of Benign Neglect

The first four decades of legal casino gambling in Nevada were characterized by minimal oversight on the part of the state. The few regulations crafted during these years were intended to maximize the state's cut of industry revenues—a substantive goal often at odds with that of establishing the propriety of proprietors. The end result was a classic case of regulatory "capture," whereby governmental officials' interests were so intertwined with those of the industry that the two became indistinguishable.

The first significant piece of casino regulation was the 1945 Tax Act, a simple bill intended to increase the state's share of industry revenues. The initial system of taxation in the state had required casinos to pay a flat annual fee to the local sheriff. The Tax Act, however, transferred authority over licensing to the state tax commission and, more importantly, shifted the basis of taxation to a percentage of revenues. The impetus behind this new policy was economic. The state legislature had passed a "One Sound State" tax package in the late 1930s eliminating all corporate, income, inheritance, and gift taxes. While federal spending in Nevada during World War II had allowed state coffers to stay solvent, the winding down of the war led to budget shortfalls.[66] Legislators saw the casino industry as a potential solution. The problem, though, was that because of the flat fee system, the state not only did not benefit from growth, it did not know the size of the industry in the first place. Robbins E. Cahill, an original member of the tax commission, explained:

> [Legislators] were looking for money for future sessions . . . a group of 'em were sitting around one time, and they began discussing the gaming, which was just starting to develop in Las Vegas in good shape . . . and so the theory began to creep around that maybe we'd better start getting something out of it. . . . Nobody knew what the profits in the business were, or really, how much is being passed over the tables in the state.[67]

The commission brainstormed a percentage-based tax, but anticipated that operators would object to it, if only because they would not wish to divulge their earnings. State officials thus opened negotiations by proposing a 10 percent tax on revenues, and subsequently allowed casinos to bargain this down to 1 percent.[68] Cahill continues:

> Somewhere in the process, [legislators] agreed to cut the ten percent tax down to one percent. They admitted it was an experiment. They said, "We don't care what the percentage is, because once we levy a percentage tax on it, after two years, we'll know what we've got to tap.[69]

Though the percentage taxation system alleviated the state's immediate budget shortfall, it soon transformed the state into a mono-economy and regulators into advocates of the industry vis-à-vis consumers, workers, and the general public.[70] By 1952, revenues from casinos surpassed those from mining to account for over half of the state's general fund.[71] Regulatory capture was further exacerbated by the fact that many state officials were personally involved in the casino business. In his 1978 ethnography of Nevada gaming control, Jerome Skolnick found frequent movement between control agencies and casino management—regulators commonly accepted positions in the industry, and vice versa.[72] Such personal interlocks, coupled with the more general economic dependence of the state upon casinos, created conditions wherein "authorities ultimately [came] to represent the interest of the industry."[73]

Regulatory capture translated into autonomy for casino operators. Besides collecting taxes, officials made minimal effort to regulate the structure or inner workings of the individual casino enterprise.[74] The tax commission, for instance, pledged to begin investigating the true identities of financiers after it was divulged that Las Vegas casino mogul Bugsy Siegel was a front man for a crime syndicate. (Siegel's 1947 murder drew attention to the questionable character of Nevada's new cohort of casino owners.) Because the syndicates were the only reliable source of investment capital to sate the growing national demand for Nevada gambling, however, investigating license applicants remained a perfunctory process.[75]

In what would become a common dynamic over the coming decades, regulators intervened in casino operations *only* where individual operators' business practices threatened the industry as a whole. During

World War II, for example, top military brass expressed concern that soldiers stationed outside Las Vegas were being corrupted by too many late nights in the city's casinos. Nevada state officials in turn convinced casinos to close down during the wee hours of the night.[76] (These voluntary curfews were quickly lifted when the federal presence in the state dissipated in the late 1940s.) In contrast, bills forbidding discrimination against black clients stalled in the state legislature during its 1939, 1949, 1953 and 1957 sessions. State officials, unconcerned that the liberal groups pushing such legislation could in any way pose a threat to the economic health of the gambling industry, sided with casinos in their fight against "consumer civil rights."[77]

State officials also endorsed and defended the interests of casino owners in the realm of labor issues. Casinos vociferously supported legislation protecting their control of the industry's labor market, including their right to hire, promote, and fire workers in the absence of external supervision or accountability.[78] Gambling regulators in turn repeatedly and unequivocally affirmed casinos' authority to fire workers "without cause."[79] But state endorsement of private (i.e., casino) control of local labor markets is most clearly seen in its approach towards the issue of unionization by casino workers. Nevada was an "early adopter" of anti-union "right to work" statutes,[80] while the state's official stance on unionization—as articulated by the chairman of Nevada's gaming commission—was that "gaming control collide[s] with the concept of a union resolution of a dispute."[81]

Markets of Capital, Consumers, and Labor in South Africa

Compared to the large secondary literature on early Nevada, little has been written about the emergence of casino industries in the black homeland states of apartheid South Africa. This reflects the extreme secrecy with which most affairs were conducted in the homelands, especially concerning their sudden metamorphosis into "casino states."[82] My analysis in this section thus draws heavily upon a handful of primary documents I was able to unearth, along with interviews I conducted with former National Party officials and homeland casino managers.

The parallels these data reveal in the histories of casino industries in the two countries are striking. In both cases, we find intense early growth financed by proprietors of dubious character. And in both we see pliant state officials unable and/or unwilling to challenge casino control of consumer and labor markets.

The initial acts legalizing gambling in each TBVC state are identical. Such standardization strongly suggests that, although the homelands were officially independent nation-states, their gambling acts were commonly authored by bureaucrats in South Africa. And in each homeland, ultimate authority over gambling was vested with the Minister of Law and Order, who was to appoint a four-person gambling board to grant licenses and monitor operators. I found no evidence, however, that these gambling boards performed such functions, or that they ever met on a regular basis at all.

The top (paramount) chief in each homeland distributed property rights personally and in line with a principle of "exclusivity," whereby licensees were granted monopolies. While these exclusivity agreements were publicly framed as a way to protect local homeland communities, they likely were designed to prevent competition from local black entrepreneurs.[83] Casino rights across the four main homeland states were initially distributed between two South African firms. The Transkei and Venda granted their licenses to a South African Holiday Inn (HI) subsidiary. Bophuthatswana and Ciskei granted theirs to a subsidiary of South African Breweries (SAB) known as Southern Sun.

The relationship among casino firms, the apartheid government, and homeland leaders has been described as an "alliance of convenience."[84] For the NP, casinos offered benefits both material (especially the alleviation of direct South African financing of homeland governments, insofar as they stimulated some taxable economic activity) and symbolic (by bolstering, through contrast with South Africa's own restrictive vice laws, the fiction of homeland political independence).[85] For South African leisure firms, the homelands were simply good investment opportunities.[86] Their labor laws banned unions and stipulated no minimum wage,[87] while the sprawling nature of the homeland system permitted access to a variety of South African urban markets. Homeland leaders in turn leveraged their license-granting powers for a variety of illicit payoffs (to be elaborated on in the next section).

How did the organization of the apartheid-era casino concern compare to that of the Nevada syndicate casino? Both were characterized by an onion-like organizational structure intended to hide the true financiers (and beneficiaries). Because apartheid statutes specified that South Africans could not be majority owners of homeland companies, Holiday Inn and Southern Sun established in each homeland a development corporation to serve as the nominal owner of the casinos (not unlike syndicate leaders' use of "clean" confederates). In reality, these corporations existed only on paper. They had no physical offices or administrative staff, and positions on their boards were filled with associates of homeland leaders. HI and Southern Sun profited from this arrangement by signing lucrative contracts to manage the properties—typically for a percentage of both profits and revenues.

Just as the Nevada casino industry underwent consolidation in its first decades, so too did the homeland industry. In 1983, Southern Sun, for reasons unclear, decided to get out of the gambling business. It spun off its casinos, selling them to a South African hotelier by the name of Sol Kerzner. Following an unsuccessful stint as a prizefighter, Kerzner had accepted a position with Southern Sun's hotel division in 1969. In the early 1980s, he left Southern Sun and founded his own firm, Sun International (SI).[88] Then, following his acquisition of Southern Sun's casino holdings, Kerzner negotiated a deal with Holiday Inn to take over its casinos, thereby gaining a monopoly on legal gambling in southern Africa.

The homeland casino industry grew rapidly in the following decade, with twelve new casinos opening between 1985 and 1995. Expansion was driven by many of the same factors that drove industry growth in Nevada. Just as the cities of California nourished the casinos of Las Vegas, South Africa's PWV metropolitan area (containing Pretoria and Johannesburg) constituted a burgeoning consumer market for casinos in the nearby homeland of Bophuthatswana. SI's "Bop" properties, strategically placed just over the border and right off major highways, were generating 75 percent of company revenues by 1995.

Figure 5.   Homeland casinos sought to display an image of racial harmony. From Sun International Bophuthatswana Limited's 1987 Annual Report.

These casinos also saw the development of novel strategies for packaging and marketing gambling. The first homeland casinos designed by Holiday Inn and Southern Sun had actually offered only a modest amount of gambling—typically a handful of tables and slot machines in the back of a hotel lounge. Kerzner, though, bucked this trend by building large and extravagant casinos with exotic themes. The homeland casinos also provided South Africans with access to other illicit—especially erotic—activities.[89] Pornographic movies and magazines (banned in South Africa proper) were widely available; an illegal but highly visible sex industry provided South African men with female prostitutes[90]; and, as the homelands were not subject to South Africa's Immorality Act, white men could appear publicly with their black girlfriends in the casinos.

A final parallel between early Nevada and the homelands relates to the casinos' treatment of nonwhite gamblers. While Nevada was cementing its reputation as the "Mississippi of the West," the homelands were striving to portray themselves (and their casinos) as places of racial harmony (see figure 5). But while local blacks were not officially barred from the resorts (one survey found that half of all adults living in the immediate vicinity of Sun International's flagship property, Sun City, had visited it), managers eventually found ways to restrict their patronage. They banned "locals" from loitering in or around the resorts; dress codes were posted prohibiting entry by anyone wearing blue jeans or sneakers; and fees were charged for parking at the resort and even for walking into the casino. The end result was a primarily white casino clientele; only a small cadre of elite blacks (typically those with ties to the tribal leaders) regularly gambled in the casinos.

Regulatory Capture in the Homelands

The homeland casino industry was also characterized by regulatory capture. In the United States, this had resulted from the fact that Nevada politicians depended so heavily on casino taxes to fill state coffers. While this was also the case in the homelands, direct corruption here seemed to play an even larger role.[91] But the result was the same, as casino operators experienced near total autonomy to manage consumer and labor markets as they saw fit.

Several pieces of evidence speak to an unscrupulous relationship between homeland governments and casino firms. One is a steady tailing off of taxes paid to these governments during the apartheid era. South African financial journalist Alan Greenblo analyzed two decades' worth of financial statements from casinos in Bophuthatswana.[92] He found that Bop president Lucas Mangope had granted firms various tax breaks, such as write-offs for investments in new facilities and the exclusion of casino revenues from value-added taxation. One company's annual report to investors even boasted that it paid tax rates "significantly lower than the norm." "Due to its ambitious building programme cushioned by abundant incentives," Greenblo concluded, "[the homeland casino industry] has paid taxes that are phenomenally low in relation to the profits generated. At no stage has it paid full tax." For several years, casinos paid no taxes at all.

Given that casinos were supposed to produce revenues for homeland governments, how were operators able to systematically evade taxes? There is no clear answer. Many have speculated that homeland leaders accepted improper favors or even bribes. An investigatory report on the allocation of casino licenses in the Transkei, for instance, concluded that paramount chief George Matanzima had accepted a two million rand payment in exchange for exclusive gambling rights and tax concessions.[93] Charges were also made that Lucas Mangope received various indulgences, ranging from free suites at casinos to "sweetheart" concessionaire contracts for his relatives.[94]

The degree to which National Party officials were complicit in—or even cognizant of—such corruption remains unknown. The NP, after all, had an interest in making homeland governments appear independent and upstanding. While it is possible that apartheid officials were simply unable to monitor the relationship between homeland governments and firms, several of my interviewees reported that NP leaders maintained ongoing communication with casino executives during these years. In an interview, one former high-ranking government official described a "cozy relationship" in which executives regularly visited NP officials at their offices and provided them complimentary rooms at the hotels. When asked if this expressed some larger pattern of complicity between the two parties, he responded, "Well, I never saw anything directly of this nature, but logic says it."

Considering these questionable relationships among firms, homeland leaders, and the South Africa government, it is hardly surprising that the casinos themselves were subject to little systematic oversight. Former homeland casino personnel today remember the properties as essentially "self-regulating." A former top manager reported that upon opening a new casino, he would submit a blueprint to the homeland's Department of Finance, who would in turn "rubber stamp" its approval. Then, every six months or so, an official from the department would notify him of an inspection and stop by for an informal "site tour." While former managers may be exaggerating their autonomy, I was unable to find any evidence that regulators ever imposed fines or sanctioned casino management. The homeland casino industry of apartheid South Africa, much like early Nevada's, was characterized by an ineffectual and largely captured system of state regulation.

CONVERGENT CONCEPTIONS OF CONTROL

Having established a set of parallels between both the political origins of the two casino industries and the organization of early industry markets (of capital, consumers, and labor), we now focus even more closely to excavate managers' practical strategies for organizing the action during the first decades of legal gambling in the United States and South Africa. In both countries, managers sought to ensure the security of the gambling transactions. To do so, they used personal networks and racial stereotypes to recruit "trusted" workers, and they secured the allegiance of these workers by granting them autonomy to "hustle" tips on the tables. In short, convergent industry origins produced identical conceptions of control: a traditional managerial habitus organizing service labor hegemonically.

Nevada: Juice, Tipping, Trust

The first generation of casino proprietors in Nevada had learned the business in the frontier casinos of the Old West.[95] After laboring behind the tables as dealers, they had saved enough to rent out a storefront and purchase a handful of tables.[96] Traditionally, casino owners had not been all that concerned with what happened on the casino floor. They would merely "rent out" tables to independent dealers, who paid losses from their own pockets and retained their nightly winnings.[97] Following the passage of the 1931 Gambling Bill, however, proprietors began running their establishments as official businesses. They maintained a central "house bankroll" and hired dealers as official employees. The legalization of gambling in Nevada thus represented both the demise of the completely independent dealer and the birth of modern casino management.

Proprietors' strategies for organizing dealing work during this initial phase of legal gambling centered upon maximizing security. Casinos were small establishments with a low overall volume of play, while the owner typically fronted the house's bankroll each night from his own savings. Under these conditions, a single loss on any large hand could spell disaster. As an operator from this era explained: "There wasn't that much play, and you couldn't afford to [lose] fifty dollars or a hundred dollars, why that was a big score. . . . [Y]ou just didn't have the players to make it up."[98] In response, owners sought to guarantee that the house won as many hands as possible, especially high-stakes ones. A dealer's speed was relatively unimportant, given the low volume of play. Nor was service (what we would today call "emotional labor") expected by the traditional (male, working-class) clientele. Security was what mattered, and only those casinos that maintained control over the outcomes of individual games survived.

Guaranteeing security was no easy matter, however. The technologies we associate with the modern casino (surveillance cameras, shuffling machines, etc.) remained distant dreams, while gamblers' strategies for cheating the house were constantly evolving.[99] The only solution was to run a "flat store," in which the house had the power to manipulate game outcomes. While a "clip joint" might use this power indiscriminately, by cheating all patrons, more respectable establishments let the games proceed fairly until a high roller or suspected cheat sat down at the table.[100] As the son of an early owner recalled: "It wasn't something that went on every roll of the dice. My dad had a philosophy that you knock out the big bet and give everybody a square roll on the small action."[101]

Flat stores depended on "sharp" (i.e., highly skilled) dealers to "knock out the big bet." In fact, casinos required a baseline degree of cheating competence from most dealers, and always employed a handful of "mechanics" who could fix a house win on any given wager. Such proficiency did not come, however, from any formal education. Dealing in this period remained a craft, with few codified standards for delivering cards and collecting chips.[102] Aspiring dealers apprenticed under a veteran, learning not only his (and, rarely, her) distinctive style, but also various "tricks of the trade," including cheating maneuvers.[103]

But this presented a new dilemma for the house: how to trust that a dealer capable of cheating clients would not use these same skills to bilk the house. Following the 1931 casino legalization bill, veteran dealers had flooded into Nevada from nearby states, where gambling remained illegal. The state was awash in "sharpers." The issue facing casinos was thus not one of labor supply but of information: how to establish that a potential employee would show a critical degree of loyalty to the house. Owners, in turn, crafted a two-pronged solution. On one hand, they deployed what we may call a "labor market fix," as owners and top casino personnel would draw upon their social networks to find and evaluate "trusted" workers. They would, for example, track down old coworkers to vouch for an applicant, or even train an existing friend or family member to deal from scratch. This system of social capital–based labor recruitment even had its own, simple, vivid moniker: "juice." A prospective dealer with personal ties to management was "juiced in," while one without connections "lacked juice."

First- and second-degree network connections allowed casino owners to build up a core nucleus of trusted "insider" staff. But as the industry grew and the size of the average tables department increased, simple social capital was inadequate for establishing the character of all workers. William Harrah, eventually one of Nevada's most successful casino operators, described the problems he encountered upon expanding his first card room into a full-fledged casino:

> Operating all the games, instead of one or two games, we had, you know, two or three Craps and six or seven "21s" and a Roulette and a horse book and things. And we couldn't watch it all. . . . [W]e couldn't be everywhere, so we did get cheated. It was from the inside and the outside. We had many crossroaders coming in. . . . But then also, we had some crooked dealers that were goin', so it was really very tough. And at times there, I wondered if we were going to make it, actually.[104]

And in the words of a veteran manager I interviewed, "As the industry took off, it was harder and harder to find good people. I mean, everybody wasn't juiced in. They couldn't have been."

Because a labor market fix alone could not guarantee security, it was supplemented with a "labor process fix." This took the form of an informal bargain negotiated between management and staff centering on the monetary tip-bets made by bettors during the games. Tip-bets (which, you'll recall, are collected by dealers only when players win their hands) were both a recognition of a dealer's agency and a strategy to win his allegiance. And these "bribes," as they came to be called, were, not surprisingly, very popular among dealers. Owners permitted tip-betting, but only as part of a larger (and implicit) bargain: dealers could utilize their skills to assist tippers when the action was light, but when stakes were high, dealers must use these same skills to the house's advantage.

This hegemonic labor compromise was regulated through a variety of institutional and normative mechanisms. Consider a 1939 law pushed through the state legislature by casino interests establishing the legal right of casinos to ban tipping on their "gaming tables."[105] There is no record, however, that any casino ever did so. The law was a form of symbolic leverage, a reminder that a dealer's ability to "hustle tips" was not a right but a privilege granted provisionally by the house. In return for allegiance during high-stakes hands, owners turned a blind eye to dealers' petty hustles and scams. "I worked with the philosophy that there's a little bit of larceny in everyone," a veteran casino manager explained to me. "And of course we had theft among our staff. My motto was always that I would control theft, cuz you couldn't ever eliminate it." There was a fine line, though, between "controlled and "uncontrolled" theft. The latter could result in dismissal or worse, as elaborated (rather graphically) by longtime Nevada casino operator, Ben "Benny" Binion:

> Naturally, some of your dealers steal a little once in awhile, you know. It's to be expected. . . . Fear will not keep 'em from stealin'. I've caught 'em, seen 'em, have 'em lay down on the floor, say "Kill me! I'm a dog. I'm no good." Damn near killed some of 'em too [laughter]. Just kicked the hell out of 'em.[106]

But bosses were not the only ones who could impose negative sanctions when the other side "broke the deal." Dealers in fact operated according to an occupational code whereby uncooperative casinos were "taxed."[107] Warren Nelson recounts his introduction to this subculture as a new dealer in the 1940s:

> One night four or five dealers were sitting there [on break] and one of them was pouring catsup on his pot roast. [The owner] came along and saw him doing this.
>
> He called a waiter over and said, "Get that catsup off that table; those are dealers sitting there and that catsup costs four bits a bottle". . .
>
> One dealer looked at another and said, "No catsup, huh? How much do you think the fine should be?"
>
> The other dealer said, "How about five hundred dollars." The others agreed, so the first thing they did when they got back to the tables was steal five hundred dollars and put it in the [tip-jar]. So that catsup went from fifty cents to five hundred dollars.[108]

Upon taking control of Nevada's casinos during the 1940s and 1950s, organized crime syndicates opted to leave in place the existing regime for managing casino labor. Network-based hiring and a hegemonic compromise with skilled dealers both fit well with the syndicate casino's decentralized structure and its need to secure the flow of money across the tables.

Syndicate casino financiers successfully kept out of public view. Based outside the state, they appointed "clean" owners and executives, even though these "figureheads" typically possessed very little knowledge about how to actually run a casino.[109] As a result, routine management was decentralized to floor-level personnel (especially pit bosses). A combination of veteran Nevada casino employees and transplants from illegal "mob" casinos in other states, these managers made most of the decisions concerning the hiring (and firing) of casino staff.[110] However, although they possessed absolute authority inside the pits, they did not yet have technologies of absolute control at their disposal. Video cameras became available by the 1960s, but they were largely ineffective until recording capabilities were added in the 1980s.[111] The syndicate casino remained by all accounts a security-focused enterprise, one in which financiers and managers obsessed upon "following the money that moved through the premises."[112]

To secure transactions, managers continued to rely on the "juice" system of network-based labor recruitment.[113] In fact, it was not uncommon for a new pit boss to fire *en masse* all of a casino's incumbent dealers to make room for his staff of confederates.[114] One important implication of managers' continued use of juice was the continuation of racial discrimination within the casino labor market. As Nevada's minority population grew during the postwar decades, casinos increasingly hired African Americans—by 1962, they represented 20 percent of the casino workforce statewide—but only in low-status, "back of the house" positions such as porters, maids, and janitors.[115] Such segregation reflected not only the pre-existing character of syndicate managers' personal networks (as Italian-American men came to dominate the pits) but also ingrained stereotypes among tables managers that African Americans should not be trusted to handle cards and chips on the tables.[116] In the coming decades, systematic discrimination against African Americans— especially as dealers—would come to constitute a serious industrial "stigma" within the field of national politics.

And how did syndicate managers organized dealing labor itself? The short answer is that pit bosses continued to rely upon the dexterity of skilled dealers to combat possible player cheating and to assist with various illicit skims and scams.[117] A veteran dealer describes standard job requirements in the 1960s:

> Every [casino] dealt single deck [blackjack] and you had to know how to manipulate cards. . . . You had to learn how to deal seconds, how to sneak a peek, how to roll the deck, how to do a straight and crooked shuffle. . . . These are all things you had to know or you couldn't get a job as a dealer.[118]

Given the industry's tremendous success during these years, managers could have simply "purchased" the allegiance of workers by paying them generous salaries (known in the academic literature as "loyalty wages") and providing them job security.[119] A dealing job could have become a casino career, regulated by bureaucratic rules and offering stable pay.

But this was a (high) road not taken. Casino managers appear to have feared that establishing formal employment contracts would interfere with their ability to "hire at will" confederates and "fire at will" workers suspected of improprieties. They instead continued to allow dealers to act as independent entrepreneurs on the tables. As a dealer explained, "All you had to do with the mob is not cheat them. And you could make your tips or whatever as long as you weren't stealing from them."[120] The late 1940s also witnessed the first serious unionization attempt by Las Vegas casino dealers. In this, as in subsequent unionization drives to this day, casinos prevailed by threatening to forbid tipping should dealers vote in a union.[121] In sum, managers treated tipping as a key component of a larger hegemonic service regime; though it entailed a conflict of interests at the level of the labor process, tipping allowed managers to maintain control of the casino labor market.

The Homelands: Expats, Tipping, and Trust

Thus far we've reconstructed the inner workings of the typical Nevada casino during the mid-twentieth century. These gambling houses were no Weberian bureaucracies, and they certainly were not Foucaultian panopticons. Even at the height of the "mob era," these were medium-sized enterprises reliant upon the eyes and ears of front-line managers to keep the action under control. Practical strategies of management during this era constituted a traditional habitus of control, in that they existed in an unregulated political environment; were localized (we could even say embodied) in the person of the pit boss; evaluated workers not in terms of formal criteria (such as years of education) but various ascriptive characteristics (especially ethnicity and network ties); and involved implicit hegemonic bargains with loyal workers. Managers in apartheid South Africa's homeland casinos deployed an identical set of strategies for regulating service work. They, too, developed and exhibited a traditional habitus of control that decentralized control to local managers and recruited workers in line with dominant racial stereotypes. Homeland croupiers were even permitted to hustle tips on the tables!

In both the United States and apartheid South Africa, an extreme spatial separation of ownership and management led to a *decentralized* authority structure within the casino enterprise. "Mafia" financiers dissimulated their true identities vis-à-vis regulators by residing outside of Nevada; in South Africa, regulations prohibiting "foreign" parties from owning businesses in the homelands meant that top casino executives had to locate their offices in South Africa proper and could make only infrequent (monthly or bimonthly) trips to the homelands. According to my sources, these site visits were treated as "working holidays"—occasions to vacation and even have a "punt" (i.e., to gamble and party). The exploits of one notorious Sun International executive remain a salacious topic of conversation among casino workers throughout South Africa today. I was told several times of his rambunctious behavior during his site inspections. He would sit at a roulette table, a bottle of Scotch at his side, winning and losing large sums of his company's own money in a night. Nor was it ever obvious what these executives were there to inspect. One former property manager whom I interviewed reported that he would prepare detailed quantitative reports in anticipation of the "big visit from corporate." But the "suits" from the head office would barely glance at them, instead spending half the night drinking and "chewing [him] out" over an overflowing ashtray in the casino lounge.

Sporadic and unsystematic monitoring by corporate translated into autonomy for property-level management. As long he stayed in the good graces of corporate executives (especially by catering to their quirks during their informal inspections), a casino manager tucked away in the Transkei or Venda remained free to run his property as if it were his own private fiefdom. In the words of the former general manager of several homeland casinos, "No one could believe the figures these casinos were generating. And as long as we kept posting the numbers, corporate could've cared less about the nitty-gritty of how we did it."

Casino managers also experienced freedom from state oversight. For instance, while apartheid labor statutes specified that homeland firms must hire and train blacks for management positions, casinos instead routinely recruited white expatriates to oversee daily operations throughout the various departments. Veteran croupiers from England were brought down to manage the tables department; white South Africans (mainly Afrikaners) with mechanical expertise would be put in charge of the slot machine division; former South African police personnel oversaw the surveillance department; and white South African women (with backgrounds in banking and finance) typically ran the accounting division. In general, the gambling departments were considered "core," sitting atop the internal hierarchy of administrative units. The other departments were considered their "support" services. Human resource units, for instance, were pejoratively referred to as "filing services," and marketing departments as "pretty girls in short skirts [who] greet gamblers at the door."

Like their Nevada counterparts, pit bosses in the homeland casinos had to guarantee a minimal degree of security on the tables, without the assistance of video cameras, shuffling machines, and the like. In response, they too developed and deployed a "labor market fix." In Nevada, the main obstacle to a complete labor market solution had been an information problem: sharp dealers were a dime a dozen, but how did one know whom to trust? In the homelands, the problem was one of supply. Around the casinos were large populations of "locals" (the managerial euphemism for black citizens of the homelands) eager for employment. And indeed, locals were widely employed in "back of house" jobs involving cleaning, construction, and food service. But managers drew a sharp and categorical distinction between gambling and "support" functions—the former were reserved for whites only. "As a rule," a former manager explained, "blacks were never to touch a [gambling] chip."

Having ruled out local blacks, whence did homeland managers find dealers? One alternative possibility was white South Africans, though they appear to have been unwilling to relocate to the black homelands just to deal cards. Whites, I was told by the former casino manager introduced earlier, would not relocate unless they were assured of a managerial position. The homeland casinos instead commenced recruiting croupiers from England, mainly young workers in their twenties. Sun International (like Holiday Inn and Southern Sun before it) subcontracted a British labor agency to screen potential workers and relocate them to southern Africa. This "expat" system of recruitment was by no means inexpensive. Nonetheless, it was deemed a great success by casino managers because it created a workforce considered entirely trustworthy. British croupiers, they believed, would have no incentive to engage in petty theft or scams. As a former pit boss explained, "UK dealers weren't gonna come all the way down here and put their careers on the line for ten bucks here or there. They wouldn't steal unless they could [get enough to] retire on."

The resulting intra-casino division of labor exemplified the notorious South African "color bar," by which blacks were excluded from skilled positions, were never to have authority over whites, and were paid only 15 to 20 percent that of white workers.[122] Toward the end of apartheid, this rule was relaxed, and some local blacks were selected to become casino dealers. But during the first two decades of apartheid gambling, the casino workforce was completely segregated. Consider the following account from "Ellen," a white South African and former human resources manager in a Bophuthatswana casino:

AUTHOR: Can you give me an overview, a sense of how you went about finding workers at [your casino]?

ELLEN: For low-level management, the bigwigs in the casino would just bring people in. We'd get a call saying so-and-so wanted to hire the nephew of his golfing buddy, and they'd be hired. If we needed unskilled help, we'd tell a couple current workers and word would spread like wildfire. The next morning there'd be hundreds of people lined up at the front gates. Sometimes we'd receive instructions that a certain friend or relative of [Bophuthatswana president] Mangope or some other government bigwig was to be put on the payroll. Often they didn't even speak English, but that's a whole other story. For all skilled casino positions, we'd run recruiting drives overseas.

AUTHOR: Was this difficult to organize, bringing them into the country?

ELLEN: No way, man, getting work permits was never a problem.

Later in the interview, Ellen claimed that Bophuthatswana's immigration office was funded and staffed by officials from her company. Though I could not verify this, her belief evidences the autonomy from state oversight that casino management experienced. The interview also illustrates several themes of this section: the surplus of local workers for "unskilled" positions, the "recruiting drives overseas" to find trusted tables staff, and illicit ties between the company and homeland leaders.

Finally, we consider strategies for organizing the action in the pits and on the tables. In brief, as in Nevada, homeland managers permitted dealers to accept tips and to engage in various entrepreneurial "hustling" games on the tables. This "labor process fix" was actually a way to buttress the expatriate labor recruitment system. In England, national gambling legislation prohibited croupiers from accepting gratuities. Tipping thus became a wage inducement to increase the supply of inherently trustworthy labor. As a casino executive explained, "We went with the tips because they were essential for the recruitment drives to get the British croupiers down here. We would consider it a part of the base salary that we advertised, and this would bring more people down." Former homeland croupiers indeed confirmed that the chance to make tips was a major factor in the decision to emigrate to southern Africa. Nikki describes why she left England in the early 1980s:

NIKKI: I was eighteen and working in a club around Manchester. We were all looking to bugger off, get a job on a cruise ship or something. At the time, South Africa was the place to come, everyone talked about it as the promised land. You made such good money. Like seven hundred and fifty bucks per month, plus two to three times that in tips. Sun paid for our housing, I had a beachfront flat . . . near Durban. All the girls had diamond earrings, all the guys wore Rolexes.

AUTHOR: But was it strange living in the homelands? In these independent black states?

NIKKI: It was like a big party! You had a swimming pool and you had a car and it was a fantasy land.

In both Nevada and the homelands, then, tipping originated *not* as a means for generating customer service. Both industries were oligopolies, and managers appear not to have asked workers to perform any emotional labor. A former homeland manager described his orientation to service thusly: "We viewed ourselves as the only game in town. If you don't like how we do things, cheers, go home." The same sentiment

Table 5 Conditions for a Traditional Managerial Habitus

	State Regulation	Industry Structure	Production Goal	Labor Market Problem	Solution
United States (1931–1970)	Minimal/perfunctory	Decentralized firms in monopolistic markets	Security	Information	Juice system + tipping (as compromise to regulate commitment)
South Africa (1970–1994)	Minimal/perfunctory	Decentralized firms in monopolistic markets	Security	Supply	Expat recruitment + tipping (to buttress labor supply)

has been documented to have characterized the managerial philosophy towards service in the early Nevada casino.[123] In sum, rather than a straightforward *service* inducement, tipping represented a roundabout way to ensure *security*.

Tipping furthermore resulted in an entrepreneurial "work-game" for dealers that was identical in both countries. Former homeland dealers reported that their nightly labor consisted of tip-making strategies akin to those employed by Nevada dealers. Nikki, introduced above, worked in all four major homelands during her career as a croupier and inspector. She described to me how she would "hustle" players:

> They loved us. These old Afrikaner men and us English girls. We English have the gift of gab, you know, and we would sweet talk them. A punter [i.e., gambler] would throw a bill down and ask for change, and we would snatch it up and announce "for the girls" [i.e., a tip] with a little wink or smile. That's all it took.

In South Africa, floor managers even received a percentage of the nightly tips collected by dealers. Homeland pit bosses thus had an added, direct incentive to endorse dealers' tip-making games.

In conclusion, this chapter highlighted *convergence* in the political origins of gambling industries in the United States and South Africa, as well as in the practical strategies deployed by managers during these early days. Security was initially their main concern; in response, they developed both a "labor market fix" (the use of networks and stereotypes to find "trusted" workers) and a "labor process fix" (granting workers autonomy to "hustle" tips on the tables). Together, these strategies both expressed a traditional habitus of control and constituted a hegemonic service regime (see table 5). This mode of managing labor and leisure, however, would come under assault, when casino industries were pulled into larger political struggles to advance the collective good by modernizing markets of labor and capital. It is to these struggles that we now turn.

SEVEN

The Birth of Regulation

STATES, STIGMATA, AND SYMBOLIC CAPITAL

Part I compared the experience of service work in the United States and South Africa at the turn of the twenty-first century. Dealing labor at Nevada's Silver State Casino is organized hegemonically, with croupiers granted autonomy to "make tips," while Johannesburg's Gold City Casino is organized despotically, as managers monitor dealers closely and deskill their labor. But these disparate service regimes of today stand in sharp contrast to the common historical origins of the two casino industries as described in the previous chapter. In both early Nevada and the homelands of South Africa, the labor of luck had been organized hegemonically, with trusted dealers permitted to hustle tips. How are we to account for these divergent trajectories? Why have managerial strategies for organizing service work remain unchanged in the united States? And why did they change so dramatically in South Africa?

The explanation is to be found in the systems of state regulation that eventually arose to oversee gambling industries. After having been sequestered for decades in the deserts of Nevada and in the desolate homelands, casinos suddenly found themselves at the center of debates taking place on the national political stage. In the United States, casinos were first pulled into the political arena during the tumultuous 1960s, as part of larger symbolic struggles over the purity of the country's economic institutions and the civil rights of minorities. Half a world away and two decades later, the end of apartheid entailed the reintegration of the formerly "independent" homeland states into South Africa proper. The question of what to do with the homeland casinos became integral to larger questions of how to craft social and economic policies for the new nation. In both cases, industry regulations were forged in fire, in the midst of political struggles to define the national good.

In neither country did casinos come under attack because of their "exploitation" of consumers. Rather, criticisms focused upon the (corrupt) character of proprietors as well as their (discriminatory) treatment of nonwhite workers. The fundamental character of the industry's capital and labor markets, we may say, became "institutional stigmata." For the managers and local state officials who depended on legal gambling for profits and tax revenues, respectively, such stigmata were a serious problem. To deal with—and disavow—them, they crafted new licensing criteria (specifying that casinos must be run by responsible corporate entities) and labor market rules (stipulating that firms must engage in equitable employment practices). This chapter describes how this process—the birth of regulation—unfolded in the United States and South Africa.

THE UNITED STATES

Remonstrance and Riposte

The decades following Nevada's 1931 casino bill were a period in which "gambling regulation was casual at best, and there was almost no attention given to the fact that many of the men who were building and operating the elaborate casinos . . . had criminal records."[1] But it was not only owners' problematic biographies (i.e., their criminal pasts) that escaped serious scrutiny, it was also the Jim Crow character of their casinos (i.e., their overtly discriminatory treatment of African Americans). Both issues made casinos potentially "discreditable" entities within an evolving national political field in which "clean" capital markets and "equitable" labor markets were becoming normative ideals. In fact, when these two issues did finally draw attention, they came to constitute full-fledged stigmata for Nevada's casinos. The consequences of this transition from discreditable to discredited status were swift and dramatic, as industry proponents moved to counter these legitimacy threats and salvage the fate of the industry.

As this overview suggests, the system of industry regulation that eventually emerged in Nevada did not derive from political dynamics internal to the state. In fact, as we saw in the chapter prior, Nevada politicians initially legalized gambling as a means for raising tax dollars, and exerted little effort to regulate operators' business practices. Benign neglect as a regulatory philosophy was only further reinforced as the industry continued to grow during the 1950s and 1960s (annual revenues during these decades increased from $39.5 million to $543.7 million). Nor did the growing state populace object to the permanent presence of casinos in Nevada. The first reliable opinion survey, in 1948, revealed that only 9 percent of Nevadans favored banning casinos; by 1962, the figure had dropped to 5 percent.[2] Public support derived from the "perception that gambling kept taxes low" because it "threw much of the tax burden upon the tourist."[3]

Instead, regulations governing casinos were forged in response to two external threats. One emanated from a classic "moral panic" concerning the presence of a shadowy foreign "Mafia" in the United States; the other from struggles to ensure the civil rights of minorities.[4] We consider first the "Mafia panic." Federal law enforcement agencies in the United States had historically focused upon high-profile crimes such as bank robberies and kidnappings, leaving the investigation of more mundane forms of criminal activity to local authorities. During the late 1940s, however, many "petty" crimes that had previously been considered unrelated (illicit gambling, prostitution, extortion, etc.) were grouped together under the rubric of "racketeering" and framed not simply as isolated local problems, but as the coordinated efforts of foreign crime syndicates. In 1947, the U.S. Department of Justice launched a "racket squad" to uncover these syndicates, while U.S. Attorney General J. Howard McGrath pressured local officials "to capture the popular imagination in a stirring campaign to crush organized crime."[5] These "highly sensationalized charges triggered a national hysteria," concurrent with and analogous to the Red Scare, as politicians crusaded to expose and excise from U.S. society not only suspected Communists but reputed "gangsters."[6]

In 1950, Joseph McCarthy, then a freshman senator from Wisconsin, lobbied to head an investigative commission on racketeering, only to be outmaneuvered by fellow senator Estes Kefauver of Tennessee. When Kefauver was appointed head of the Special Commission to Investigate Organized Crime in Interstate Commerce, McCarthy turned his attention to fighting Communism. From the start, Kefauver considered gambling to be the most dangerous of all racketeering-related crimes, as revealed by his statement of the commission's purpose: "A full and complete study and investigation of interstate gambling and racketeering activities."[7] In fact, it was only through pressure applied by Nevada's longtime senator Pat McCarran that the commission's scope was broadened to include not just gambling but other forms of criminal activity.[8]

Both the methods used and the conclusions reached by the Kefauver Commission were dramatic, even sensational. There was, Kefauver stated in his final report, "a shadowy, international criminal organization known as the Mafia, so fantastic that most Americans find it hard to believe."[9] Based out of Italy, the well-organized Mafia had infiltrated the political and economic institutions of the United States. And though it had bases in New York and Chicago, the "mob" used Nevada as the hub for its criminal activities. In a paradigmatic case of a "political witch hunt," Kefauver held a hearing in Las Vegas on November 15, 1950. In front of national television cameras, he chastised Nevada politicians and casino personnel for undermining American values.[10] "As a case history of legalized gambling," Kefauver declared, "Nevada speaks eloquently in the negative." Not only was gambling an activity that "produces nothing and adds nothing to the economy," but Nevada's casinos were run by mobsters, its government corrupt and inept. Here Kefauver uncovered an "alliance of gamblers, gangsters, and government" serving only to lend the Mafia a "cloak of respectability."[11]

Nevada politicians tried to counter Kefauver's accusations. They argued before the commission that insofar as the state needed experienced gambling operators to run their casinos, and insofar as theirs was the only state in which gambling was legal, they'd had no choice but to license "criminals."[12] Kefauver's opinion of this argument is expressed well in his final report:

> When Counsel Halley asked [Nevada Tax Commission member William Moore] how the Tax Commission could possibly have licensed a certain Detroit gambler named Wertheimer, who had a flagrant record for illegal operations in other states, Moore replied: "Sure, but . . . that is no sign he shouldn't have a license in a state where it is legal." Halley incredulously asked: "It makes no difference to you whether he gambles in a state where it is not legal" "No," drawled Moore, "how else was he going to learn the business?"[13]

Although much casino financing during this era did originate with known crime syndicates, the historical consensus is that Kefauver greatly exaggerated the extent to which these groups constituted a coherent, much less international, organization controlling America's key institutions. Nonetheless, Kefauver's inflammatory rhetoric had immediate and (from the point of view of Nevada politicians) ominous consequences. In the aftermath of the hearings, a flurry of legislation was drafted to increase federal authority over gambling in the United States (read: Nevada). In 1951, Congress passed the Transportation of Gambling Devices Act, requiring manufacturers of casino equipment to register annually with the Department of Justice; in 1952, the American Bar Association disseminated a "Model Anti-Gambling Act" for fighting organized crime.[14] Most significantly, Kefauver proposed a 10 percent tax on all casino transactions in the country, "enough to discourage most customers and effectively destroy the industry in Nevada."[15] While the proposed tax did not make it through Congress, Nevada politicians took the federal threat very seriously. As Kefauver's nemesis, the "drawling" William Moore, recalled, "It became obvious . . . that, if somebody didn't get control of this business, sooner or later there would be no business."[16]

Making Gambling a Privilege

The dilemma facing Nevada following the Kefauver crusade was "how to maintain revenue generated by the gangsters while dissociating the state from their disrepute."[17] State officials responded by crafting a privilege theory of licensing, whereby the state assumed the power to investigate potential proprietors and deny property rights to questionable applicants.

The legal groundwork for a privilege theory had actually been in place since 1931. In that year, the Nevada Supreme Court had established that "gaming as a calling or business is in the same class as the selling of intoxicating liquors in respect to deleterious tendency. The state may regulate or suppress it without interfering with any . . . inherent rights of citizenship."[18] This judgment was referenced periodically in the following two decades, for instance, by state officials to justify the 1945 casino Tax Act,[19] and by the Nevada attorney general following the 1947 murder of Bugsy Siegel (in a published opinion that the state should consider "the character of applicants" when issuing licenses).[20] But only in the wake of the Kefauver hearings was the philosophy of privilege translated into concrete administrative procedures, when Nevada's legislature codified for the first time standards for evaluating license applicants: they could not be foreign "aliens," could not have had any felony convictions within the previous five years, and must be free of ties with suspected organized crime syndicates.

The casino industry initially resisted new regulations, culminating in a showdown before the Nevada Supreme Court. The backlash was spearheaded by two prominent casino operators, Marion Hicks and Clifford Jones (the latter of whom was also the state's lieutenant governor). The men co-owned a Las Vegas casino called the Thunderbird, and in 1955, they had received notice that their license was being revoked due to widespread suspicions that the establishment was secretly bankrolled by notorious crime boss Meyer Lansky. Hicks and Jones successfully sued the state in district court, arguing that regulators had not produced sufficient evidence of illicit financing to revoke their license. The Nevada Supreme Court, however, agreed to hear the state's appeal, seizing the chance to definitively "[fix] the jurisdictional area within which the courts shall act in this field of gambling control."[21]

The case boiled down to a single issue: do regulators have unfettered autonomy to grant and deny licenses, or must they adhere to the evidentiary standards of a criminal trial? If the former, the decisions of regulators would be considered final, applicants would be denied the right to appeal, and the privilege theory of licensing would be validated. The Nevada Supreme Court, in its 1957 decision, did indeed affirm the state's position concerning the ultimate authority for licensing:

> For gambling to take its lawful place in Nevada it is not enough that this state has named it lawful. We have but offered it the opportunity for lawful existence. The offer is a risky one, not only for the people of this state, but for the entire nation. Organized crime must not be given refuge here through the legitimatizing of one of its principal sources of income. . . . Not only must the operation of gambling be carefully controlled, but the character and background of those who would engage in gambling in this state must be carefully scrutinized.[22]

That the ruling was not simply a technical clarification for industry insiders but a strategic move to buttress the industry's image in the larger field of national politics is suggested by its tone and imagery. The court even adopted much of Kefauver's own rhetoric regarding, for example, the danger that the state could provide "refuge" for "organized crime," as well as the association of "controlled" gambling with the well-being of the "entire nation."

The state now moved to build the bureaucratic infrastructure to administer its privilege theory of licensing. The leading figure in this movement was new Democratic governor Grant Sawyer, elected in 1959

on a platform of strict "casino control" (one that played well to a citizenry anxious about the fate of its cash cow). In a famous speech, Sawyer
articulated his regulatory philosophy thus: "My feeling, to state it briefly,
is this. Get tough and stay tough. A gambling license is a privilege—it
is not a right."[23] Sawyer's administration pushed the state legislature to
pass the Gaming Control Act of 1959 (the first significant piece of casino
legislation since the 1945 Tax Act), which established a full-time Gaming
Commission as "the ultimate authority on all gaming matters" in the
state and charged it with "sole responsibility for issuing licenses." The
act also created a Gaming Control Board to serve as the commission's
enforcement arm.[24] Both commission and board members, furthermore,
were to be appointed by the governor and granted a full-time salary, so
as to insulate them from political and economic pressures.

The Gaming Control Act also specified new criteria for casino licensing. These were broadly defined, to give the commission wide discretion
in its decisions. A licensee had to be a "person of integrity, honesty and
good character" who would not constitute "a threat to the public health,
safety, morals, good order and general welfare of the state." Even rumors
of "association with unsuitable persons" could constitute case for denial
of a license.[25] As a member of the commission explained, "The law [was
set] so broad that you probably could deny a license, if you expressed the
reason, because a guy had blue eyes."[26]

To publicly signal the tenacity with which they now evaluated
potential casino owners, officials designed a series of "regulatory rituals." Casino applicants were required to appear before the Gaming
Commission and publicly avow that they had never had personal
dealings with the Mafia (a ceremony echoing one performed by Joe
McCarthy's House Committee on Un-American Activities, in which
prominent Americans were required to avow that they were "not and had
never been a Communist"). The commission also published an annual
"black book" containing mug shots and aliases of notorious mobsters
permanently banned from the state's casinos. Many of these rituals drew
upon dominant racial, ethnic, and religious stereotypes. For instance,
Mormons constituted a disproportionately large percentage of Gaming
Commission and Gaming Control Board members.[27] Jerome Skolnick,

based upon firsthand fieldwork inside these regulatory agencies, argued this to be an intentional symbolic maneuver targeted towards actors at the national level: "When a Mormon presides on a board regulating an industry stigmatized by . . . the notorious history of gangland connections in Las Vegas, the Mormon projection cleanses."[28] Regulators also promulgated an image of the disreputable gangster/gambler as Italian, even though Jewish Americans had constituted the majority of early casino financiers.[29]

How successful were these initial efforts at "cleansing" the industry? Despite the great fanfare with which regulators went about investigating applicants, they were unable to detect and eliminate the influence of crime syndicates. The reason was simple: effective regulation of the industry's capital market conflicted with the state's long-standing tradition of guaranteeing employers control over labor markets.[30] Syndicate investors remained out of state (and behind a wall of fictive firms and figurehead owners), but still coordinated skims and scams through their personal ties with confederates on the casino floor (the pit bosses and their dealers).[31] The state literally could not *see* this influence, insofar as it had no authority to do background checks on workers or to demand that casinos dismiss suspect staff. That regulators nonetheless *sensed* the presence of "improper" elements is implied by the recollections of a former Gaming Control Board member:

> We found it very difficult to extend authority much below the level of ownership. We couldn't really determine who was qualified to work for an owner, nor were we in a position to go to an owner and demand that he fire somebody just because we didn't happen to think that they were proper people.[32]

Widespread suspicions that Nevada's casino industry remained under the secret control of crime syndicates provoked a second, even more serious threat from federal officials. It was spearheaded by Robert F. Kennedy, who had been appointed U.S. attorney general in 1960 by his brother, President John F. Kennedy. Like Kefauver, Robert Kennedy viewed the Italian Mafia as a serious and imminent threat to the American way of life. He had first gained renown as chief counsel to the Senate Labor

Rackets Committee, exposing connections between labor unions and organized crime. From this came a book, provocatively titled *The Enemy Within*.[33] Like Kefauver, Kennedy considered Nevada to be the Mafia's main source of legitimacy and financing. He publicly chastised the state as "the bank of America's organized crime."[34]

As attorney general, Robert Kennedy publicly pledged to "press Congress to close down gambling."[35] He tripled the number of FBI personnel in Las Vegas and began preparations for a massive raid on Nevada's casinos. Unlike state-level regulators, however, Kennedy understood that to fully expose secret syndicate owners would entail first learning more about the true identities and illicit activities of their confederates on the casino floor. In collaboration with FBI director J. Edgar Hoover, he ordered the wiretapping of homes of department heads, pit bosses, and even dealers. But this (illegal) surveillance program was discovered and exposed in the press, causing considerable consternation among Nevada politicians. Governor Sawyer publicly accused Robert Kennedy of "domestic espionage" and "harassment against the state of Nevada."[36] Sawyer, whose intense campaigning had helped John F. Kennedy carry Nevada by the slimmest of margins in the 1960 election, personally appealed to the President to forestall the raid.[37] President Kennedy intervened, negotiating a temporary truce between the two sides, and following the 1963 assassination of his brother, Robert Kennedy left the attorney general's office to focus his energy on a New York senate run. This afforded Nevada some breathing room, and once again the federal threat to the casino industry moved to the front of the state's political agenda.

Sawyer's successor to the governorship, Republican Paul Laxalt, not only ran on a platform to "erase the image that we are in bed with hoodlums,"[38] he proposed a new tack to the problem: rather than attempting (futilely) to *police* organized crime figures out of the industry, the state should *replace* them with publicly traded firms. Independently regulated by the Securities and Exchange Commission, publicly traded firms would have an incentive to "avoid negative publicity" and "would stand to lose more should they be caught cheating."[39] They would also have access to large pools of investment capital. Nevada politicians, in short, saw a fully "free" capital market as the panacea to the state's image problem. How could the mob compete with modern, well-funded corporations?

To make a "free market" is, perhaps paradoxically, always a political project, one requiring active and ongoing intervention on the part of the state.[40] Laxalt's administration had to engage in two such interventions. The first was a reform of existing licensing procedures, which specified that all stockholders in a casino firm must be personally licensed by the state. This 1955 policy had been an attempt to preclude hidden ownership by organized crime figures. Besides being an abject failure, it had had the unintended consequence of excluding from the industry publicly traded firms, whose thousands of shareholders were unlikely to make the trek to Carson City for personal appearances before the Gaming Commission. Laxalt lobbied the state legislature, which was easily persuaded to rewrite the law. Nevada's 1969 Corporate Gaming Act thus required the personal licensing of only those owning 10 percent or more of the stock in a casino firm.

A second and less tractable problem was that publicly traded firms had long expressed wariness about acquiring a stake in the industry. (This was in fact the reason why policy makers had not foreseen the issue in 1955.) Accepted wisdom on Wall Street held that casinos, though potentially profitable in the short term, were on the whole a risky investment, given frequent federal crackdowns.[41] Again, Laxalt skillfully intervened when an opportunity presented itself. In 1966, Howard Hughes, the aging but still well-respected American entrepreneur, had relocated to Las Vegas.[42] Laxalt befriended Hughes and, when he expressed interest in the casino industry, encouraged him to invest. The governor and state Gaming Commission then fast-tracked the purchase by Hughes of several of Las Vegas's "problem" casinos. By 1970, Hughes's Summa Corporation controlled one-seventh of the state's casino revenues.[43]

Although the Summa Corporation was privately held, the presence in Las Vegas of "the amazing Howard Hughes" (as he was called in a 1977 biopic) sufficiently quelled the concerns of several publicly traded leisure firms. The Hilton Corporation was the first to invest in Nevada. It purchased two casinos in 1970 and set Wall Street abuzz in 1976, when the firm reported that these properties now accounted for 43 percent of its total revenues.[44] Holiday Inn, Ramada, and others soon followed suit, such that by the end of the decade, publicly traded firms controlled over half of the Nevada casino market.[45]

The project to displace "mob" owners with corporate ones was a success. If anything, the "cleansing" of the capital market occurred more quickly than could a concomitant restructuring of the labor market. As of the early 1980s, "hundreds of high-level executives in various casinos still had ties to or experience with the mob."[46] Several skimming scandals were even uncovered at major casinos in that decade,[47] though these appear to have been isolated events, not coordinated efforts of national crime syndicates. And there is no doubt that the industry's new corporate image satisfied federal authorities. In 1976, Congress ordered a national overview of gambling policy; the tone of its final report could not have differed more from that of the Kefauver and Kennedy crusades. It concluded:

> During the 1960s, syndicate control over casino operations began to be replaced by large corporate investments in gambling properties . . . a situation the Gaming Commission believes has resulted in the weeding out of undesirables. . . . Scrupulously controlled private enterprise has proven successful in Nevada.[48]

Nevada's casinos, in sum, were now corporate and thus clean.

Equal Enjoyment versus Equal Employment

Overt discrimination against racial minorities also came to constitute a stigma for Nevada's casinos within the national political field. At the same time that Robert Kennedy was targeting the industry's corrupt capital market, federal agencies and activist groups, as part of a larger civil rights struggle, were pressuring casinos to modernize their labor practices and to fulfill affirmative action requirements. Casino management resisted such intrusions, while regulators refused to make "equal rights" a precondition for property rights.

The struggle to desegregate casinos was waged on two fronts. The first, focused upon consumers, was a swift success. The Nevada branch of the

Figure 6. Governor Sawyer and civil rights leaders strategize how to pressure casinos to integrate. Courtesy of UNLV Libraries, Special Collections.

National Association for the Advancement of Colored People (NAACP) had for decades pressured the state legislature to outlaw consumer discrimination. Bills ordering integration were introduced in 1939, 1949, 1953, and 1957, though none passed.[49] With the election of governor Grant Sawyer in 1958, however, the NAACP had for the first time a powerful ally in the state government. Sawyer swayed conservative members of the legislature by arguing that segregation would generate adverse publicity during the 1960 winter Olympic games in northern Nevada. The NAACP, meanwhile, organized several public actions, including a march along the famous Las Vegas Strip. The Nevada Resort Association (NRA), the trade group representing casinos, responded by pledging to desegregate their facilities. In 1960, it signed a written agreement to this effect and, by all accounts, subsequently ceased discriminating against minority consumers.[50]

The second front in the fight against discrimination focused on employment. Although African Americans had migrated to the state in large numbers during the previous two decades, as of the early 1960s, there were no blacks employed in the industry's most visible (and lucrative) occupation: dealing.[51] Governor Sawyer and the NAACP attempted to recreate their success in ending consumer discrimination, but the same tactics provoked even stauncher resistance and ultimately failed. It would take direct intervention by the federal government to compel casinos to commit to equitable labor market policies.

From the start, Governor Sawyer recognized that the most effective way to pressure casinos would be to make fair hiring practices a precondition of a gaming license. As he explained, "There are some broad, generic terms in the gaming regulations, such as 'unsuitable methods of operation' that can be used in calling up [i.e., summoning before the Gambling Commission] a licensee. . . . Denial of employment rights could be determined to be not in the best interests of the state."[52] But the commission refused to tie "employment rights" to its new privilege theory of licensing. In a 1960 opinion, the state attorney general settled the dispute between Sawyer and the commission, ruling definitively that "civil rights" lay beyond the purview of gambling regulation:

> [Nevada law empowers] the Commission to attach conditions [to a state gaming license] only when those conditions are directly related to licensing and controlling gaming within the State of Nevada. . . . For the Commission, as an administrative agency, to pronounce what civil rights must be observed by state gaming licensees is to extend the Commission's authority beyond the sphere of gaming.[53]

Sawyer responded by creating a state Commission on the Equal Rights of Citizens (CERC) to monitor the hiring practices of employers (widely understood to mean casinos) and to handle complaints of discrimination. However, "the legislature assured that the commission would be powerless to fulfill its mandate by providing it with no staff and almost no money."[54] (Staffed by volunteers, the CERC's annual budget was less than that of the state's taxi cab authority.)[55]

As a last resort, Sawyer confronted the casinos directly regarding the conspicuous absence of African Americans behind the tables. But managers were obstinate. In a series of informal meetings with the governor, they defended their labor market practices. They argued that black dealers would scare off white gamblers, and even that blacks lacked the innate capacity to perform the numerical calculations necessary to deal. As Sawyer later recounted:[56]

> The personnel director of one of the [casinos] told me . . . "We have a black boy that we just think the world of. . . . We'd all love to see him get ahead. We've spent a lot of time and money on him, and we tried to make a 'Twenty-One' dealer out of him. . . . But," he said, "there's just one thing that you can't overcome . . . you've got to be able to count up to twenty-one. And," he said, "this boy just couldn't do it."[57]

The NAACP also attempted to reproduce tactics successful in fighting consumer segregation to achieve employment desegregation. In early 1963, it planned a public picket line on the Las Vegas Strip, this one to draw attention to employment discrimination in the casino industry. This caused sufficient concern among casinos to elicit a pledge to commence training and employing blacks, especially as dealers.[58] In contrast to their behavior with respect to the consumer desegregation agreement, however, casinos dragged their feet. In fact, not until three years later, in 1966, was a black dealer hired on the Las Vegas Strip.[59] An inspector for the Gaming Control Board described the situation as of the late 1960s: "There were [black] waiters and there were even black cocktail waitresses. . . . [The casinos] were hiring blacks to do everything but deal."[60]

Unsatisfied with the snail-like pace at which casinos were moving to integrate their dealing staffs, the NAACP filed a complaint with the National Labor Relations Board.[61] Casinos responded with further pledges to hire black workers and agreed to a series of remedial measures such as diversity training for white managers, targeted job recruitment in black neighborhoods, and a $75,000 grant to the Nevada branch of the NAACP.[62] Again, though, progress was slow. By 1971, a full decade after the initial pledge to integrate African Americans behind the tables, they made up just 4.9 percent of Las Vegas dealers and less than 1 percent of floor managers (far below their representation in the local labor market).[63]

Like the invisible presence of corrupt "mob" owners, the visible absence of black dealers would attract unwanted attention to casinos on the national stage. It was a time of intense civil rights struggles across America, the crowning achievement of which was the 1964 Civil Rights Act banning discrimination in various spheres, including employment. In the decade following the passage of the act, the federal government received thousands of complaints from workers across all sectors of the economy.[64] To most efficiently use their limited resources, officials practiced a form of "regulatory pragmatism."[65] This entailed, for instance, forgoing costly litigation against every suspected discriminator and instead negotiating consent decrees with select, high-profile companies. The purpose of these decrees was twofold: not only to remedy labor practices in that particular industry, but also to make a more general statement about the rights and responsibilities of private firms in America.

Nevada's casinos were a perfect test case for the consent decree mechanism. Las Vegas was in the national spotlight because of both its glitzy image (several books and films had recently been released on "Sin City") and Robert Kennedy's recent crusade on the casino industry. The latter, in particular, was assumed to have made casino managers especially sensitive about their public image. Also, the current transition to corporate ownership offered an opportunity to transform traditional business practices. The successful imposition of a consent decree upon Nevada's casinos would thus represent more than an attempt to alter the demographics of a single service occupation; it would be a symbolic statement that equitable labor market practices were an essential component of good corporate citizenship.

On June 4, 1971, the U.S. Department of Justice filed a formal complaint against the Nevada Resort Association alleging multiple violations of the Civil Rights Act.[66] The complaint stated that although blacks fill 18 percent of total industry jobs, they "are limited to the lowest-paying, less desirable duties and occupations."[67] Three long-standing business practices were pegged as responsible for this state of affairs: first, the personalistic "juice" system of recruitment whereby casinos "hir[ed] employees for certain jobs by relying upon word-of-mouth referrals and personal contacts of incumbents"; second, the placement of workers into jobs based on their ascriptive characteristics rather than their objective qualifications; and third, a failure "to provide opportunities for training, advancement and promotion to black applicants and employees equal to those provided white[s]."[68]

In preliminary meetings with the Justice Department, lawyers for the NRA sought to temper the tone and terms of the decree, with mixed success. On one hand, casinos succeeded in inserting language specifying that in signing the decree, they admitted no past wrongdoing: "This decree . . . shall not constitute an adjudication or finding on the merits of the case and shall not constitute or be construed as an admission by the defendants."[69] On the other hand, they pressed unsuccessfully for permission to hire other minority groups besides African Americans.[70] As a party to the negotiations recalled, "Basically, [the Justice Department] set the percentages of jobs in each category that had to be [filled]. Now, they abandoned all pretense of making it a *minority* compliance . . . they just came right out and said *black*. They have to be black people not minority people."[71]

The consent decree, signed in 1971, specified concrete steps to remedy discrimination in the pits.[72] Regarding hiring, the juice system had to end. Each casino was to "establish and thereafter maintain a central personnel office" to evaluate applicants, and information on job openings had to be advertised in local newspapers (including those with predominantly black circulation), rather than through "word of mouth."[73] The decree also specified precise hiring quotas: for every two new dealer openings, one black must be hired until blacks constituted 12.5 percent of a casino's tables staff. And should the local labor market not supply enough black dealers, special "in-house" dealing schools had to be run for new black hires. As for job placement and promotion into supervisory positions, personal networks and subjective assessments were no longer appropriate mechanisms. Notifications of vacancies had to be posted "near the time clock or other location[s] to which employees have regular access." In addition, all black workers were to complete a skills inventory with which casino executives would "engage in affirmative recruitment of black persons for future vacancies [as] 'Officials and Managers.'"[74]

But the most significant aspect of the consent decree was its specification of concrete, comprehensive procedures for state monitoring of casinos' labor market practices. Firms were required to submit quarterly reports to the federal government detailing the racial composition of all job categories. The decree also stipulated that managers must keep detailed records on all personnel decisions, records that could be audited on site by government officials, "provided requests for such documents shall not be so frequent as to impose a burden or expense on defendants."[75] Finally, the decree named the terms by which a casino could be released from monitoring. If, after three years, all jobs had reached the 12.5 percent goal, a casino could petition for release.[76]

From 1972 to 1974, casinos sent their "quarterly labor reports" to the U.S. Justice Department. In response to an inquiry from a University of Nevada professor, the department described how it processed them:

> Copies of the quarterly reports from the resort industry are filed with this office, where they are given close attention and analysis. The reports themselves are keyed to Section VI of the Decree, which . . . provide[s] a comprehensive picture of the employment practices of the respondents. . . . In addition, we keep in close contact with the hotels concerning their performance under the decree.[77]

In May 1974, responsibility for monitoring the decree was transferred to the new Equal Employment Opportunity Commission (EEOC), created specifically to enforce Title VII of the Civil Rights Act.

By the late 1970s, then, a very different gambling industry had emerged in Nevada. No longer autonomous, it was now governed by regulations intended to "clean up" both its capital markets *and* its labor markets.

SOUTH AFRICA

Purifying the Past

The formation of industrial policy in Nevada was not a natural and inevitable step in the "life course" of the industry. Rather, regulations were a political response to challenges emanating from outside the state. Local politicians and proprietors, who for years had used casinos to generate taxes and profits, scurried to defend their industry. They had to convince external audiences that casinos were owned and operated in accord with the public good. Coincidentally, an identical dynamic took place in southern Africa. The end of apartheid gave rise to the question of what to do about the homeland casinos. In fact, the question of gambling policy became central to larger debates about how to advance the national good in the "new South Africa." For incumbent casino operators and other industry advocates, such debates constituted legitimacy threats; in response, they, too, crafted regulations to ensure "clean" corporate ownership and "equitable" labor market practices.

We begin in South Africa where we left off in the United States, with efforts to reform long-standing race-based strategies for recruiting casino dealers. In South Africa, though, these efforts at reform were initiated by casino firms themselves. During the late 1980s, top executives at Sun International began speculating informally among themselves about the fate of their homeland casino monopoly if and when apartheid should fall. The general sentiment was that the ruling white regime would not be able to hold onto power much longer. "We could see the writing on the wall," one executive recounted to me. The group also came to the consensus that it would be difficult to maintain their licenses once the African National Congress came to power, as the homeland casinos were widely seen as a corrupt appendage of the apartheid system. The company's founder, Sol Kerzner, had recently fled the country in response to accusations that he had bribed homeland leaders. Plus, for decades the casinos had staffed their most important positions (dealers, pit bosses, etc.) with British expatriates, not "local blacks."

The company took steps to proactively improve its image in the eyes of a new black South African government. It formally removed Kerzner from its board. More significantly, it moved to reform its labor market practices. I was able to locate and interview the executive charged with coordinating this transformation across SI's homeland casinos, whom I will call "George Hunter." He described his initial assessment of the job: "It was as though we had fourteen different companies working in fourteen different governments. . . . Nothing was standardized. I thought it was utterly hopeless." From his office in Johannesburg, Hunter drafted and express-mailed to each casino a set of guidelines directing managers to begin hiring blacks as dealers (and in other key gambling positions). The pits were to be "localized."

But while easily drafted into a memo, orders to reform employment practices were hard to enforce in practice. Like the floor-level managers in Nevada, homeland casino bosses initially resisted directives from outsiders to "fix" their established system of recruiting trusted dealers (from the United Kingdom). As Hunter stated, "[The expat system] wasn't broken to them, and they sure as hell didn't want to fix it." Their arguments against hiring black dealers even echoed those of Nevada's pit bosses. They protested that "blacks were untrainable as croupiers" because they lacked the capacity to perform complex calculations regarding odds and payouts. The casino bosses also argued to Hunter that black dealers would repel white gamblers, that "a Dutchman [Afrikaner] would rather lose his money to a white man. He will not stand to see a black take his bet off the table."

An opportunity arose in 1988 for Hunter to implement his labor localization plan. In that year, Sun International announced the opening of a new casino, the Morula Sun, in the homeland of Bophuthatswana. Hunter arranged to set up and oversee an "experimental" dealing school for local "Bop" citizens. Corporate human resource personnel were dispatched to the site, where they selected 160 local Tswanas and designed a "special" curriculum to compensate for their supposed deficiencies. "Blacks," Hunter explained, "have good retention skills if you keep it simple." So rather than requiring the memorization of formulas or written tests, the trainers emphasized spatial and color-based methods for calculating payouts.

The experimental dealing school was a complete success. While the first course was scheduled to take three months, all of the trainees were judged ready for live action within six weeks—thus disproving pit bosses' arguments that blacks lacked the innate ability to deal. Nor did white gamblers flee when the new cohort of black croupiers took their place behind the tables. "There was no problem at all," Hunter recounted. "If anything, the Afrikaners didn't mind the blacks as much as the English, with their cockney accents!" Such was the beginning of the end of the expat recruitment system. For the next five years, British

croupiers were brought down only to plug short-term labor shortages
(for instance, in the event that not enough local labor could be trained
in time for the opening of a new casino); the hiring of black dealers was
otherwise the norm. By 1995, blacks constituted an estimated one-third
to one-half of all tables staff in the homelands.[78]

While casino managers initially resisted this "localization" program
foisted upon them by "corporate," its implementation actually allowed
them to maintain control over the labor market. Consider the mechanics
of hiring and training. Attrition rates in the dealing schools were high
(between 60 and 80 percent of all trainees, Hunter estimates, did not
make it through to completion). Nor was attrition voluntary, as managers used the schools to sequester, study, and weed out workers. Helen,
the Gold City Casino pit boss whom we met in chapter 4, was one of
the first Tswana dealers hired in Bophuthatswana. She described her
experiences in one of the first training schools:

HELEN: I was raised in Garankuwa [a village in Bophuthatswana] by
          my grandmother. We were very poor, and there was nothing,
          no jobs where we were. In 1990, I finished matric and had a
          baby, saw they were recruiting at the [casino]. I told my grand-
          mother I was gonna get a job. When I got to the gate there were
          hundreds and hundreds of people there, lined up outside look-
          ing for work. A white man came out, taking our envelopes
          with the matric certificates. He grabbed my arm and said they
          are hiring for croupiers and would I be interested? I didn't
          even know what that was, but it was a job was all I was need-
          ing to know. . . . So we were sent to Mabatu to train for six
          weeks.

AUTHOR: Tell me about the school.

HELEN: There were twenty trainees, all of us black.

AUTHOR: Were they all women?

HELEN: Oh no, about half-and-half. Every Friday we were given a test
          on what we learned that week. So on Thursday nights we
          would all pack our bags, because on Friday they announced
          the results at eleven, and the bus left at one for the flunkees.
          It was like *Big Brother,* and you didn't know who would be
          voted out.[79] I called my grandma to tell her to pray for me

every Thursday night. On the last week, [the trainer] gave me these hard bets and I messed up, and he yelled, "What's wrong with you? Are you fucking stupid?" I broke down crying because I thought I had flunked. But he said afterward that I was one of the best and he had just been testing me and I had made it. I ran and called my grandma and said, poverty is out of the house now!

Casinos responded to the imperative to hire "local labor" by imposing stringent entry criteria—if blacks must be hired, they would first have to go through an intensive screening process. So while the color of the tables staff began to shift, the underlying "labor market fix" remained the same: managers were able to secure a critical mass of "trusted dealers."

Managers also retained control over the internal labor market, that is, over job placement and promotions. For instance new black workers were not allowed to deal to high rollers until they'd accumulated a year of seniority. Casinos, in turn, rarely promoted experienced black dealers to pit boss, let alone to higher levels of management. In the words of Precious, one of the first black croupiers: "If you were black it was so hard to get promoted, even if you were the best dealer. I mean, if you ever saw a black inspector, you had to rub your eyes, because it must be a mirage!" It was understood, according to Precious, that the only blacks to be promoted were those who did not "appear too clever or well-informed. Oh my lord, if they saw that you were smart or asked a lot of questions!"[80] Evidence of white-black differences in promotion rates can be gleaned by examining the work histories of those current tables managers at Gold City Casino who began their careers in the homeland casinos (about 90 percent of the managerial staff at Gold City Casino). Whites worked an average of 3.2 years as dealer before promotion to inspector, and another 3.1 before moving to pit boss. Blacks spent nearly twice as long in each position: 6.2 years as a dealer, 5.0 years as an inspector.

Finally, homeland casino managers retained absolute power to fire workers for any reason. Black croupiers, in particular, had few legal protections and certainly no claims to job security. In an interview, a (white) former pit boss explained to me how managers dealt with mistakes or errors on the part of black dealers: "Back then, if [they] fucked up, they got fired. We called them in, read them the riot act, and that's it, out the door."

As this quote illustrates, new black croupiers received harsh and unequal treatment vis-à-vis their white coworkers. One conspicuous manifestation of this inequality was found in the system of worker accommodations. Whites were given furnished apartments on the complexes of the resorts themselves, while blacks were forced to commute— often long distances—to work. So while white croupiers could walk from their swimming pools down to the casino, Solomon, hired as a dealer in 1991, had to commute three hours each way from his home village, walking and hopping on and off a series of buses.

Nonetheless, former black dealers recall life on the tables as a positive experience, on the whole. Because the casino could retain control of the labor market, managers made no major changes to the dealing labor process. Even after blacks started working behind the tables in the late 1980s, croupiers were permitted to shuffle by hand and to keep their tips. New black croupiers, in their tuxedos and evening gowns, deftly handled playing cards and exercised no small amount of authority over gamblers. They also ate their meals in a special dining room reserved for tables workers, rather than the shabby cafeteria used by the general staff. The homeland casino, in short, remained a hegemonic service regime—identical in broad outline to that which existed (and still exists) in Nevada. For former homeland dealers (such as Helen) who are still employed in the industry today, those days are remembered fondly—especially in comparison to the despotic panopticon that is the South African casino today.

A Society in Transition

Sun International executives strategized to remake their image ahead of the anticipated political upheaval. Most significantly, they "localized" their tables staff. But they did not anticipate how swiftly and dramatically the homeland casinos would be pulled into the national spotlight following the fall of apartheid. The National Party had commenced negotiating a peaceful transfer of power with the African National Congress as early as 1990. This culminated in a quick and "bloodless" revolution, with the country's first democratic election in 1994. Although the ANC emerged victorious in the voting, it formally shared power for the following three years with both the NP and the Inkatha Freedom Party (a Zulu nationalist party) in a Government of National Unity (GNU). A chief goal of the GNU was to pen a new constitution, and one of the issues to be considered was what to do about the brewing "casino controversy."[81] The government would eventually embrace gambling legalization, with specific regulations to ensure free consumer markets, clean capital markets, and equitable labor markets (the precise policy goals that emerged in the United States).

Gambling policy in post-apartheid South Africa was not written upon a *tabula rasa,* but amid various "entrenched interests," each seeking to maintain (or gain) the right to operate casinos. There was, of course, Sun International, anxious about the fate of its casinos now that the homelands had been officially reintegrated into South Africa (where gambling remained illegal per the 1965 National Gambling Act). But there were also new players to the game. During the late 1980s, when the capacities of the police were stretched fighting the uprisings against apartheid, a large illicit gambling industry had sprung up in South Africa's cities.[82] These small "joints" were operated by civic organizations and private entrepreneurs, and by 1994 there were an estimated 4,000 of them throughout the country.[83] They even formed their own advocacy group—the Gambling Association of South Africa (GASA).[84] Significantly, GASA casino operators represented the full spectrum of South African racial groups. Around Durban, street-corner casinos were run by Indians; blacks operated betting parlors in the townships around Johannesburg; while "competitions" in Cape Town were often overseen by coloured South Africans.[85]

Political maneuvering by the National Party during the transition era also shaped the terrain on which struggles over gambling policy were played out. During the late apartheid era, the NP had made one final attempt to buttress the homeland casino industry by launching an assault upon the new urban casinos. South African President F. W. de Klerk publicly denounced them as a threat to public order,[86] and in 1991, he ordered Minister of Justice Kobie Coetzee to draft legislation increasing penalties for violations of national gambling law.[87] The resulting Gambling Amendment Act of 1992, however, generated backlash in the media and from opposition parties, who saw it as evidence of corrupt ties between the apartheid state and homeland casino operators. They labeled it "The Kerzner Bill," calling it a bald attempt by the NP to protect Sun International's monopoly.[88]

To deflect such criticism, De Klerk called for an independent Commission of Inquiry to study the gambling problem. Commissions, political scientist Adam Ashforth has argued, were a standard device used by NP officials to produce "coherent schemes of legitimation" for their racist policies and reframe them as technical means for pursuing the "common good."[89] For instance, in an attempt to stifle growing black militancy during the 1970s, president P. W. Botha had authorized the Riekert and Wiehahn Commissions, both of which recommended granting strategic concessions to urban black workers. The NP now invoked the commission instrument one last time, when De Klerk and Coetzee asked James Allen Howard, a respected Afrikaner judge, to investigate the gambling issue.

Howard's subsequent report conceded that gambling prohibition in South Africa had been a failure, as evidenced by the "massive demand" now satisfied by the "illegal" casinos.[90] But it denied that urban casinos operating in accord with free market principles were best for the nation. Consumers must be protected from operators, who will "tempt people of modest means to squander the little they have," with "disastrous" social consequences. Casinos should be located at least an hour's drive from cities, and their overall number limited to ten to prevent an "overstimulation of demand."[91] The Howard Report, in brief, recommended legalizing casinos in South Africa, but as a restricted, rural industry catering to the urban middle class. Though couched in an objective tone, these recommendations would certainly have preserved intact the homeland casino industry. A GASA official complained, "Sun International could end up with all ten licenses," and SI's Managing Director later admitted, "The recommendations were very close to what SI proposed. . . . We were pleased with the outcome."[92]

But by the time the Howard Report was released in 1993, talks between the NP and the ANC were well under way. The report was, in the words of its author, "a dead duck," as NP leaders decided that to radically overhaul national gambling policy at the last minute would have weakened its position in negotiations for the transfer of power. The party thus "punted" on the sticky casino question, leaving it to the new government to sort out.[93]

What, though, were the interests of the ANC in gambling policy? Movement leaders had historically voiced criticism of the homeland casinos, and especially of Sun International.[94] In addition, the ANC had long espoused a socialist vision for economic and social policy in South Africa—a philosophy seemingly at odds with privatized gambling.[95] But during the GNU period, gambling was put into the portfolio of Deputy Minister of Justice Chris Fismer.[96] Labeled in government circles the "Minister of Gambling," Fismer worked closely on casino policy with two other ANC officials: Trevor Manuel, the finance minister, and Alec Erwin, head of the Department of Trade and Industry.[97] (In our interviews, Fismer stated that his group also remained in contact with the ANC executive—both President Nelson Mandela and Deputy President Thabo Mbeki—during its deliberations.)[98]

Fismer's group came to advocate an extensive, well-regulated casino industry as best for South Africa.[99] The simplest way to understand what appeared on the surface to be an unexpected move is to recognize how the ANC perceived its own stockpile of material and symbolic assets at the time. On one hand, it was assumed that legal gambling would generate revenues for the government. The immense success of both the homeland and urban casinos had demonstrated a significant demand for gambling among South African consumers. The turmoil of the transition era, meanwhile, had taken a toll on the economy. Upon assuming power, the ANC faced high levels of unemployment, a huge informal economy, and the systematic hiding of assets overseas by wealthy whites.[100] Civic organizations and new provincial governments, meanwhile, were pressing the central state for financial help. It was in this context that gambling came to be imagined and spoken of not as a matter of ethics or justice, but as an economic issue. [101]By 1994, casinos were routinely referred to in government circles as a "form of taxation."[102] And insofar as provinces could regulate casinos directly, gambling came to be seen as, in Fismer's words, one of the "few original sources of income for provinces," a means to "enable them to generate maximum income for State coffers."[103]

Though capable of generating economic revenues for the state, casinos still came with potential political costs. The Fismer group was aware that legalizing mass gambling in a developing country could generate a backlash from citizens and civil society. The only survey conducted during this period on attitudes toward gambling revealed that less than 10 percent of South Africans were "in favour of legalised gambling." In addition, the public perception of casinos (especially among black citizens) was still negatively colored by the apartheid regime's corrupt "casino states."[104] But such negatives were not in themselves sufficient deterrence. Although Fismer recognized that legalizing gambling would be controversial, he also understood that the party, having just won national elections by landslide margins, possessed "extraordinary legitimacy."[105] In short, key policy makers recognized that the new South African state possessed a relative surplus of political capital vis-à-vis a dearth of economic capital.

Gambling with Empowerment

The initial crafting of casino regulation in the United States had two distinct moments: one centered upon the character of owners (i.e., Nevada's privilege theory of licensing), the other upon their labor market practices (the Consent Decree). In South Africa, these two moments were compressed into a shorter time frame—the three-year transition period following the fall of apartheid—and into a single policy domain—a new gambling commission. Nonetheless, symbolic struggles over casinos in the new South Africa centered upon the same two stigmata as had those in the United States. And similarly, casino proponents ultimately prevailed by responding to external legitimacy threats with regulations to ensure clean owners and equitable labor practices.

Upon being tasked with planning a new gambling policy for South

Africa, Chris Fismer discovered that de Klerk's original legislation authorizing the Howard Commission remained in place, and he used it to call a new Commission of Inquiry. He and Erwin recruited Nicolas Wiehahn, a retired high court judge, to head the gambling commission. Wiehahn had headed a commission of inquiry in 1979 recommending the recognition of black trade unions and, as a result, had gained respect among black leaders as a *veligte* (enlightened) Afrikaner.[106] (He proudly displayed in his office a framed photo of himself shaking hands with Nelson Mandela.) Fismer and Erwin understood that Wiehahn, as a veteran commission head, could be counted on to not only translate their general ideas into a concrete set of policies but also justify them as in the best interests of the nation. In early 1994, they sent him a detailed brief outlining their objectives.

Over several interviews with Wiehahn, I sought to reconstruct the process through which he researched the subject of gambling policy and compiled his final report on the matter.[107] He explained that upon receiving the brief from Fismer, his first step had been to get a sense of who the "players" in the debate were. Public opinion was clearly against mass gambling, but this was not in itself considered a major obstacle, especially since there would be no popular vote on the issue. Of greater importance was the matter of where various interested constituencies stood. As organized bodies within the political field, their concerns and ideas would have to be taken into account.

Wiehahn thus issued a public call for "submissions" concerning potential new casino legislation. Excluding those from individuals, thirty-five were received from three main groups: nonprofit organizations, Sun International (and related corporate interests), and the GASA casinos. (Fortunately, these documents were preserved by one of Wiehahn's former colleagues.) What is most striking about the submissions is that the vast majority argued that gambling *should* be legal in post-apartheid South Africa, but regulated so as to advance the goal of black empowerment. The three groups, however, advanced very different definitions of empowerment and thus proposed vastly different industry rules.

Multiple civic organizations submitted proposals to the Wiehahn Commission. Only one, the South African Communist Party, advocated a complete ban on gambling, arguing that it is an industry that preys upon the poor and fosters an ideology of individualism.[108] The remainder of these submissions concurred that gambling is potentially deleterious, but argued that it is also a necessary evil . . . and one only they themselves could operate so as to protect society! For example, the South African Federation of Mental Health wrote:

> It has to be accepted that today only 30 percent of the population will contribute voluntarily towards a welfare project and that we cannot afford to disregard those who want something in return. This, however, means that provision must be made for prizes. . . . This council would recommend as follows: That competitions be permitted, but that they be rigidly controlled by registered charities to prevent dishonesty and profiting by commercial concerns.[109]

Corporate casino interests were represented by Sun International, as well as several new business consortiums headed by former SI executives. (There was not at this stage any formal representation by U.S. casino firms, for reasons to be discussed in the following chapter.) They advocated what was essentially a continuation of the apartheid policy framework: a limited number of casinos confined to rural areas and catering to the upper classes. Such regulations, SI argued in its statement, would both protect the urban poor and create jobs in impoverished provinces "where they are needed most."[110]

Urban entrepreneurs proposed as best for South Africa an entirely different industry structure. They argued that small, privately owned casinos would achieve maximum market penetration and generate the most jobs. And while Sun International had for decades staffed its properties with expatriate white dealers, GASA casinos hired and trained South Africans: "An overriding factor to be taken into account is employment. Most of these [urban] gaming clubs employ predominantly South African citizens. . . . Why are so few South African citizens, white and black, trained in [Sun International] casinos?"[111]

Wiehahn thus faced, on one side, sponsors in the federal government eager to maximize tax revenues, and on the other, multiple constituencies vying for the right to run casinos in accord with the larger postcolonial goal of "empowerment." This is the context in which Wiehahn's final report must be read—as a technical document, a blueprint for local governments to use casinos as an alternate form of taxation, and also as a symbolic statement, an attempt to justify legal gambling as in the best interests of the nation. The common denominator would be its final conclusion that "clean" corporate casinos should "empower" black citizens as workers.

The Complete Wiehahn Report on Gambling in South Africa opens by posing the general question of whether gambling should be legal in South Africa.[112] The answer is a resounding yes, a declaration arrived at through particular constructions of the nature of gambling, previous policies of prohibition, and the desires of the populace. To start, gambling is defined broadly as "any activity engaged in for the sake of a return of which the outcome is uncertain." This definition, however, obscures the statistical reality of commercial gambling: the outcome for the gambler is in the long run not "uncertain," but a loss of money to the house.[113] Yet defined as any form of risk taking, the urge to gamble becomes a motivation inherent to human nature, and we may label as a gamble practically any activity, such as playing the stock market or even existence itself: "Life," the report declares, "is and always will remain a gamble." It follows that the apartheid regime's prohibitory policies were undemocratic and reflected the morality of but a conservative minority:

> Government policies of the mid-60s reflected what it believed to be the moral viewpoints of the White population. The Board is of the opinion that . . . the majority of people in the new South Africa, even if not strongly in favour of gambling, would certainly not be opposed to it.[114]

This discursive construction of prohibition as political violence renders it unnecessary to report any empirical measures of the public's current views on gambling.

Having established that gambling should be legal, the report next addresses the question of how to structure a casino industry.[115] The issue is addressed through a cost-benefit analysis: we must identify casinos' various effects upon society, maximize the positives, and minimize the negatives. Acknowledged are the potential negative effects for consumers emphasized by nonprofit groups in their submissions: exploitation of the indigent, family decay, neighborhood deterioration, and so on. Such deleterious social effects, however, derive not from gambling *per se*. Rather, they are all symptoms of an underlying disorder known as "pathological gambling." The report states that while "normal" gamblers play for fun and risk only what they can afford to lose, medical specialists have documented that a certain percentage (though small; typically under 1 percent) of any population will suffer from a psychological abnormality in which they are driven by "inner urges" to gamble uncontrollably. Because this is a psychiatric condition, specialist care and treatment are required: "The gambling industry [must] establish an institute or clinic for the treatment and rehabilitation of pathological gamblers."[116]

In addition, any negative effects for consumers are offset by positive benefits for workers. Casinos, as labor-intensive service enterprises, would create an estimated 100,000 new employment opportunities. In addition, they would provide for the "reparation of imbalances in society," especially those resulting from past discriminatory practices. The report states precisely who should be "uplifted":

Disadvantaged and underprivileged persons and communities in South Africa who have become so due to historical and political reasons. This happened because of a lack of opportunities caused by unfair discrimination against them in law, policy and practice. The Board believes that the gambling industry offers an ideal opportunity for the upliftment, advancement and economic empowerment of these peoples.[117]

By hiring and training them as workers and managers, casinos could empower "previously disadvantaged individuals."

To the extent that casinos offer a net positive benefit for society, it follows logically that regulations should maximize the size of the industry. (Note, too, that the medical program for treating the discrete population of "pathological gamblers" was to be funded as a percentage of revenues, such that the mitigation of negative effects was linked to *increasing* the supply of gambling opportunities.) But what sort of rules would facilitate a vibrant and dynamic casino industry? Concerning the "supply side" (the number and placement of casinos), the report's philosophy was that "market forces will be the major determining factor with regard to the allocation and distribution of casino . . . licenses." It estimated—by factoring in population size, disposable income, and expected per capita gambling expenditures—that South Africa could sustain forty international-standard casinos. (The fact that over a decade later, only twenty-eight casinos have been built—despite attempts to find takers for all licenses—attests to Wiehahn's decision to err on the side of oversupply rather than undersupply of the market.) As for the location of casinos, they should not be confined to rural areas, as this would place them further from dense urban markets, negatively impacting revenues:

> The Board deliberated whether some "mild form" of "affirmative action" could be applied in the allocation of casino licenses per province. This would have the effect that . . . licenses be taken away from the "haves" and be given to the "have-nots" of provinces. . . . However this, in the board's opinion, is a political-economic consideration. The Board's calculations are based on scientific and empirical research.[118]

Market forces should also govern the "the demand side." The state must "allow as little interference as possible with the gambler's freedom to gamble," for the choice to wager is not only voluntary—"no one is compelled to gamble"—but a basic right denied under apartheid. Nor should the state restrict the ability of proprietors to stimulate or sate demand. Regarding advertising and marketing, the report "strongly supports the notion of a self-designed, self-formulated and self-imposed code of conduct which the industry could develop with time."[119]

While the Wiehahn Report endorsed "free" consumer markets, it did impose restrictions upon several other key markets. As discussed above, the formal goal of empowering the previously disadvantaged implied substantive regulation of the industry's labor market. Caveats were also voiced with regard to the industry's capital market, as the report elaborated specific criteria for the granting of property rights. First, licenses for the existing urban casinos were vehemently denied, a move that was, on the surface, somewhat surprising. The report had until that point echoed GASA's submission to the commission by equating empowerment with black employment and calling for policies to maximize industry revenues. Nonetheless, the urban casinos were framed as a dangerous presence in South Africa:

> The illegal [sic] casinos presented, and still do so, a serious problem . . . for the government and most South Africans. These casinos started operating in South Africa approximately five to six years ago in flagrant violation of the law—a serious and dangerous phenomenon in any society. . . . This can be construed as nothing else but a rape of the law . . . and a sure sign of the loss of freedom is the compassion which extends pity not to the raped but to the rapist.[120]

These thousands of operators, despite the ambiguity surrounding their legal status during the waning years of apartheid, were declared ineligible for casino licenses in the new South Africa. But the urban casinos did not go gently into the night. Upon the release of the Wiehahn Report, GASA staged rallies in cities across the country to protest their exclusion and filed suit against the government.[121] Such organized resistance was in vain, however, as the Rand Supreme Court ruled definitively against GASA, and the organization disbanded in 1996.

But to whom should property rights be granted? With the small entrepreneurs ruled out, the remaining candidates were civic organizations and private firms. While not adjudicating directly on the matter, the report proposed licensing criteria that seemingly endorsed the latter. Casino applicants must have first, a track record of "knowledge, skills and experience . . . in the casino industry"; second, a sound financial history with access to large capital funds; and third, minimal ties to the government.[122] All of these criteria obviously favored private firms over charities and other civic groups.

Parliament approved the Wiehahn Report as the National Gambling Act (NGA) of 1996. It must be emphasized that, unlike the Howard Report produced at the twilight of apartheid, the Wiehahn Report was not intended to reproduce the homeland casino industry. Nor was its goal the preservation of Sun International's monopoly. An executive with SI recounted to me the company's reaction upon first hearing of the new industry rules: "I'll put it to you this way, we all felt that Wiehahn's a bastard, a lackey of the ANC. His calculations were horrible, the result of politics." This assessment, while overblown in its rhetoric, is correct in that "politics" did play a role in the Wiehahn Report, despite its "scientific and objective" tone. Fundamentally, it reflected the interests of state officials in using gambling to generate tax revenues. Thus, while GASA's proposal to link casinos to black worker empowerment was endorsed by the report, and while small urban casinos arguably could have maximized industry revenues, these casinos were nevertheless denied property rights. Thirty or forty large corporate casinos, given the state's limited regulatory resources, represented an easier pool of operators to monitor and tax than did thousands of small "illegal casinos."

The report was also "political" in that it served as a symbolic statement to key constituencies within the larger political field, one justifying corporate gambling as in the best interest of the nation. In my interviews with industry regulators, I found that the Wiehahn Report occupies a prominent place on their desks and bookshelves. It even felt as though they were often quoting from it directly. For instance, the rhetorical figure of the pathological gambler was repeatedly invoked in response to suggestions that gambling might have negative social consequences, while the number of jobs created for PDIs was regularly cited as evidence of the industry's positive developmental impacts. Consider as well the following public exchange between industry representatives and critics in 2001:

> "I wonder whether it is not time to have another look at our policies on gambling, especially casinos," social development minister Zola Skweyiya told Parliament earlier this month, a call that has won backing from churches and other groups. Money that should have been spent on food, or to build stable families, was going on gambling . . . he said.
>
> [But only] about 1 percent of gamblers crossed the line from "social to problem gamblers," said Trisch McDonald, a psychologist from [a] Gauteng casino.
>
> "We found the prohibition route did not work and the best response was to regulate the industry properly," said Sfiso Buthelezi, the chief executive of the National Gambling Board. Buthelezi said the industry has created about 50 000 jobs . . . "in the hands of those from previously disadvantaged communities," boosting black empowerment.[123]

One cannot but conclude that the report continues to provide legislators stock answers and explanations with which to defend the casino industry from its various critics.

This chapter has told the story of how casinos, for decades sequestered in the American desert and the desolate South African homelands, were eventually pulled into larger debates over how to define the national good during times of turmoil. During its postwar "age of affluence," the United States grappled not only with the question of how to defend itself from imagined "enemies within," such as the Mafia, but also with that of how to extend the American dream to its racial minorities. Following the end of apartheid, South Africans debated how to cleanse the country of its discriminatory past and how to empower the "previously disadvantaged." In both cases, there arose critiques that existing casino industries violated the principles behind, and thus impeded the attainment of, these goals. The specific regulations crafted to govern casinos were direct responses to these external legitimacy threats. They represented, in short, maneuvers to symbolically erase prominent industrial stigmata. And although these processes took place in different policy domains, the underlying field dynamics were the same, and they resulted in identical outcomes: regulations to foster free consumer markets, clean capital markets, and equitable labor markets.

EIGHT Of Dice and Men

DIVERGENT MODES OF MANAGEMENT

What happens when "modern" industry rules encounter a "traditional" managerial habitus? This is the question posed in chapter 8. In chapter 6, we saw that early casino financiers in both the United States and South Africa sought to conceal their true identities by physically basing themselves far from their gambling palaces in Nevada and the homelands, respectively. This entailed leaving control over day-to-day operations to property-level managers, who used networks and racial stereotypes to recruit trusted workers. On the casino floor itself, decentralized control combined with an effective labor market fix to produce hegemonic service regimes—that is, skilled dealers who were permitted to hustle tips from customers. But these systems eventually came under assault from without. Chapter 7 showed how in both countries, disreputable owners and discriminatory hiring practices came to constitute stigmata in the larger political field, in response to which regulators put in place policies to cleanse the industries' capital and labor markets.

But how can identical policy aims produce divergent outcomes in practice (the continuation of a hegemonic service regime in the United States versus the transition to a despotic one in South Africa)? The historical and ethnographic research in this chapter will reveal that despite a formal convergence of policy, divergence occurred in terms of how new regulations were implemented. Nor was this divergence random. As agents of the state moved to enforce new industry rules, they encountered resistance from entrenched managers. Regulators' ability to overcome this resistance in turn derived from the configuration of the larger political fields from which they drew their authority and resources. In the United States, moral entrepreneurs succeeded in defining a healthy, beneficent gambling industry as one in the hands of "good corporate citizens." Civil rights groups, in turn, failed to link fair hiring practices to a larger conception of the national good. Such dynamics are characteristic of America's *neoliberal political field,* wherein regulatory energy focuses upon ensuring the integrity of proprietors while leaving corporate control of the labor market unquestioned. The opposite pattern characterizes the *postcolonial field* of contemporary South Africa, where the state rigorously regulates firms' labor practices yet must by necessity relax standards for granting property rights. In brief, regulatory goals concerning capital and labor markets possessed widely different valences across the two countries, resulting in mirror-opposite patterns of regulation.

While the ultimate cause of divergent service regimes is the differential configuration of national political fields, we must still consider precisely *how* new regulations translated into concrete "games of work" for croupiers. Described herein are the two mechanisms through which this occurred: the effect of capital market regulations upon the centralization of authority within the service firm, and the effect of labor market regulations upon managerial trust in workers. The rapid entry of "clean" corporate entities into the U.S. gambling industry buttressed decentralized control within the casino, while the failure of the state to enforce employment equity allowed floor managers to maintain trust in workers. Pit bosses, as a result, remain in charge and espouse fidelity to the "traditional" (i.e., hegemonic) organization of service work. (The interaction rituals observed by Erving Goffman while dealing in the early 1960s thus remain alive and well in Nevada today—a reproduction of social form resulting not from inertia but from managers' success at warding off external threats.) In South Africa, in contrast, property rights were defined to allow "competent" operators (former homeland casino personnel) to retain control of the industry, so long as they adhere to affirmative action quotas for front-line service workers. These new titans of the industry in turn experience a sharp rupture with the past. They distrust the "previously disadvantaged" workers they are required to hire, and so centralize power and impose despotism. This argument—and that of the book as a whole—is summarized in figure 7.

UPSTANDING INC.

"Clean" Owners, Decentralized Control

My first fieldsite, Nevada's Silver State Casino, is part of the publicly traded leisure corporation Upstanding Inc. I found the overall distribution of authority and flow of information throughout this firm to be highly decentralized. Casino-level personnel—typically the general manager, in conjunction with the heads of the gambling departments—handle the daily labor of organizing and overseeing production. They decide what sorts of technology and equipment to use on the tables, they define standard operating procedure for dealers, and they handle the myriad minor crises and predicaments that arise throughout the night. This tier of casino management also exhibits a standard career biography across the entire industry. Of the fifteen property-level managers I formally interviewed at various Nevada casinos, all were veteran casino workers with twenty-plus years of experience in the industry, and all but three had commenced their careers as dealers.[1] It may be an overstatement to proclaim, as one executive did, that "after fifty years, the industry still suffers directly and indirectly from its illicit origins and the management culture that evolved."[2] But my interviewees certainly

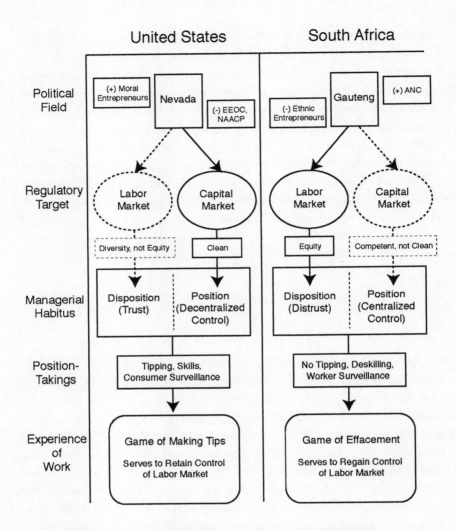

Key: Dashed lines denote weak enforcement. Power of groups in political field indicated by (+) and (-).

Figure 7. Linking political fields, managerial habitus, and games of work.

did view their place in the casino world as very much in line with that of their predecessors during the industry's "golden days."

Decentralized control within the contemporary Nevada casino firm derives from regulators' success at precipitating, within a relatively short period of time, a shake-up of casino ownership during the 1970s and 1980s. Following the Kefauver and Kennedy crusades, the state of Nevada had to rely on stringent investigation of proprietors as the "mainstay of the control apparatus."[3] The governor, legislature, and Gaming Commission reconfigured policy so as to both force out corrupt "mob" owners and bring in legitimate leisure firms. This shake-up, however, created a vacuum of industry-specific expertise at the apex of the new casino concern. As Albert Balboni argues, "The rapid turnover was typical of the gaming industry as a whole [and] brought about the entry into gaming of executives from lateral positions in other industries."[4] Executives of hotel firms such as Hilton and Ramada, many of whom had never set foot in a pit, suddenly found themselves in charge of casinos grossing millions of dollars. Their general sentiment was well summarized by a manager in one of the first publicly traded corporations to invest in Nevada: "These guys in gambling for twenty years have a sixth sense. We haven't got enough time in our lives to learn what they know."[5]

This new cohort of executives could have attempted to collect, codify, and centralize the tacit knowledge of floor managers. But they eschewed such Taylorist tactics, choosing instead to leave "casino ops" to the veteran pit bosses: "[C]orporations did little to alter the internal management structures of the casino . . . the biggest changes in the casino resort that the new ownership groups brought were ones of scale rather than substance."[6] The rapid expansion of legal gambling during the 1980s and 1990s only further institutionalized this decentralized intra-firm division of managerial labor by distracting the attention of top executives from the casino floor itself. Commencing with a 1978 public referendum in Atlantic City, New Jersey, states and localities across the United States began debating the desirability of casino gambling. Executives with gaming firms were active players in these debates. They lobbied against legalization where it was detrimental to their interests (as with efforts to allow casinos on Native American tribal lands) and for expansion where they could compete for new licenses (as they did in Detroit, Michigan). In addition, executives were kept busy raising investment capital from new sources on Wall Street to finance projects in Nevada and across the country.

The history of management regimes at Silver State Casino illustrates this pattern. The original founder of the company was forced out in the 1970s over allegations that he had engaged in illicit dealings with the Mafia. A sale was arranged to a new ownership group, with the understanding that they would take the firm public and appoint a head officer from outside the industry. The differences in styles between the founder and the new head were stark. The former had been known as an eccentric and patriarchal figure, one who would occasionally even walk the floor of the casino to joke with—or scold—individual staff (a management style much like that of executives with the homeland casino firms). Upstanding Inc.'s current head officer, in contrast, was originally trained as a financial analyst. Though each morning he glances over a summary of the casino's wins and losses from the previous day, he avoids the hubbub of the pits. His energy is spent on public relations and dealing with investors on Wall Street.

Responsibility for organizing and overseeing the action at Silver State Casino resides with the casino manager, "Joe Rossi." Joe comes from a casino family. His father worked as a dealer at an illegal casino in the U.S. South, but following a police crackdown in the 1950s, he moved his family to Nevada, where he legally plied his trade and taught the craft to his son. He even arranged for Joe to be hired to work alongside him in a well-known Las Vegas property. There, Joe was eventually promoted to pit boss, and then to assistant casino manager. In 1994, he was recruited by Upstanding Inc. to manage their flagship property, Silver State Casino. During our interview, he leaned back in his office chair and deftly shuffled a deck of cards while he talked. He tells me how, upon taking the job, he decided to "clean house" by making multiple changes to the policies of his predecessor. For example, he raised dealers' base pay rate slightly to improve company morale, and he increased the ratio of single-decks to shoes on the blackjack tables to entice in more gamblers.

Joe's authority to order such changes stands in sharp contrast to that of his counterpart at Gold City Casino. In South Africa today, it is corporate executives, not property managers, who make all decisions with regard to tipping, technology, and surveillance. We can in fact index and compare the centralization of authority across the two firms by looking at the variations in dealing procedure across their casinos. Among the casinos owned by Upstanding Inc. there are slight variations—for instance, while all allow dealers to make tips, some (such as Silver State Casino) require dealers to share their tips with coworkers, while others permit workers to "go for their own" tips. Such diversity derives from the autonomy of property-level managers to determine the nuances of policy. Within Empowerment Inc., however, there is no variation at all, as dealing procedure is strictly standardized across its properties. (Decentralized control is generally considered typical of U.S. firms, wherein "strong managers," rather than "weak owners," direct production.)[7]

Labor Control Retained

Success in "cleaning up" Nevada's capital markets was not reproduced in the realm of labor markets. We saw in the previous chapter that the Gaming Commission refused to make civil rights a precondition for a license "privilege." The NAACP and EEOC in turn imposed a Consent Decree upon Nevada's casinos. It not only required substantive changes to long-standing hiring practices (especially the elimination of the nepotistic "juice system"), it also required each casino to submit a quarterly report detailing the demographics of its workforce. However, in terms of its stated goal of increasing the number of African Americans behind the tables to 12.5 percent, the Consent Decree must be judged a failure. In 1971, African Americans constituted approximately 5 percent of Nevada's dealers; as of 2005, they made up only 6 percent (even though their share of the state's population remained constant).[8] More generally, my field-work revealed that managers continue to view the state as largely impotent, incapable of regulating their labor practices. Why were state officials unable to sustain their regulatory energy past the civil rights era?

We pick up the story in May 1974, inside the West Coast office of the EEOC. The Nevada Consent Decree had been placed in the portfolio of Jennifer Gee, an attorney with the commission's compliance unit. For several years, Gee had maintained contact with several civil rights groups in Las Vegas, including the Nevada NAACP. These organizations complained that the commission was being too lax in enforcing the decree, and reported ongoing complaints from African-American job-seekers and workers. Especially troubling were charges that casinos were employing African Americans only temporarily so that the casinos could list them in the quarterly reports, after which the workers were fired without cause. Nor could these allegations be proven through the quarterly reports alone. As Gee stated, "A black individual could be hired into a position . . . and be fired a week later and his employment would still be reported."[9]

The EEOC needed to gather more detailed information on casinos' labor market practices. But the commission possessed a woeful lack of resources. It faced a deluge of complaints from workers throughout the country; its California office was in San Francisco, 400 miles from Las Vegas; and its budget did not allow for regular on-site visits to the casinos, let alone a permanent presence in Nevada. The only realistic option was to attempt to expand the original reporting requirements of the Consent Decree. In the summer of 1974, the agency mailed each casino forty-eight "interrogatories" requiring additional information on how managers hired, promoted, and dismissed workers.[10] An idea of their extensiveness is conveyed by a representative example:

Interrogatory 15: Identify all job vacancies that have arisen in the jobs listed in Section II, Paragraphs 2, 3, and 4 of the Consent Decree since June 4, 1971, and for each vacancy state:
(a) The date the vacancy arose;
(b) The date the vacancy was publicized to the employees;
(c) The date the vacancy was filled;
(d) The name, address, race, previous job, and date of hire of the person hired or upgraded to fill the vacancy;
(e) Whether the person who filled the vacancy was promoted, newly hired or had changed jobs;
(f) How the person who filled the vacancy learned of the vacancy;

(g) The name, address, position held at that time, and the date of notification of each Black employee notified of the vacancy;

(h) Whether the person who filled the vacancy was related in blood or kinship to another employee in a supervisory or managerial position.[11]

Casinos balked at these new reporting requirements. In August 1974, attorneys for the Nevada Resort Association filed a motion for protection from the EEOC in Las Vegas District Court. They argued that to compile the detailed information requested in the "overly broad" interrogatories would be "oppressive and burdensome."[12] Casinos already provided the government "detailed and voluminous records" through the quarterly labor reports, NRA attorneys claimed.[13] These records should constitute proof that managers are in compliance, with additional information required only through a "prima facie showing by the aggrieved party of disobedience of the order."[14] The EEOC in turn filed a countermotion to compel casinos to answer the interrogatories.

There followed a year of legal wrangling between the NRA and the EEOC, culminating in a decisive victory for casino management. On May 9, 1975, magistrate Joseph L. Ward granted the casinos their motion for protection. In his ruling, Ward endorsed the argument that requiring casinos, as private businesses, to regularly submit to the government anything more than summary workforce statistics would constitute an onerous burden. The state's attempt to systematically collect procedural information on casinos' labor market practices, in sum, was rebuffed.

At this point the EEOC essentially gave up the goal of integrating the pits. Throughout the 1970s, a representative of the EEOC would make a brief annual visit to Nevada, but after that, inspections ceased.[15] And there was no attempt to add the new casinos opened during the 1980s and 1990s to the Consent Decree. The only source of information on the demographics of casino workers today are the general "EEO-1 reports," submitted annually to the EEOC by all private businesses employing at least a hundred workers in the United States. These reports consist of a single table documenting the race and gender composition of nine job categories within the firm (ranging from service workers to administrative support staff to executive management).

Casino managers today, however, do not consider the EEO-1 reports to be a serious factor in their decisions regarding whom to hire and promote. On one hand, they themselves are responsible for estimating and reporting the race of their employees, which even EEOC officials admit allows firms to "do quite a bit of fudging in order to make themselves look as diverse as possible."[16] As a tables manager explained, "dealers stick out like a sore thumb" on the reports because they constitute such a large percentage of the casino's workforce. But, he continued, "you can cover up just about anything. Play with [the EEO-1 forms], make it look neat. Plus, the EEOC isn't based here. They're out of California, and they have enough to take care of there."[17] On the other hand, it is widely known that data culled from the EEO-1s are not used to systematically monitor particular firms. According to an attorney with the EEOC, "The forms are not used proactively. . . . We don't pore over them and go, 'Hey, this particular company's entry level workers are really skewed.'" Rather, data are stored for potential subsequent use as evidence in individual lawsuits; if a worker complains to the EEOC that he or she has suffered discrimination, the agency will issue a right to sue and make the data available to the complainant. Each year, however, the agency receives approximately 100,000 complaints, of which only several hundred are successfully litigated.[18] In short, the odds that any individual act of discrimination on the part of an employer will be prosecuted are long.

It is not the case that the demographics of Nevada dealers have remain unchanged during the past three decades. A casual visitor to my fieldsite, Silver State Casino, would see not legions of Italian American men behind the tables, but rather men and women of various races and ethnicities. Nor does an aspirant croupier today rely on "juice" alone to achieve a first job; one must first attend one of the state's official dealing schools. Yet such changes have been cosmetic in nature. Seemingly novel employment practices are in fact analogous to—and in many ways natural extensions of—the long-standing system of labor recruitment based on workers' ascriptive characteristics and managers' networks. These new practices permit the ongoing actualization of traditional schemata of control and, as importantly, project a public image of casino firms as

Table 6 Demographics of Nevada's Tables Workers in 2005
(percent)

	White	Asian	Black	Hispanic/ Other
Dealers	55	34	6	5
Floor Managers	73	16	6	5

modern and fair employers. "Juice," we may say, has survived, though in transfigured and legitimated form.

Firms have formally modernized employment practices while preserving substantive control over the labor market through two specific mechanisms. First, they have countered demands for employment *equity* (i.e., a workforce representative of the local community) by recruiting a staff of dealers displaying *diversity*.[19] Most notably, rather than take remedial steps to integrate African Americans, entrenched (mainly white and male) managers have recruited Asian immigrants to work the tables. While whites constituted 95 percent of dealers and 99 percent of pit bosses in Nevada's casinos in 1970, in 2005 the figures were 55 percent and 73 percent, respectively. And while African Americans have made no significant gains, the percentage of Asians employed as dealers and floor managers increased from practically nil in 1970 to 34 percent and 16 percent today (and even though their representation in the state's population increased only modestly, from 1 percent to 4.5 percent). Table 6 summarizes the racial demographics of tables employees in Nevada in 2005.[20]

Why have casino managers settled upon Asian immigrants as the preferred substitute for white dealers?[21] One possibility is that this was a strategy to lower labor costs—perhaps immigrant workers were willing to work for less than native-born workers. The evidence does not support this argument, however, as dealers' wages have remained constant (i.e., at or near the federal minimum) for decades. A second possibility is that changing worker demographics reflected a changing consumer market (i.e., managers cater to certain categories of clients by hiring workers of the same race). But less than 3 percent of visitors to Nevada today are of Asian heritage, far below their representation in the casino workforce.[22] A third hypothesis is that Asian immigrants best fit some pre-existing stereotype on the part of managers as to what constitutes a "good dealer." This is the explanation that best fits my field data. When asked directly why they hire so many Asian dealers, managers repeatedly invoked these workers' "extreme company loyalty," how much "trust you can put in them," and their "reliability."

The result is a system that can be seen as entirely analogous to the substitution of "local" black homeland workers for British dealers in South Africa during the late apartheid period. In both cases, casinos 'diversified' their internal labor markets in response to an external political threat by hiring ethnic workers treated as "honorary whites."[23] And in both cases, network-based hiring systems (expat recruitment in South Africa, "juice" in Nevada) were replaced with formal training institutions—dealing schools. That is to say, Nevada's dealing schools do more than just provide technical instruction in the craft. They serve as labor market intermediaries through which managers evaluate, screen, and sort potential employees.

Recall my experience of "breaking into" the Nevada casino industry, described in chapter 2. Initially, I found it puzzling that the students at the Sure-Thing Dealer Academy were ranked according to their "personalities" rather than their aptitude for handling cards and chips. Eventually I came to understand that Paula, the head instructor, was a former dealer with active personal networks throughout the industry. Through such informal channels, she would hear about job openings before they were advertised publicly (if they ever were at all) and prearrange with pit bosses auditions for students possessing "good personalities." In the industry today, "personality" is a euphemism for character and general trustworthiness.[24]

This primary though concealed function of dealing schools came into full relief when I arrived in Nevada for a second round of fieldwork. This time, despite two years of experience behind the tables, I did not receive a single callback after applying at over twenty major casinos in

Las Vegas. And it was the start of the busy season! Frustrated, I returned to the Sure Thing Dealing Academy. Unfortunately, Paula had recently retired from the industry, and the school had closed. There was another school not far from my new apartment, however, so I stopped by and explained my plight to the head instructor, Gloria. She laughed and told me that my problem derived from my dearth of connections:

> You will never get hired that way, by walking in and applying. This industry's like a big octopus, because everyone knows everyone. My school's been around for fifteen years, so I know so many of the pit bosses out there. Many even got their start here in the school. . . . I am in contact regularly with about twenty casinos that do hiring through us. They will call me up looking for people. Tell me right away what they are looking for. We need two white girls and a Chinese man, or whatever. And that is what I send over, and as long as you do not screw up your audition, the pit boss will give you a note on a piece of paper to take to the personnel office to hire you.

While we were chatting in her office, I glanced at the class roster sitting on her desk. Instead of evaluations of dealing proficiency, next to each name was jotted remarks such as "possible drug problem," "comes in late half the time," and "friendly personality." I in turn was told that I was "sure to get a job because [I] look clean-cut." And so, despite knowing how to deal all of the casino games, I reenrolled in dealing school. I went in each day to practice my dealing and establish rapport with the instructors. A month later, Gloria, confident in my character, contacted two casinos to which I'd previously applied "cold." I was sent back to apply again at their personnel offices, and within a week I received calls inviting me in for auditions.

There is a saying among casino personnel today: "Juice may be on life support, but it ain't dead." A pit boss explained the ongoing importance of personal connections:

> Some people complain about "juice" and how you have to know someone to get a job in this business, but there is a reason why this is done. You hire people . . . because you know you can trust them. No one trusts a stranger when it comes to handling money. So it really isn't favoritism, it's about hiring people who are not going to cheat you.[25]

To further supplement this system of underground referrals, casinos have been early adopters of new technologies for establishing the character of potential workers. Credit histories, drug tests, and occasionally even personality tests are required by casinos today.[26] Casinos were also exempted from state laws prohibiting employers from sharing personal information on workers in order to establish "blacklists," when the NRA argued to state regulators, "[Our] employees handle large sums of money and [we] need to check the past honesty . . . of applicants."[27] And at no point in the past thirty years has there been a serious attempt to curtail managerial authority to fire employees at will.[28]

As a consequence of the foregoing developments, Nevada managers today experience a sense of continuity with the past. In decades prior, pit bosses operated in line with a traditional habitus of control, an essential condition of which was a perceived freedom from government oversight. My fieldwork among contemporary managers revealed an orientation entirely in line with this traditional habitus, insofar as they speak of regulators as unwilling and/or unable to monitor their labor practices. Consider the following statement from a Las Vegas casino boss:

BOSS: We have a working relationship with the state here. I can run my business as I need to.

AUTHOR: What about the state's Equal Rights Commission? Do they ever apply pressure to hire certain categories of people as dealers or other workers?

BOSS: They're a joke. Completely inept. At [my casino], the only pressure I ever get to diversify comes from above, from corporate. They'll tell me, you have three white guys as shift bosses already, can't you find a black or a woman? But I always take the most qualified applicant. I just call the president and say so and so is the most qualified and he says go head and hire him. And I always do.

Continuity on the Casino Floor

How does continued control of the labor market, coupled with a decentralization of managerial authority, affect specific decisions for organizing casino labor? In general, contemporary managers espouse

Table 7 Technology in Nevada's Casinos in 2005

	Automated	*Manual*
Shuffling	23% (shuffle machines)	77% (hand shuffling)
Card Delivery	49% (shoes)	51% (hand pitching)

a fidelity to tradition that translates into continuity regarding their choices for structuring service work. Consider their orientation toward their tables staff. Managers throughout Nevada's casinos repeatedly pronounce confidence that dealers are trustworthy and "on our side." The comparison with South Africa further demonstrates that such assessments are not derived directly from the structural position or economic dependency of workers. Managers at Gold City Casino pointed to workers' poverty and lack of education as evidence of their propensity to pilfer; in contrast, Nevada managers view these same conditions as proof that their workers are trustworthy. Consider the following two statements:

> Nobody steals here. If you have no college education, why would you risk a good job like this for, at most, a couple grand?

> I trust the people here. Granted, some small dealer scams and thefts surely go on, but it's too hard these days to get away with a big score. The tips are great, you can make a couple hundred on a good weekend night. Why would you screw that up?

Free from state oversight and full of trust in their staff, managers make decisions regarding technology, surveillance, and tipping that are in line with traditional principles of control. Consider their feelings toward the various technologies for automating gambling transactions that have become available over the past several decades (see table 7). Shuffling machines, a Taylorist technology *par excellence* insofar as they maximize speed and security, are used on only one of every four black-jack tables in the state. As remarkably, managers permit dealers to deliver cards by hand (i.e., by pitching them, rather than through a shoe) on half of the state's tables.[29]

In my interviews, I asked managers *how* they decided whether or not to automate dealing. Two rationales were repeatedly invoked. On one hand, shufflers and shoes were viewed as incongruent with tradition; on the other, they were assumed to be unpopular with clients. The following statements are representative:

> Shuffling machines? No way. Their main advantage is that they're faster, but this is [Silver State Casino]. They would be out of place, too gimmicky. The people who come here don't want to see that.

> We've never used shufflers in my casino. Everyone hates them. I like the personal approach.

> Shufflers are pricey, not worth it. They already had a few when I got here, and I wish I could get rid of them. . . . As for speed, well, I'll give them that, they do speed things up. But players like the shuffle time. It gives them a chance to ask, "What's showing tonight?"

Interviewees admitted that shufflers speed up the games, but felt that this was irrelevant insofar as the tipping system kept the games moving at an adequate pace anyway. (In fact, not a single manager reported regularly monitoring dealer speed through technical evaluations of "hands dealt per hour.") The casinos that do use shufflers extensively are exceptions that prove the larger rule. They install the machines not due to fears about dealers cheating or working too slowly, but out of concern that card counters may be targeting the casino.

Confident that their dealers can be trusted, Nevada managers make technology-related decisions with regard to the gambler (as a consumer market to attract and as potential cheaters to protect against). Thus, on approximately half of the tables in the state, croupiers deliver cards by hand rather than from a shoe. Hand-dealing is perceived by managers not as a security risk, but as a savvy marketing move. Many even use computer software to estimate the optimal ratio of hand-dealt to shoe games based upon their popularity with gamblers. "The market will decide," is a typical explanation. "The key is to find the right mix of

Figure 8.   Single-deck (i.e., hand-shuffled) blackjack as marketing device. Photo by
the author.

games, to monitor the utilization of different setups around the casino."
Managers thus evaluate the single-deck pitched game in terms of its
popularity with players, and despite its greater potential for dealer
manipulation. It serves, as figure 8 shows, as a mechanism of product
differentiation and an advertising lure.

A telling illustration of managers' consumer-focused mind-set is provided by the current transition in Nevada from "classic" to "6 to 5" blackjack. In the former, a winning hand of blackjack earns the gambler a 3 to 2 payout. Over the past decade, however, as average gamblers have become more adept at rudimentary card counting, the casino's hold percentage on the game has decreased. One easy and obvious solution to this problem would have been to make shuffling machines standard on the tables—new models completely eliminate the threat of card counting. Instead, managers continue to allow hand-dealing but have changed the long-standing blackjack payout to 6 to 5. Although this has evoked protest from gambling "purists," it has proved quite popular with the general gambler. In explaining why he didn't simply install shuffling machines to combat card counting, a manager stated, "The players like it; they like holding the cards. It represents the real Las Vegas."

The same underlying principles influence managers' decisions regarding surveillance. Risk and danger are imagined to emanate not from dealers, but from gamblers. As a pit boss stated, "We're like a candy store. Your counter staff may steal a gumball now and then, but it's someone from the outside who's gonna go for the 5-pound box." So in contrast to South Africa, where surveillance energy is directed toward monitoring dealers (especially through the worker audits known as target reports), in Nevada, surveillance operates through the space/time targeting of clients. Camera operators and pit bosses, that is, decide where to hone their gaze based upon the size of a gambler's bet and the degree to which his or her play betrays a card counter.[30] In short, because managers trust their dealing staff, surveillance obeys a consumerist logic.

The durability of a traditional habitus of control also explains the ongoing importance of tipping in the industry. To start with, managers are not unaware of dealers' various hustling games. Nor do they view tipping as the optimal method for structuring casino labor. "Dealers maximize tips, which is different from maximizing profits," I was told by Joe Rossi, the manager of the Silver State Casino. Nevertheless, they continue to allow tipping on the tables for two reasons. First, top casino managers (such as department heads and shift bosses) continue to identify with and maintain networks with staff in the pits. As Joe explained during our interview, when he receives a call from the floor informing him that someone has won "fifty grand" on the tables, "The first thing I ask is, 'Did they take care of [i.e., adequately tip] the boys?'" He repeated again, with a solemn look on his face, "Did they take care of the boys?" The mere fact that he refers to his dealers, over half of whom now are women, as his "boys" illustrates both Joe's self-image as a benevolent patriarch of the casino family and his sense of continuity with the casino world he broke into thirty years ago. For Joe, as it is for all of the managers I interviewed, tipping is very much an inviolable emolument.

In addition, managers view tipping as a means of forestalling unionization among staff.[31] I would often describe to managers in Nevada the decision by South African casino firms to eliminate tipping in their casinos. This would invoke a look of shock and a grimace, along with the following sort of reactions:

> There's no way we could ever do that here. The unions would come right in.

> It'd be terrible for morale. Shame on them. If we did that, the unions would be beating down our door for sure.

Managers believe that allowing workers to accept gratuities, despite the immediate inefficiencies that the dealers' "game of making tips" entails, precludes unionization by creating high levels of inter-casino mobility as workers constantly "chase tips."[32] Rather than think of themselves as being tied to a single employer, Nevada dealers experience work as analogous to "having your own little business. If you take care of business and everything, no one bother[s] you."[33] Such an entrepreneurial self-concept works to the benefit of management, since unionization in the United States occurs at the firm level, not at that of the industry or occupation.

In Nevada, tipping continues to represent a hegemonic compromise with skilled labor. But it also provides a powerful tool of coercion should workers decide to collectively organize. Namely, managers hold the elimination or curtailment of tipping as the ultimate "trump card." As a table department manager related, unionization drives are the time to "make it about the money":

MANAGER: At the [X Casino], we told them, if you let that union in here, do you know the first thing they'll go after? That's right, your tokes. They will take 25 percent of your tokes for your union dues.

AUTHOR: Is that true? Was the union going to do that?

MANAGER: I don't know, probably not. But that's what you have to do, make it about the money.

In sum, tipping serves as a mechanism for retaining control of the labor market, not in relation to the state but to the omnipresent threat of unionization.

EMPOWERMENT INC.

"Competent" Capital, Centralized Control

Regulators in the United States succeeded in displacing "corrupt" mob owners with "clean" corporations. New corporate executives in turn decentralized control over daily operations to property-level managers. In South Africa, the opposite dynamic took place. Figure 9 depicts divergent patterns of managerial authority in the two countries. Because regulators in South Africa were unable to recruit "clean" firms to take over casino licenses, they redefined property rights to privilege "competent" proprietors. Concretely, this entailed licensing several new consortiums headed by former homeland casino personnel. These actors proceeded to centralize power within the casino firm, so that they now make all production-related decisions from their offices high above the streets of Johannesburg. This section describes the process through which this occurred.

Empowerment Inc., the subject of my South African fieldwork, is one of three firms that collectively dominate the national casino market. This "Big Three" holds eighteen of twenty-eight total licenses in South Africa; in Gauteng, they operate three "mega-casinos" (including my fieldsite,

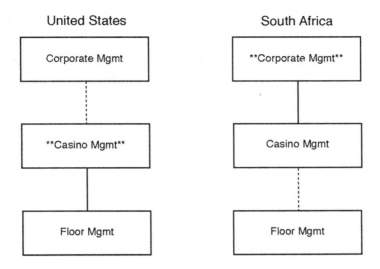

Stars denote locus of decision-making. Dashed lines denote weak ties.

Figure 9.   Cross-national differences in managerial authority, networks.

Gold City Casino) that together generate over 70 percent of the province's total gambling revenues. All three firms, furthermore, are headed by former Sun International employees, and all have staffed their corporate offices with veteran personnel from the company's homeland properties (including a large number of former English croupiers).[34] These common origins were repeatedly invoked in my interviews: "We all worked for Sun at some time"; "So many people at this company came from Sun"; "It's a Sun culture." In sum, while top executives in Nevada's new casino firms were neophytes to the industry, in South Africa, they are all veteran "casino men."

How were these former employees of Sun International—a company widely demonized for alleged unscrupulous dealings during apartheid—able to obtain property rights in the new South Africa? To answer this question, we must consider in detail how individual provinces allocated casino licenses. The 1996 National Gambling Act established the general principles of gambling regulation for the country; but left administrative responsibility for granting licenses to the provinces. In Gauteng, a provincial Gambling Board (the GGB) was formed, staffed primarily with accountants and lawyers. The board's first task was to decide whom to award casino licenses to. Several categories of applicants, such as nonprofit organizations and the former GASA casinos, had already been ruled out by the Wiehahn Report. This essentially left the board with two potential candidates: foreign gaming companies and domestic proprietors. By all accounts, board members and the provincial government strongly preferred the former. "The use of gaming as a means to drive economic growth," an early policy document stated, "will only succeed where there is significant foreign investment."[35]

There would, however, be no significant foreign investment in South Africa, not even in Gauteng, the country's wealthiest province (with 40 percent of national personal disposable income). In 1997, the GGB issued an "Invitation to Apply for Casino Licenses."[36] Altogether, twenty-three applications were submitted for six possible licenses; only one came from a U.S. gaming firm (the company was granted a license, but it sold off its South African interests a few years later).[37] Foreign firms appear to have eschewed the Gauteng market due to concerns about profitability and stability. Industry publications, for instance, warned potential investors to be cautious of the country's volatile currency and high crime rate. Nor would there appear on the horizon a figure along the lines of Howard Hughes, blazing a trail into the South African market and quelling mainstream concerns. As a Nevada executive stated, "There was initial interest, especially for licenses around Johannesburg and Cape Town, but in the end we all concluded that when it came to South Africa there were just too many hard yards."

Gauteng Gambling Board officials were forced to decide among various domestic applicants. Small and medium-sized operators were excluded from consideration *de facto,* as only those capable of building "international-standard casino complexes" and paying an application fee of R570,000 (about $100,000) could apply. The remaining applicants fell into two camps. The first group consisted of the consortiums headed by former SI employees, which proposed several new casinos in working and middle-class, mainly white suburbs. Because of the racial composition of the executives sponsoring these plans, these were referred to informally by GGB members as "white" applications. In contrast were several "black" bids. These were proposals by black businesspersons to build casinos in the urban townships. There appeared, furthermore, to have been a strong desire among many in government not to grant property rights to former SI personnel. As a board member stated, "Some of us were very critical of Sun and their history in the former homelands. We wanted to outright ban them from getting licenses. 'They must take the knock,' was the feeling."[38]

Former SI executives had anticipated that their homeland pasts would constitute a stigma in the eyes of regulators, so they took proactive steps to cleanse their image. They contracted academics, economists, and consultants to testify that their companies were forward-looking and modern, not racist and traditional. They proposed casino themes referencing the United States and Europe; several, like Gold City Casino, were replicas of famous Las Vegas properties. And in their application materials, they addressed their unsavory pasts head-on—though without admitting culpability. This entailed distancing themselves from SI's questionable dealings during apartheid, often framed as the personal doings of Sol Kerzner alone. As one company argued in its proposal to the GGB:

> [This] firm is not run or owned by Kerzner. To derogate [our] present aspirations to contribute to the development of a successful gaming industry in South Africa on the basis of one individual's alleged past would be unfair, unrealistic and not in the interests of the country.

Such efforts appear to have allayed the concerns of board members. An executive with one of the new casino firms recounted the following:

EXECUTIVE: We had to deal with the baggage of our past, the association that came to mind between us and the old apartheid regime.

AUTHOR: How did you do that?

EXECUTIVE: By going and sitting down face to face with the Gambling
             Board. And sure, they had a chip on their shoulders, you
             could tell. But we said, look, that was Kerzner and he is not
             a part of this company. He isn't even in the country. Would
             we be sitting here with these empowerment plans and all
             these banks willing to finance us if we were racist?

AUTHOR: How did they respond to this? Was your argument
             successful?

EXECUTIVE: Well, we got the license, didn't we?

Although the actual process of adjudicating among casino applicants
took place behind closed doors, it attracted a great deal of attention. It
was watched closely by civic groups claiming to represent the public
interest (many of whom had had their own casino proposals denied by
the Wiehahn Report), and the media did their best to turn the process
into a public spectacle through daily reports on "the Gauteng casino
uproar" and the "casino license scramble."[39] And though the GGB could
recommend licensees, it had to both explain its decisions publicly and
obtain final approval from the province's executive council. We may
even say that the process of granting casino licenses constituted a key
early act of defining the national good within the new South Africa.

In a series of policy documents, the GGB explained how it adjudicated
among casino applicants.[40] It stated (in line with the Wiehahn Report)
that projects were judged according to two general criteria: their potential economic impact and their plans for black empowerment. This first
criterion was defined as an operator's "potential to successfully and prof-
itably manage the proposed casino."[41] It was, in short, an evaluation of a
project's revenue (and thus tax) potential. The specific measures used to
rank applicants on this dimension were straightforward and amenable
to quantitative evaluation:

- The applicant's financial resources and initial capital investment
- The total number of job opportunities
- The commercial viability of the project
- Management competence, as demonstrated by international
  experience

The second general criterion was a casino's potential to "empower" local communities and "persons disadvantaged by unfair discrimination." But how was this more abstract notion of black empowerment operationalized? And to what extent did it conflict with the first (exclusively economic) criterion?

Controversy surrounding this issue came to a head regarding the "Township Casino," a proposal by a prominent black businessman to build a casino in a predominantly black urban area. The board had assigned each of the twenty-three casino applications to one of six geographical areas inside the Gauteng province. This meant that the overall licensing process boiled down to a series of smaller contests among three or four applicants in each area. The Township Casino competed against three other proposals (all submitted by established South African leisure firms, labeled here Casinos A, B, and C). The applications themselves were immense documents, hundreds of pages long and full of details on every conceivable aspect of the proposed casino.

In its evaluation of these four projects' potential economic impact, the board gave the Township Casino low marks. It ranked last on capital investment, both because it was the smallest of the four and because "there may be an element of risk in [the casino] being able to raise its R100 million share capital from the local community." The board also considered each casino's projected contribution to provincial gaming tax revenues, with the largest project, Casino A, coming first. Regarding management, the board stated that Casinos A, B, and C were all "well-known operators," while Township operators "have limited experience" and so merited the lowest ranking. As for employment, the board again ranked Casino A, the largest project overall, first.

The Township Casino fared somewhat better on the board's evaluation of each project's empowerment potential. Those measures were "softer" and less quantitative than those used to gauge economic impact. For instance, officials considered the project concept—the theme and message of the overall complex. The Township Casino proposed to build a museum commemorating black history in South Africa, while the other proposals offered themes referencing international locales. Yet though the board lauded the Township bid for offering attractions of "historical significance," on the whole, Casino A offered "bigger convention facilities and a wider range of other leisure facilities." Themes and concepts, the board argued, should be judged simply by asking whether "[they] cater for the needs for the markets [the casino] is targeting." Casino A thus ranked first on project concept, and the Township Casino last. The Township Casino did, however, achieve high rankings for its proposed location—a site that "strongly meets the objective of investment in a previously disadvantaged and declining area"—and equity participation in the project by PDIs.

The Gauteng Gambling Board, in its final report, ranked Casino A as the top applicant. In doing so, it prioritized the overall size of the project as well as the management team's past experience in the gambling industry. Other factors (such as community revitalization or cultural facilities) were either accorded less weight or reframed as mere marketing matters. In effect, the board defined property rights so as to favor "competent" operators (namely, former Sun International managers) rather than "clean" local black entrepreneurs.

The board's refusal to grant a license to any of the "black bids" did cause controversy. At a provincial council meeting, several members of the Gauteng government publicly criticized the board's decision.[42] An official with the Board stated:

> The township bids weren't as strong as the others, and to have granted them just because they were best on the equity criteria would not have been good. As for [Township Casino,] we weren't gonna give it to him just because he was black. . . . And no one would have gone to the township if it'd been granted a license, as they would have preferred to drive even farther to a safer casino.

The Gauteng minister of welfare responded, "Has the board considered, for example, that putting a casino in [a township] can change the perceptions and influence the market to start investing in [the townships]?"[43] The final allocation of licenses was delayed for a month due to ongoing disagreements between the Gambling Board and the provincial government. In the end, the board prevailed, but not before the resignation of one council member in protest.

DIVERGENT MODES OF MANAGEMENT

It was in this contentious environment that the notion of worker empowerment came to bridge the chasm between a casino's economic benefits (as defined by the board) and its contribution toward black upliftment (as demanded by government officials and civic groups). Each successful casino applicant was required to provide the Gambling Board an "Empowerment Mission Statement" describing how it would advance the interests of black employees. Empowerment Inc.'s Statement for its new Gold City Casino centered upon "three pillars" of empowerment.[44] The first was that of job creation: the firm pledged to create 2,000 permanent jobs for the province. The second involved affirmative action: the company would engage in "positive discrimination" such that within five years of opening, previously disadvantaged individuals would hold 80 percent of total jobs. Concretely, this entailed a strict quota system for hiring PDIs. The third pillar focused on human capital development: the casino would train PDIs in various technical and managerial skills. It would also engage in "succession planning," whereby PDIs would be prioritized for promotion into managerial positions.

Only the first two of these three pledges have been fulfilled. Five years after its opening, Gold City Casino employs 2000 workers, over 80 percent of whom are considered PDIs (refer to table 4). But despite the explicit promises made in their succession plan, the former (white) Sun International personnel who head Empowerment Inc. have not ceded control over any major managerial decisions to new PDI managers. In contrast to Nevada, where corporate executives continue to decentralize authority to pit bosses, Empowerment Inc. executives actively centralize power within the leisure firm. They monopolize financial and other types of information, make all important production-related decisions, and, as we saw in chapter 3, structure the labor process despotically. How were corporate executives able to sidestep this key third pillar of Gold City Casino's Empowerment Statement?

As was the case with the U.S. government's failure to implement labor market reforms, South African regulators possess neither the will nor wherewithal to fundamentally alter underlying structures of capital and control. Drawing upon my ethnographic data, I can specify three reasons why the spirit of empowerment policy was not translated into substantive changes in practice. First, the Gambling Board granted Gold City Casino an exception regarding the promotion of blacks into upper management. The Empowerment Statement had divided the casino's workforce into three categories: general staff (front-line workers such as dealers), floor management (pit bosses and supervisors), and upper management (shift bosses and department heads). And while the firm proposed an 80 percent PDI quota for both of the first two categories, its target for upper management was only 40 percent. (This latter target was further diluted by the fact that the board agreed to count white females as PDIs for these positions, because women of all races had been excluded from managerial positions during apartheid.)

In its Empowerment Statement, Gold City Casino justified the ongoing underrepresentation of blacks in upper management through appeal to the principle of "realism." It asked the Gambling Board to acknowledge "the particular difficulties of achieving the required mix of employees at the higher levels within the organization—owing to historical imbalances in skill availability." (That these "historical imbalances" were a result of their own hiring policies during apartheid goes unmentioned.) In addition, the company argued that affirmative action must be balanced against economic realities. Should social equity conflict with the need to ensure competence at the executive level, the latter imperative should take precedence: "Empowerment policy . . . will be pursued relentlessly with exception only for the maintenance of operational standards and integrity." Gambling Board officials, in granting Empowerment Inc. a casino license, effectively endorsed these qualifications on the integration of blacks into upper management.

Second, Gold City Casino operationalized empowerment so as to obfuscate the horizontal distribution of power within upper management. Inside the casino, decision-making authority resides with the heads of the gambling departments (i.e., the casino manager, two tables managers, and the slot department head). These four positions, furthermore, are staffed by white men (two British expatriates and two Afrikaners). In contrast, the only three blacks in upper management head the departments of Human Resources (HR), Industrial Relations (IR), and Community Relations. These positions have nowhere near the authority and autonomy of the gambling positions. I frequently lunched with the HR director, a Tswana man named Timothy, and during these lunches, he would complain about the lack of respect accorded his department. Although HR was referred to in the company's Empowerment Statement as the "driving force of the organization," Timothy pointed to corporate's decision to place it in a small building across the street from the casino itself as evidence of his department's marginalization within the firm. "Not once since I started here three months ago," he told me, "has [the casino manager] come over to the HR building. Not once!" Four months into my fieldwork, Timothy resigned from the firm. Similar grievances were voiced by Samuel, the IR director. He complained that his main duty was that of performing the organizational "dirty work" of disciplining and firing workers.[45] "Howzit?" I asked him one afternoon. "They're happy with me this week," he responded, "We fired ten people. That is productivity!" Samuel, too, soon resigned from the company.

Third, numerical empowerment quotas did not reflect the vertical distribution of power within the firm. Empowerment Inc. managers, faced with the imperative to hire PDIs as workers and floor managers, have simply shifted the locus of decision-making upward (a phenomenon referred to as a "floating colour bar").[46] Pit bosses, department heads, and even the casino manager himself no longer make major decisions regarding the organization of the casino floor. All production-related issues are settled by executives in Empowerment Inc.'s head office. This is, of course, not entirely in the interests of (largely white) casino managers, who have experienced a loss of authority compared to their early experiences in the homelands. For example, I found that the Gold City Casino tables manager, Steve, had been arguing for months with the company's gaming director over shuffling policy. Steve wanted an exception to allow hand-dealing in the casino's "private area," where wealthy (and sometimes foreign) gamblers complained about the shuffling machines. Upon losing the argument, he called the policy "ridiculous" and the gaming director a "dinosaur" for being so intractable on the matter.

Despite animosity toward individual corporate executives, casino managers such as Steve identify with the company more so than they do with their floor staff. In general, dealers and even pit bosses at Gold

City Casino were despised by upper management, who considered them to be incompetent and untrustworthy. This orientation stands in contrast to that of Nevada managers (see figure 2), and results from the state's success at enforcing significant labor market reform in the industry. It is to this process that we now turn.

Labor Control Lost

Though lax regarding the issues of ownership and control, state officials do keep close watch on firms' hiring and dismissal practices for front-line staff such as dealers. The labor of regulation in South Africa, in short, entails the regulation of labor markets. In doing so, state officials meet the mandates of the original National Gambling Act, as well as those of individual firms' Empowerment Statements. But on a more general level, labor market regulation constitutes a key form of symbolic labor within the larger political field. In the decade since the passage of the NGA, casino regulators and even the ANC itself have been frequently criticized for the country's new gambling policy. Casinos, in particular, are condemned as a regressive form of taxation, and as an industry favoring large corporations over small businesses and entrepreneurs. In response, proponents regularly cite the number of jobs created by casinos, along with their adherence to affirmative action quotas, as evidence of casinos' net positive effect for society. By ensuring that firms empower black workers, regulators maintain a critical amount of legitimacy for the industry (and thus the survival of their own cash cow).

The Gauteng Gambling Board ensures worker empowerment through reference to a list of concrete "deliverables." These were specified by firms in their original applications and are monitored through regular submittal by casinos of quarterly manpower reports (the preparation of which constitutes the bulk of the work done by a casino's Human Resources staff). The reports provide numerical data by which regulators may judge progress toward the various components of black worker empowerment. In some areas, quantification is relatively straightforward. Regarding job creation, for instance, casinos report simply "the total number and distribution of job opportunities" (i.e., the number of workers on the payroll, broken down by department). To prove compliance with affirmative action requirements, casinos provide charts detailing the number and percentage of PDIs working as general staff and as floor managers in each department. In this regard, the reports resemble those submitted by U.S. firms to the EEOC (i.e., the EEO-1s). In South Africa, however, casino firms must supplement basic quantitative data with procedural information on how they go about hiring and dismissing workers (of the sort requested by the failed Nevada "interrogatories" discussed in chapter 7). Casinos include in their reports the names and demographic characteristics of all workers hired and fired during the quarter; and for terminations, they must supply additional documentation on why the worker was fired and how the dismissal was handled.

To verify the accuracy of the reports, the board conducts surprise on-site audits, during which officials perform head counts, interview workers, and inspect HR files. Should inspectors find that a firm is failing to meet its empowerment commitments, they can impose fines and even revoke the casino's license. The Gauteng Gambling Board's monitoring of casinos' labor market practices, in short, is tenacious. Nor can the seriousness with which managers take such regulation be overstated. This was driven home for me one morning when I arrived at work to find the tables department in a state of panic. Management had just learned that board officials were on their way to perform a labor audit. I walked over to the office of the casino manager, Rob, who was on the phone with head office going over the most recent quarterly report. It seemed the Gambling Board was suspicious that the casino had been over-reporting its staffing levels and listing training classes that hadn't actually occurred. Rob mentioned several times his concern that they could be fined tens of thousands of rand. And during the week following the audit, he spoke to the board several times each day, arguing that new employee initiation classes should be counted towards training, and that the casino should be excused for dipping below its staffing target because of a business downturn that month. He would prevail on the first argument but not the second, and the casino was forced to pay a small fine and hire workers to bring staffing levels back to the targets specified in the Empowerment Statement.

Executive managers acknowledge that stringent regulation of the labor market is a "fact of life" in South Africa today. Yet state power, while respected, is greatly resented. During the course of their daily labor of running the casino, they compare the new rules with those of the past, especially the "golden age" represented by the unregulated homeland casinos. For example, when reflecting upon the new constraints on their autonomy to hire, veteran casino managers frequently complain about what was euphemistically labeled in the Empowerment Statement as "relaxed entry and evaluation criteria for PDI" service workers. While in the homelands they had various screening mechanisms at their disposal to establish the character of new hires (the expat recruitment system for white dealers, prolonged dealing schools for local blacks), hiring decisions are today dictated by the state. "Before, we could pick and choose our dealers," the tables manager lamented one morning, "but now we just have to take people off the street."

Particularly telling was a failed attempt by Empowerment Inc. executives to redefine the very definition of a "previously disadvantaged individual." In their initial application, they had defined a PDI as any "individual who being a black South African citizen, is socially and economically disadvantaged." This was in fact a strategic move on the part of veteran managers to staff the new Gold City Casino with black croupiers imported from the former homelands. "Local" black dealers, as we saw in chapter 7, were first rigorously screened by homeland managers and then treated as "honorary whites." The Gambling Board, however, rebuffed the firm's attempt to define as a PDI any black South African, insisting instead that the label be applied only to black citizens of Gauteng residing within a 10-kilometer radius of the casino.

Managers also resent new constraints on their ability to dismiss workers at will. "I miss the old days," I overheard a shift manager reminisce to colleagues one night. "You just took a dealer in the back room and fucked them up and sent them out the door." This loss of firepower is widely mourned by managers, who must today provide extensive documentation (such as the specific offenses precipitating the decision) for all dismissals. In addition, a plethora of regulations guarantee workers recourse to challenge a termination order. Two senior executives expressed their views toward this new arrangement as follows:

> When someone is caught cheating and fired, nine times out of ten they ring up the Gambling Board or CCMA [the Council on Conciliation, Mediation, and Arbitration, a national board to which workers from all industries can appeal dismissals]. I then have to go, stand there, and act like a lawyer to argue our case!

> If a dealer gets caught, they go before a magistrate who gives them a slap on the wrist and sends them back to us, his attitude being that why should [Empowerment Inc.] worry about a couple thousand rand?

Change on the Casino Floor

In Nevada today, control resides with veteran floor managers. Free from state oversight (especially of their employment practices), they continue to put into practice their traditional habitus of control (through the choices they make concerning tipping, technology, and surveillance). In South Africa, veteran "casino men" have also managed to stay in control of the industry, and they too still possess a traditional habitus of control. It is not that the basic principles through which they see and act upon the world are different than they were during apartheid. Rather, as the worlds around their casinos have been reconfigured, the same principles of decision making now generate different choices regarding the organization of service labor. Such is the framework within which we may make sense of the radical reorganization of the South African casino in the immediate post-apartheid period, that is, as an ultimately futile attempt by entrenched executives to reestablish the world in which they commenced their careers.

Vigilant state enforcement of new labor market regulations has produced a deep sense of distrust toward workers. Managers' official meetings and informal conversations were dominated by gossip concerning petty scams purportedly performed by new croupiers, slot attendants, and food servers. PDI dealers in particular were considered not only duplicitous but also incompetent. One early morning when I was coming off my shift, an Afrikaner shift manager pulled me aside to complain about his staff. Sweeping his hand across the pit, he declared: "They shouldn't be here. Ten years ago, you would not have seen them on the floor of a casino." Along with PDI workers, PDI floor managers were viewed with odium. "Maybe fifteen of the fifty-two inspectors on the floor right now are at all competent," Gold City Casino's tables manager told me. "The rest know fuck-all. Now, in the old days, if you weren't up to par, they would pull the dealer off the table. Inspectors were assertive; they wanted to correct dealers and provide an example. Not anymore."

But it would be incorrect to say that the managerial worldview divides the casino floor into white/trustworthy versus black/untrustworthy workers. The real principle of classification was revealed most clearly by the casino's few black pit bosses, who had been part of the original cohort of dealers hired in the Bophuthatswana homeland. These managers went to great lengths to distinguish themselves, the "Bop people," from the new urban "township workers." For instance, Helen held harsh opinions of township dealers. "[They] have no pride," she informed me one evening, "Look at how they stand, with their legs spread out and leaning against the table. In Bop, we learned that a croupier should stand at all times at an angle and with your chest out. But these township people, if you tell them about it they look at you like you have no right to correct them. Talking to them is like talking to a wall. Or a tree." Senior white managers also distinguished township dealers from prior cohorts of black workers. Nikki, for example, regularly contrasted the "terrible work ethic" of the new PDI dealers with that of the homeland dealers, who were "excellent workers, the best." This constituted proof for her that the inadequacy of the "township dealers is not a genetic thing."

Managers' fond memories of the "good old days" and their complaints concerning current croupiers do not just represent grouchy "shop-talk" on the part of overworked executives. Rather (and as demonstrated by comparison with Nevada, where veteran managers experience continuity with the past), such reminiscing derives from a particular trajectory traveled through the larger field of South African politics during the past two decades. This trajectory guides decisions on structuring casino labor—that is, managers' "position takings" regarding technology, surveillance, and tipping. The despotic panopticon can, in this sense, be read as an attempt by managers to deal with the wresting away from them of control of the casino labor market. It is, in short, an organizational structure particularly well-suited for centralizing control and maximizing security.

Empowerment Inc. executives imagine the casino floor as populated not with clients to be served, but with incompetent dealers looking to steal from the house. They obsess, in short, about security. "Compared to the casinos in Las Vegas," the Gold City Casino general manager told me in our first meeting, "we have to practice constant and intense supervision of our workers." (Based upon my fieldwork in both countries, I would argue that the technical competency of dealers in South Africa is on par with those in the United States. And while it is an open question whether the former are more likely to steal than are Nevada dealers, managers themselves possessed no instrument with which to measure and compare croupiers' "propensity to pilfer.") Management's reorganization of the post-apartheid casino must be understood as based upon a "gut feeling" that PDIs, if given the proverbial inch, would rob them blind.

Corporate decisions concerning the use of technology to routinize work and monitor workers were made in relation to such suspicions. Empowerment Inc. executives made shuffling machines, microphones, and computer screens standard issue for all tables, while company policy was rewritten to permit no deviation from procedure on the part of workers (recall, for example, the extensive displays of "clean hands" now required of all croupiers at Gold City Casino). One executive even explained to me his ambition to make his casino the most technologically advanced in the world: "That's the big thing. It eliminates the opportunity for theft, the scams. Anything that can be automated, we'll automate." This reflects both a distrust of PDI workers and an antipathy toward state regulations expropriating from managers control of the labor market. "It's excessive, no doubt," he continued, "but keep in mind it never used to be this way. It's an empowerment thing, you know."[47]

The same principle underlies the ban on accepting tips. This was a choice made by a handful of Empowerment Inc. executives shortly after the company was formed in the mid-1990s. A member of this group described to me the genesis of this new policy:

> When putting together an operating plan for [Gold City Casino], we had a meeting in which tipping policy was discussed. I was the only one to argue that we should continue to allow it as we'd done in the homelands. But [the company CEO] was dead set against it. He would not even discuss it. It would produce widespread cheating, and that's that.

The no-tipping policy is today wildly unpopular with floor managers, who feel that it undercuts employee morale and, in the words of one, "sucks the life out of" interactions on the tables. However, the veteran croupiers and pit bosses who now head Empowerment Inc. view the policy through categories of perception formed in the homeland casino—PDI workers, unlike the British expats and the thoroughly screened "Bop" dealers, would be unable to resist the temptation to assist tipping clients, thus compromising security.

This fixation upon security for workers creates constant problems for producing adequate levels of speed and service for consumers. We could even say that management's quest for complete labor control renders the games dysfunctional for gamblers. Consider the decision to prohibit tipping. Managers admit that the policy hurts service in the casino, but they also insist that players do not desire service anyway. "Service is shit everywhere in South Africa," was a common response from managers when asked directly why they refuse to use tipping as a mechanism of product differentiation in a competitive market. But such explanations were contradicted by my fieldwork in the pits, where gamblers, many of whom had regularly patronized the homeland casinos, voiced displeasure that they could no longer provide gratuities to workers.

Executives would also claim that PDI dealers do not want to work for tips. "Blacks," I was told by an Empowerment Inc. executive, "view having to give service as demeaning, especially with tipping, where it is solely based on the player's wealth." Another claimed that black croupiers were unable to perform customer service: "It's their culture. These workers just don't have the tools to give service." Yet at multiple

times, I witnessed workers challenging such framings of their preferences and abilities. At a monthly staff meeting held in the large arena
usually reserved for concerts and boxing matches, a female dealer asked
the casino manager: "Where do our tips go? They should be mine!"
The rest of the dealing staff clapped and shouted their support. The
casino manager took the microphone and explained that tip income is
quite volatile, while the company's flat wage provides a stable income.
The no-tip policy, he reasoned, was actually in their best interest. The
young woman was not satisfied, however. She stepped back up to the
microphone and declared, "But I am here to be a service professional.
This policy makes me unhappy, and if I am not happy, then the customer
is not happy."

As with service, the extreme automation of casino labor produces
ongoing problems for regulating the speed of play. Shuffling machines,
for instance, increase dramatically the average plays-per-hour on each
table, thereby accelerating the pace at which the casino "grinds" money
from clients. The end result for the gambler is that temporary experiences of good fortune are quickly overshadowed by his or her cumula-
tive losses. Managers thus had to constantly battle the perception that
their games were "tight" or even "rigged." During my fieldwork, they
implemented a comprehensive plan to "build in slowdowns" for each
game in the casino. Slot machines were reprogrammed to "lock up" more
frequently (requiring a floor manager to verify winnings and restart the
machine). On the blackjack tables, meanwhile, the casino would play a
short clip of rock music after a player received a twenty-one. Dealers
would then pause for a few seconds to delay the start of the next hand
and thus slow the pace at which players depleted their bankrolls.

Intense surveillance, the confiscation of tips, and the automation of
labor are all defensive maneuvers to prevent the theft of cash, chips,
and other valued goods. But in addition, the casino-as-panopticon represents an attempt by executives to regain control over the labor market.
According to Gambling Board regulations, the only reason allowed for
firing a worker is "conduct detrimental to operational integrity" (i.e., a
security-related infraction). By setting impossibly high standards and
then constantly documenting failures to meet them (especially through

the nightly target reports), managers produce for each worker an extensive dossier of infractions. Should they then decide to fire a particular worker, the dossiers are used to justify the termination to the Gambling Board. The panopticon, in other words, not only *prevents* infractions, it *produces* them, thereby restoring (some degree of) managerial authority over the internal labor market. (In turn, the stress and degradation associated with working in a panopticon produces an inordinately high rate of voluntary resignation. The annual labor turnover rate at Gold City Casino is 15 percent, two-thirds of which is due to voluntary resignations rather than outright dismissals.)

A despotic service regime characterizes not just Gold City Casino, but all of the casinos in the Gauteng province. Given that the situation is dysfunctional for consumers, why does no individual firm move to break free of it (by, for example, returning to hand shuffling or allowing dealers to make tips)? This would seem to represent a viable strategy to gain an advantage in a competitive (and many say overcapitalized) market. Again, though, we must situate managerial "common sense" not in relation to some ideal type of instrumentally rational action, but within the biographical trajectories of concrete individuals. Top decision makers at South Africa's three main casino firms all commenced their careers in Sun International's homeland casinos. They stay in close contact with one another and imagine the industry to be a unified body struggling against the state and its new empowerment regulations. "We're all mates," a regional director for Empowerment Inc. explained to me. "We all came up together with Sun, and we still have that mindset." Just as Nevada floor managers conspire to *retain* control of the labor market, South African executives act collectively in an attempt to *regain* control over it. That industry rules intended to "empower" the country's long oppressed black majority in practice produce a despotic service regime is a profound and sad irony of the post-apartheid condition.

Conclusion

CASINO CAPITALISM AND POLITICO-PERFORMATIVITY

The twentieth century witnessed not simply a liberalization of gambling policies across nations and states but also the emergence of a novel model of structuring casino industries, what we may call the Nevada model. The essential characteristics of this model, as it originated in the Mojave Desert, consist of a radical affirmation of the consumer's "right" to gamble, property rights defined to favor dynamic industry growth, and complete control by the "house" over the labor market. And while these gambling regulatory principles were historically new, they were not at all inconsistent with Nevada's long-standing "One Sound State" policy philosophy. Since the late nineteenth century, state politicians have attempted to attract outside investors through low tax rates, minimal spending on social services, and other pro-growth economic policies.[1] In what Richard Siegel has labeled an "ironic convergence," these key elements of Nevada's extreme neoliberal policy prescriptions were adopted by policy makers across the United States and, indeed, the world.[2]

The fundamental tenet of this new neoliberal paradigm was that markets of all sorts should be allowed to self-regulate. Any attempt by governments or other entities to restrict their natural functioning would impede efficiency and lead to deleterious effects for society as a whole. Financial markets, the thinking went, must facilitate the free flow of capital so as to encourage investment and entrepreneurship. Consumers should be free to maximize individual utility by purchasing whatever goods and services they desired, and flexible labor markets would allow businesses to hire and fire workers as is necessary to meet the demands of an ever-changing global marketplace. How exactly was American-style neoliberalism globalized during the late twentieth century? And what is its future in light of the crises currently roiling the world system?

Of course no single study can provide a definitive answer to these questions. This conclusion therefore adopts a more modest goal: to use the case of casino legalization to evaluate several more general theories of globalization.[3] First, in addressing *why* gambling policy converged upon the Nevada model, I reject both coercive and normative explanations. The Nevada casino model was not forced upon unwilling governments, nor did it suddenly become taken for granted globally as a legitimate business enterprise. Instead, it was strategically adopted by entrepreneurial state officials in response to fiscal crises, as a transposable technology for extracting tax revenue from consumers. Second, my field data revealed that the formal convergence of casino policy concealed divergence in *how* gambling is produced and consumed on the ground. Rather than a natural process of "decoupling," the gulf between models and practice must be understood as itself a form of symbolic politics, one played out between performing firms and regulatory audiences within a national political field. The confluence of these two arguments constitute what I call a politico-performative approach to studying work, management, and markets in an era of neoliberalism and beyond.

FROM DIFFUSION TO POLITICS

The integration of nations and cultures into a single global order has long been presumed to drive a convergence toward templates of organization based upon those developed in the United States.[4] In *The Protestant Ethic and the Spirit of Capitalism,* Max Weber famously argued that a rationalized ethos of everyday life first emerged in the U.S. colonies among insecure Calvinists seeking signs of their own salvation.[5] (As we saw in chapter 6, gambling, like gluttony or gloating, constituted for the Puritan evidence that one was predestined for damnation.) This rational and abstemious ethos in turn found a home in the bureaucracies that came to dominate commerce in nineteenth-century capitalist America. As they came into competition with these new administrative structures, traditional organizational forms either bureaucratized themselves or perished. According to Weber, the end result would be a society of ruthlessly efficient though cold and impersonal "iron cages." (He would have undoubtedly interpreted the extreme routinization and joylessness of work at Gold City Casino today as validation of his dystopian vision.)

In the twentieth century, Weber's argument concerning "American exceptionalism" (i.e., the country's dubious distinction as birthplace of modern, rational capitalism) was carried forward, most notably by business historian Alfred Chandler. Chandler argued that capitalism developed and thrived in America not because of religiously inspired dispositions, but as a necessary adaptation to the vast territorial expanse of the North American continent. To coordinate production, large bureaucracies emerged and served as a "visible hand" guiding industrial development.[6] This peculiar brand of competitive national capitalism, the argument goes, has prevailed in the United States—and likely will on a global scale as well. The literature predicting a "McDonaldization of society" has in turn applied Weber's and Chandler's efficiency thesis to the modern service economy.[7]

Contemporary scholarship, however, maintains that while convergence may be occurring, it has little to do with the inherent efficiency of large bureaucracies.[8] The hand (visible or otherwise) of the market is no longer sufficient to transform the world into an iron cage. The perfectly rational organizations theorized by Weber are here just ideal types—rare in reality, given the multiple forces buffering firms from market pressures (state bailouts, oligopolistic trusts, etc.). Nonetheless, a wide variety of empirical studies have found around the globe "a pronounced tendency to copy . . . American forms" of organization.[9] So what is driving convergence?

Sociologists Walter W. Powell and Paul J. DiMaggio, in their seminal paper "The Iron Cage Revisited," specify three mechanisms driving the diffusion of U.S. forms: coercive external pressures, modernizing norms, and mimetic copying in response to uncertainty.[10] The global diffusion of the Nevada casino model, however, cannot be explained through reference to these three usual suspects. Consider the coercion hypothesis. It would predict that the Nevada model for regulating gambling has spread via direct pressure from powerful global elites.[11] But there is no evidence that the International Monetary Fund, World Bank, or other international agencies have pressured states such as South Africa (or the United Kingdom, or Singapore, or the Sioux Nation) to liberalize casino policy. Nor can we single out expansionist strategies on the part of Nevada "gaming" companies, most of whom in fact fought tooth and nail against the spread of casino gambling. This was due in large measure to the state's 1959 Foreign Gaming Rule, which "clearly prohibited Nevada casino licensees from being involved in gaming activities outside of the state."[12] Even when this rule was repealed in 1993, Nevada firms would often bankroll anti-casino campaigns elsewhere. This resistance proved futile, and many of these firms have since acquired licenses in new jurisdictions. But it would be incorrect to view direct coercion by international organizations or private firms as the driving force behind the liberalization of gambling law globally.

Neoinstitutional theorists such as Powell and DiMaggio argue that coercive pressures are increasingly less important anyway than are processes of normative and mimetic isomorphism. State officials, for instance, in the face of complex and rapidly changing environments, may borrow (or simply download) political constitutions, school curricula, and mission statements.[13] "American forms," more legitimate because they are perceived to be more "modern," here serve as templates for elites lacking the time and expertise to reinvent the wheel.[14] These arguments concerning normative and mimetic processes are grounded in a conception of action labeled "macrophenomenological." It is macro in that it is opposed to micro-oriented accounts that emphasize the emergent, *sui generis* character of social life. Actors, in the neoinstitutional view, are constituted by larger structures, not the other way around. And it is phenomenological in that it opposes realist accounts that analytically privilege power and interests. In short, individuals are, in the words of John Meyer, "enactors of scripts rather more than they are self-directed actors. The social psychology at work is that of Goffman or Snow, emphasizing dramaturgical and symbolic processes in place of the hard-boiled calculation of interests assumed by rationalist actor-centric approaches."[15]

As the above quote suggests, neoinstitutionalists use Goffman to theorize both the substantive *content* of new global templates, and the *mechanisms* driving their diffusion. Regarding content, Goffman argued that the social glue holding together modern American society is a ritualistic respect for the individual; the "world society" thesis, in turn, argues that the common content of emergent models is a respect for individual rights (recall the Wiehahn Report's insistence upon citizens' "freedom to gamble"). As for mechanisms, opinion polls and voting patterns can make politicians aware of liberalizing values.[16] New norms can be championed in the political arena by powerful advocates such as professional groups.[17] In the end, however, national elites are embedded in a global culture which negatively constrains but, more importantly, positively guides action by functioning as a "generalized other" in relation to which action is oriented.

Normative pressures cannot, however, explain the globalization of mass gambling. Most fundamentally, it is not the case that the Las Vegas casino has achieved the status of a taken-for-granted, legitimate template. There certainly has occurred no significant shift in public opinion regarding casinos. While surveys do reveal a modest increase in popular tolerance of gambling in the abstract, citizens generally oppose the construction of casinos in their own communities—the famed NIMBY ("not in my backyard") syndrome.[18] Meanwhile, influential professional communities within law, medicine, and economics all remain deeply divided on the question of whether legal gambling is on the whole beneficial for society. But perhaps the strongest evidence against normative and mimetic arguments is that only rarely are casinos legalized by popular vote, relative to executive or legislative decree. (Consider that in 2003, only three out of forty-five gambling expansion referenda in the United States prevailed; the remaining forty-two encountered substantial opposition and were defeated.)

Considering continued public antipathy toward mass gambling, as well as the acrimonious debate that decisions to legalize casinos stimulate, it would be hard to label these moves as merely mimetic. To legalize casinos is neither a coerced nor a free choice, but a strategic decision made by concrete political actors in specific local circumstances. It undoubtedly entails costs for those perceived as responsible for doing so. But in exchange for what sorts of benefits? It is in this vein that I argue that the globalization of Nevada-style casinos represents a dramatic alteration in long-standing calculi used by state actors to evaluate legal gambling. In brief, perceived economic benefits increasingly outweigh political costs. Insofar as casinos retain some degree of social stigma in the community, political actors who opt to legalize them still risk running afoul of important constituencies. Yet, since approximately the late 1970s, officials have demonstrated a willingness to forgo symbolic profits of prohibition, and for several reasons.[19]

First, the well-documented "crisis of the tax state" created new incentives for policy makers of all stripes to find alternative sources of revenue.[20] Over the past several decades, standard strategies of achieving (or even approximating) solvency through taxation have proved ineffectual due to an ever-growing demand for social services, the threat of "capital flight" from high-tax jurisdictions, and popular movements that have obtained legal codification of taxation restraints. Meanwhile, the conservative revolution of the 1980s and 1990s ushered in the "rebirth of [a] liberal creed" hostile to Keynesian-style deficit spending.[21] In this context, casinos and other forms of mass gambling were increasingly evaluated in terms of their potential to generate economic revenues for the state in the short term, rather than their various social costs, real or perceived.

Second and relatedly, the revenue potential of gambling industries grew tremendously due to changes on the demand side. Casinos are part of a rapidly growing sector of the economy known as leisure and recreational services. Although these "nonessential" activities—eating out, watching films, having one's hair styled—were once the sole province of the wealthy, they now constitute taken-for-granted "needs" of average citizens.[22] Between 1970 and 1990 (the initial two decades of casino expansion), expenditures on recreation increased 500 percent among U.S. consumers, while recreation expenditures as a percentage of total consumption doubled.[23] Various reasons have been specified for this growth, including an expansion of the middle class, increases in leisure time, and widespread availability of consumer credit.[24] These changes all magnified the economic potential of legal gambling for states: casino "spend" came to constitute not merely a luxury tax upon the rich, but a large-scale levy to be culled from the middle, working, and even underclasses.

Third, as "no new taxes" became standard mantra for candidates and incumbents alike, and as the size of potential consumer markets grew, the Nevada casino model emerged as a viable and transposable tool with which to capture revenues. Nevada politicians and firms did not actively promote this model. The IMF and the World Bank did not strong-arm states into adopting it. Policy makers worldwide, however, could not fail but notice the success of the Nevada economy, widely assumed to derive from its wide-open gambling policy.[25] As was regularly reported in the popular, academic, and business presses, the state achieved rapid population growth, low unemployment figures, and regular budget surpluses, even during recessionary years for the United States as whole. Hard numbers implied the Nevada miracle was not a mirage, and the former moral pariah became an economic paradigm.

Debate exists over how unique and historically contingent the Nevada case was, and thus over how replicable its experience may be. Perhaps it, as an early adopter, had merely captured a temporary monopoly, and new casino states will pursue an increasingly smaller piece of the overall revenue pie. Perhaps Nevada was successful because of its lure as a tourist destination; less desirous (and sunny) locales will attract not tourist dollars but "local spend." And perhaps new casinos will not stimulate local economies but suppress them, via a "substitution effect" whereby any new jobs created merely displace existing forms of employment. These are all valid concerns, risks to be weighed, and many states continue to decide that they are too great. Others, however, take the chance, wagering that the Nevada model can be picked up and placed down anywhere, in Detroit or Durban, Manchester or Macau.

To understand the issue this way is to move from a vision of American models smoothly diffusing globally to a contextual and processual vision of local politics as exhibiting a game-like character. As the rules, constraints, and incentives of the game change, so will the strategies of the players within the field. And as is the case in any field analysis, to understand the nature of an institution is to specify what sort of translation, or conversion, of different species of capital it accomplishes. The Nevada casino, in this sense, is less an abstract template implemented from above than a specific technology used strategically to extract revenues from below. A gambler sets a ten-dollar bill on the blackjack table and, as Goffman documented, experiences a sense of drama and excitement. He or she has action. Seen from above, however, as a statistically average transaction, the casino each time hands that gambler back nine dollars, pockets 50 cents for itself as revenue, and hands 50 cents to the state as a tax. Seen in this light, a casino is but a mechanism for euphemizing taxation. And though the long-term consequences of this technology are still very much unknown, its success in generating revenues in the short term is undeniable.[26] In the United States, for instance, 3 percent of all governmental income now derives from gambling taxes, while state officials report feeling "drunk on gambling revenues."[27]

FROM DECOUPLING TO PERFORMANCE

The Nevada casino model is diffusing globally through processes political in nature. But convergence is only half the story. While state actors worldwide encounter common economic incentives to legalize casinos, rarely are they able to simply enforce their will when it comes to policy. Organized groups within a given political field—such as communities of faith, business firms, or trade unions—may possess the power to block or undermine liberalization policies.[28] From the point of view of those wishing to harness the fiscal potential of legal gambling, such opposition represents a legitimacy threat—one, furthermore, typically countered by offering concessions to hostile constituencies. Such concessions will take the form of concrete regulations placed upon the industry and its relationship with various categories of relevant agents—upon, that is, particular markets. Historically, regulations focused upon consumer markets (e.g., restrictions on a casino's operating hours). Such restrictions, however, tend to dampen revenues, and so prove unpalatable to gambling proponents. As a consequence, regulations increasingly focus less on consumer markets than on capital markets (property rights specifying who may own and operate casinos) and labor markets (employment policies detailing how workers are to be treated).[29]

But how do symbolic politics as they play out in political fields affect the action on the casino floor? In the introduction, I argued that Erving Goffman erred in refusing to consider the larger political context in which interactions are embedded. But dominant theories of globalization too often commit the opposite error, forgoing systematic study of everyday life inside firms. Differences between global scripts and local practices are simply dismissed as a case of decoupling, a residual category used to account for the lingering effects of history, power, and interests. As an ontological principle, however, Goffman argued that reality resides at the level of *verstehen*, wherein individuals negotiate and make meaning of organizational structures. So while the blackjack games in the United States and South Africa look identical, the action on the tables could not be more different.

Gamblers in Nevada believe game outcomes result from an individual's adherence to the "book" of basic strategy; in Gauteng, they believe that wins and losses derive from collective decisions made by "the table." Nevada dealers experience work as a world of autonomy in which they make tips; dealers in Gauteng experience work as alienating and seek to produce the impression that they are in no way responsible for game outcomes. Managers in Nevada envision the pits as populated by their trustworthy "boys"; in Gauteng, managers gaze out over the casino and see nothing but untrustworthy "PDIs" handling chips, cards, and cash.

Rather than assuming a convergence of organizational forms and dismissing as decoupling any divergence at the level of the lifeworlds within them, we took the latter as a starting point for problematizing the former. A multisited, global ethnography was the method best suited for this task of "tracing and describing the connections and relationships among sites previously thought incommensurate."[30] So while divergent service regimes at Silver State Casino and Gold City Casino could be traced to a single proximate cause—managerial trust or distrust in workers—these relations of trust were located within a historically constituted managerial habitus, itself shaped by two distinct forms of state regulation regarding markets of capital and markets of labor.

The formal goals of these two pillars of policy are distinctly "modern" in character. The two industries, in their incipient phases, had been characterized by minimal regulation, overt discrimination, and extensive corruption. And in both cases, a state bureaucracy for monitoring firms emerged to ensure that casinos as legitimate business enterprises adhered to principles of purity (proprietors are clean and responsible corporate citizens) and equity (achievement, not ascription, structures the labor market). Such convergence no doubt reflects the integration of both countries into world society—in line with what could be called a consolidation of global standards of symbolic capital—coming as it did in the context of the civil rights era in the United States and the end of apartheid in South Africa.

But why were these new regulations implemented so differently in practice? Neoinstitutional theory argues that national actors will "make valiant efforts to live up to [the new global] model."[31] Failure to do so despite their good faith efforts is then attributed to either a lack of resources or contradictions among the various goals elaborated in world society scripts. But, one may ask, are actors always sincere in their efforts to meet new global role expectations?

Goffman argued the opposite. Performers, he claimed, are not always taken in by their parts; they can be cynical about them as well. Indeed, cynicism rather than sincerity best characterizes the orientation of both U.S. and South African managers toward new values concerning employment equity, as well as their responsibility as modern employers to redress past wrongs by adhering to affirmative action. As a Nevada manager stated to me regarding the Las Vegas Consent Decree: "Like in sports, we figured the rules do sometimes change, and you have to adapt." Adaptation to changing rules in this case entailed not hiring African-American dealers to achieve equity, as the decree specified, but employing Asian immigrants to display diversity. The key audience for firms' labor market "performance" was not a "generalized other" within world society, but underfinanced and ill-equipped regulatory agencies (the EEOC and the Nevada Equal Rights Commission). In this scenario, Nevada casinos fit Goffman's definition of a cynical performer and the state that of a "weak audience."[32] The balance of power between regulators and the regulated in the United States is contextualized through comparison with South Africa. Casino executives there, though equally cynical regarding their role as responsible employers, nonetheless were unable to stage a perfunctory performance (i.e., employ groups other than local township blacks as dealers) due to the presence of a "strong audience," the Gauteng Gambling Board.

The overarching "scripts" disseminating globally, in this perspective, not only provide rules and values to guide action, they also reshape the terrain upon which struggles among groups take place. As Randall Collins has argued, interactive rules may constitute not only normative constraints upon behavior, but strategic resources as well.[33] It follows that while we may find consensus concerning broad values, there will also occur contestation over how adherence to these goals is defined and displayed. Support for this "realist" reading of Goffman comes from my analysis of the genesis of casino regulations. While all parties in the newly democratic South Africa recognized the legitimacy of the value of "black economic empowerment," they debated how progress toward the goal of BEE should be operationalized. The casino industry was an early flashpoint for such debates. Apartheid-era managers negotiated with regulators over the definition of a PDI (for example, whether white women would count as PDIs in upper management), the proper percentages of PDIs for each staffing level, the format of the quarterly labor reports, and so on. These negotiations were, in essence, struggles to establish the institutional "setting" for presenting and proving empowerment. The quota charts that constitute the bulk of the quarterly labor reports submitted by Empowerment Inc. to the Gauteng Gambling Board, for instance, obscure the tokenization of black employees, who experience a gulf between their dramatic and their real power within the organization. Formally adhering to norms of equality, rather than openly flouting them, signifies not the integration of Empowerment Inc. into world society but rather a more insidious form of reproducing historical patterns of inequality within the new South Africa.

To purify controversial casino industries entailed implementing divergent patterns of regulation on the ground. The end result was not dual instances of decoupling, but two different ways of managing the neoliberal condition—of dealing with globalization. The ultimate cause for divergence lay in the logic of what counted as symbolic capital in the two political fields, in how gambling industries would display an image of adherence to the larger social good. In the United States, threats to the legitimacy of the industry were countered through a process of individualizing and personalizing corruption. New, clean owners were brought in to replace old, desecrated ones, and the industry was declared righteous. The end result was not unlike that described by Mary Douglas in her account of ritualized pollution and purification: "His legitimacy being in doubt, he must be removed, and to remove him, his antagonists accuse him of having become corrupt. . . . The accusation is itself a weapon for clarifying and strengthening the structure."[34] In South Africa, the opposite occurred: the head remained intact while the structure of the body was transfigured. Unlike the initial cohort of casino proprietors in the United States, former homeland operators retained their positions as captains of industry, their "sins" essentially forgiven by new regulators. But they now look upon their own bodies with distrust and disgust, obsessively self-monitoring with the latest technologies of surveillance and control. A shuffling machine, seen in this light, is more than just a means for randomizing a deck of cards.

Rather than an imposition of legitimate scripts from above, this study revealed a highly dynamic process of legitimating new organizational forms from below. Politics and performance, not diffusion and decoupling, drove the making of the global gambling industry. The Nevada casino model, a novel technology for euphemizing taxation vis-à-vis consumers, generated backlash from various groups claiming to represent the public interest. Successful symbolic ripostes to these challenges—that is, a particular constellation of regulations placed upon consumer, capital, and labor markets—in turn generated nation-specific ways of manufacturing the gambling "product."

Are the regulatory dynamics described herein unique to the casino industry? To address this question, we can make one final revisit to Goffman, this time to his classic work, *Stigma*. While standard readings of the stigma concept assume an objective division between the stigmatized and a separate class of normals, Goffman's concept is in fact a relational one:

> [It is] possible to restrict the analysis to those who possess a flaw that uneases almost all their social situations. . . . This report argues differently. The most fortunate of normals is likely to have his half-hidden failing, and for every little failing there is a social occasion when it will loom large, creating a shameful gap between virtual and actual social identity. Therefore the occasionally precarious and the constantly precarious form *a single continuum, their situation in life analyzable by the same framework*.[35]

By analogy, examining the dynamics of state regulation of gambling can inform our understanding of more "mainstream" industries, all of which have skeletons in the closet, detractors in civil society, and socially constructed costs and benefits. The handling of ongoing corporate scandals through the demonization and replacement of top executives—while leaving organizational structures untouched—characterizes industrial policy across the United States, while in post-apartheid South Africa the trope of Black Economic Empowerment is key for justifying a wide array of existing and emergent institutions.

THE FUTURE OF CASINO CAPITALISM?

Both neoliberalism and the Nevada casino model disseminated across the globe during the final decades of the twentieth century. The timing was not coincidental. The fall of communist regimes removed one of the few remaining ideological barriers to legalizing mass gambling. Structural reforms in both developed and developing economies produced large budget deficits at the same time that Keynesian principles fell into disfavor. And a market mania swept the globe, according to which markets of all sorts should be allowed to self-regulate. Free markets of labor, capital, and consumption, the emerging consensus held, would maximize flexibility, encourage innovation, and lead to the greatest good for all.

The first decade of the twenty-first century draws to a close with these assumptions cast in doubt, and many now wonder whether the neoliberal fantasy was just that: a fantasy. Rather than generating efficiency and equality, free markets seem have to produced grave crises in a variety of spheres. Left to their own devices, equity markets introduced myriad opportunities for malfeasance and incentives for exuberant speculation. Lacking resources and momentum, the fight to end discrimination against minorities in the labor market stalled. Unbridled consumption, meanwhile, may even have put our planet in peril.

The response to these crises has been just as dramatic. We have witnessed a swift, organic reaction to these negative effects of rapid marketization from publics and their representatives the world over. When I finally left the casino floor in 2005, staunch advocates of neoliberal casino capitalism controlled the federal government in both the United States and South Africa. But a mere three years later, as I put the finishing touches on this manuscript, both regimes have teetered. The United States has just elected as president Barack Obama, who ran on a platform of reviving governmental oversight of a variety of economic and social spheres. And in South Africa, President Thabo Mbeki (a staunch advocate of neoliberal policy in general and new gambling laws in particular) was recently ousted by a resurgent faction within the ANC. In fact, a decade of single-party rule in South Africa may be coming to an end with the emergence of a new party, the Congress of the People (COPE), who seek to capitalize on public anger at the ANC's embrace of neoliberal principles that have benefited a select few and left far too many behind.

Only time will tell whether such developments will have a lasting effect upon dominant principles of governance in the two countries. Neither the ANC nor the new COPE party has yet articulated a clear alternative vision for reconciling the goals of economic growth and social empowerment in the new South Africa. President Obama's inauguration speech, meanwhile, was notable for both its affirmation of the market ("Its power to generate wealth and expand freedom is unmatched") and its blaming of individual failings for the country's current crisis ("Our economy is badly weakened, a consequence of greed and irresponsibility on the part of some"). Nor can anyone predict with certainty whether the Nevada casino model will still be with us a decade or a century hence. Herein, however, lies the value of a politico-performative perspective. It recognizes that social and economic policies are not written *de novo*, but at particular historical junctures and in relation to very real material constraints that tend to favor the status quo. Yet material realities are never absolutely determinative. They are amenable to symbolic framings and counterframings by challengers in political field games who, much like gamblers at a blackjack table, experience each round of action anew, confident in their belief that, after all, the house can't prevail every time.

Methodological Appendix

COMPARATIVE ETHNOGRAPHY AND REFLEXIVE SCIENCE

The essence of participant observation is self-immersion in the lives of those we study. Ethnographers seek to know firsthand their subjects' worlds and to thickly describe these worlds to others. But it is also true that ethnographers, like all social scientists, begin their research weighted down by assumptions and categories of analysis formed through engagement with extant bodies of knowledge. Managing the tension between these two ways of knowing—between a subjectivist description of everyday life, and an objectivist analysis of its conditions of possibility—is the essence of the ethnographic condition.[1]

For this project, I sought to nurture a dialogue between the "folk theories" of those with whom I worked and established sociological theory. I thus cannot deny that I began fieldwork armed with prede-termined ideas and expectations, "scholastic concepts" that served as valuable tools with which to make sense of the initially bewildering world of the casino. These concepts, however, soon proved inadequate to describe the full range of workers' motives, motions, and emotions. It was through minding this gap between the logic of theory and the logic of practice that I began to reflect upon and reconstruct my own presuppositions. There is a saying among veteran pit bosses that the gambler "never leaves the casino with what he came with." This is true of the ethnographer as well.

Though trying in terms of selecting cases and negotiating access to multiple sites, a comparative study of the same job in different societies offers exceptional analytic leverage.[2] When comparing dissimilar occu-pations, tried-and-true scholastic concepts provide a handy frame for discerning commonalities and building an argument. Both McDonald's workers and insurance salesmen must control their clients; both flight attendants and bill collectors will have their emotions manipulated by their employers. Differences between jobs may then be brushed aside as residues of idiosyncratic production imperatives. But if the organization and experience of work differ across two otherwise similar workplaces, we have a puzzle—a puzzle, furthermore, that must be solved by extend-ing out from the workplace to the larger context in which the work is embedded.

So it was that I spent four years bouncing back and forth between the United States and South Africa. Half of this time I spent behind the tables, documenting games of service work that were both different (entrepreneurial for U.S. workers, despotic for South African croupiers) and divergent (insofar as casinos in the two countries were originally organized identically). The other half I spent behind the scenes, conduct-ing primary research among managers and regulators. These data were mobilized to explain why service regimes have diverged in the two countries.

Throughout this fieldwork I operated in line with a reflexive concep-tion of science as elaborated by the extended case method.[3] Reflexive science differs from its counterpart, positive science, in four respects.

First, rather than neutralizing our influence on those we study, it recognizes that our interventions "create perturbations that are . . . music to be appreciated, transmitting the hidden secrets of the participant's world."[4] Second, reflexive science seeks to aggregate multiple points of view into a single picture of social process, that is, of how action unfolds over space and time. Third, it seeks not to establish the representative of a particular case vis-à-vis a universe of similar cases, but to delineate the external forces structuring one's research site. And fourth, it entails using one's empirical findings to problematize and reconstruct a particular theoretical paradigm.

How does one put these principles to work in comparative ethnography? This is the question addressed in this appendix. I first describe how the principle of reflexivity aided me during the process of gaining entrée to my two research sites. In both countries, I started off a student and ended up a dealer; the different paths traveled between these two roles, however, revealed much about the social worlds I was studying. I then explain how the principle of reflexivity allowed me to transform different subject positions across the two sites (as a national versus a foreigner, and a covert versus overt researcher) from a liability into an asset.

REFLEXIVITY AND ENTRÉE

The process through which one gains entrée to one's fieldsite can reveal much about the nature of the site. All social worlds are saturated with webs of power relations; they are, we may say, always preconstituted politically. And whether researchers like it or not, they will be treated by those they study as a party to these relations—as a coconspirator or competitor, a resource or threat. Rather than seeking to minimize or deny such reactions, the reflexive ethnographer embraces them in order to put them to use. By paying close attention to how one is received during the key moment of gaining entrée, much can be revealed. In my case, the different ways in which I maneuvered around barriers to entry portended my final argument concerning divergent political structurings of the global casino (though I did not realize it at the time, anxious as I was about getting in at all).

In the United States, I first attempted to study casino workers by directly asking permission from executives at several large firms. This proved to be an exercise in futility. Upon arriving in Nevada, I phoned the head office of each of the state's main casino firms and introduced myself, explaining that I was a graduate student doing a thesis on the "gaming" industry. I was straightforward about my purpose: to do a case study of a casino (the identity of which would be kept anonymous) and to write about the work of dealing. Responses to my queries were cold, to say the least. In some cases, I was sent through a dense thicket of phone trees, directed to call a marketing director, who directed me to call an assistant vice president, who directed me to fax my résumé to a secretary, from whom I never heard back. In others, I was simply told no from the start.

Though frustrating at the time, the resistance to my research was, in retrospect, revealing. I had initially assumed that corporate executives were concerned about the potential rigmarole associated with clearing my research with the state—that getting official permission to let a student study the casino floor might be a complicated, time-consuming process for them. But I phoned up the Nevada Gambling Control Board and found that this was not the case. As far as they were concerned, as long as I had no criminal record, I was free to work on the floor.

At this point, I realized that corporate executives simply had nothing to gain from allowing an outsider into their properties. Their casinos earn great profits and are in good standing with the state. If nothing is broken, what could I have helped them fix? On the contrary, it was possible that I would renege on my pledge to keep secret the identity of my research site and produce a muckraking report of some sort. And even had I gained the trust of executives, securing access would not have been a "done deal," insofar as they are not the true gatekeepers. As I showed in part 2, the intra-firm division of labor in Nevada entails a gulf between corporate and property managers, the latter of whom still control entry into the pits, just as they did in the heyday of the "juice" era.

I had no choice but to go covert and work my way into the casino from the ground up. I enrolled in dealing school, presenting myself as a college grad unable to find work in his major field of study (my bachelor's degree in sociology did nothing to blow my cover). I trained hard and mastered the requisite skills, but more importantly I cultivated connections and built up a reputation as an eager understudy. This meant making the rounds each night to the "break-in" casinos in town, betting small stakes on the tables and engaging in small talk with the dealers and pit bosses, to make sure they came to know my face and name. Most importantly, I got on the good side of the dealing school instructors so that they could vouch for my competence and "personality." In other words, I built up my "juice."

These myriad strategies paid off when I was called in to audition at Silver State Casino. Once Rick, the shift manager, decided to hire me, the rest was *pro forma*. I filled out a job application in the human resource office and secured a gaming license from the sheriff's department, neither of which were problematic from the point of view of pit bosses. In sum, the process by which I gained entrée to Silver State Casino illustrates two key characteristics of the industry: a decentralized structure of authority within the firm, and a high degree of managerial control of the labor market.

The process by which I became a croupier in South Africa entailed a very different set of strategies. This of course reflected the fact that I was a foreigner. But the trials and tribulations involved in gaining entrée to Gold City Casino also revealed much about the industry itself.

My initial historical research on South Africa's gambling industry revealed that the apartheid-era homeland casinos had regularly hired foreigners to work as dealers. I thus initially harbored hopes of again working covertly in the pits. And, mentally grounded as I was in the world of the Nevada casino, I even attempted to reproduce my earlier job search strategies. I conducted site visits to various properties in Johannesburg, playing blackjack and making small talk with the pit bosses. I would mention that I was a visiting student at the University of the Witwatersrand, had dealt cards in Nevada, and was interested in finding work while in South Africa. They would listen and nod. But when I would ask (rather casually I thought) if they could help me find a job, the response was laughter. Hiring was completely out of their hands,

I was told, not just for me as a foreigner, but for all new workers. Such decisions were made by top managers in consultation with the gambling board. If I were to get into a Jo'berg casino, it would have to be from the top down.

And so gaining entrée was again a process of trial and error—and one that was the converse of my Nevada experience. Having failed to make headway by building up juice with floor-level employees, I phoned the head office of Empowerment Inc. early one Monday morning. After a few minutes of conversation with a company secretary, I was able to set up a series of appointments with executives for later that week. Unlike the corporate executives I'd contacted in Nevada, these were all veteran "casino men" (most were British, and all were former dealers). I was particularly impressed with how involved and informed they were concerning the day-to-day operations of their individual properties.

As I sat in the office of Empowerment Inc.'s regional director, I prepared for the worst. He had spent the majority of his career working in the homeland casinos. I assumed he was used to keeping a low profile and would be suspicious of a potential "muckraker." On the contrary, he seemed quite enthusiastic about my research plan. Why was this? At the time I was so elated at having found a sympathetic gatekeeper that I didn't fully consider the reasons behind his enthusiasm. In retrospect, however, it makes perfect sense. First off, I, a student from the United States and a former Nevada dealer, represented for him a source of legitimacy, especially in the eyes of the gambling board. Any association with the "clean" casinos of Las Vegas could only assist his company in purifying itself of its unsavory apartheid origins. Second, from the start, he trusted me, a fellow white male, fully. I would, he insisted, see things as he did, especially concerning the problems presented by "these new dealers" (i.e., the township blacks the company is required to hire according to new empowerment laws). And third, though he now sat atop the country's largest gaming firm, he was a croupier at heart. Confined to his high-rise office, miles from the nearest casino, he thirsted for—craved, even—information about what was going on in the pits. As he sat there gazing at me from behind his oversized executive desk, I could sense the wheels spinning in his head. His eyes lit up as I brought up the idea of me working in his new property, Gold City Casino. I could work as a dealer, he said, as long as I agreed to be his "eyes and ears" on the ground. (I subsequently found various ways to neglect my "duty" of submitting regular written reports to head office.)

While executives with Empowerment Inc. granted me free roam of their Gold City Casino, they warned that the final okay must come from the state. I figured this would be no problem, as I had by this point already had several amicable meetings with top officials at the Gauteng Gambling Board. Yet I'd underestimated the seriousness with which board members view their duty of regulating the industry's labor market. While it had taken just under three hours to process my dealing license in Nevada, it ended up taking three months for the board to approve my temporary work permit. This delay, I subsequently discovered, resulted from a dispute within the board over whether I would be considered a "non-PDI" for the purpose of calculating affirmative action quotas, and was resolved based on the fact that I would not be paid by the company (a provision on which I'd insisted in order not to take work away from current employees at the casino). Gaining entrée in South Africa was a top-down process, reflecting both the greater centralization of authority within the casino firm and the more active role played by the state in regulating the labor market.

THREE ETHNOGRAPHIC EXTENSIONS

Why did I find the experience of service work at Silver State Casino to differ so thoroughly from that at Gold City Casino? To answer this question, I first had to take a step back and consider how my subject position varied across the two sites, and how this might have affected the manner in which I collected and interpreted my field data. Perhaps I experienced dealing in Nevada as an entrepreneurial game of making tips and dealing in Gauteng as an onerous game of effacement not because of any real differences between the two sites but because of my own personal experiences in each workplace. Perhaps the fact that my Nevada fieldwork was my first foray into the strange and exciting world of the casino explained why work there felt engaging. Maybe, too, my covert status made Nevada workers' "tricks of the trade" more accessible to me. In turn, living in South Africa was often a strange and alienating experience for me; perhaps this made work there alienating as well. Being open as a researcher could in turn have produced an insurmountable breach between my own experiences and those of Gold City Casino's "real workers." However, as my days behind the tables turn into weeks, and the weeks into months, innumerable conversations with and observations of coworkers convinced me that I wasn't the only one playing these two particular work games. They were collective endeavors, experiences of service work shared by all at each site.

At this point, I was confident that my finding of disparate service regimes had nothing to do with how my subject position varied across my two research sites. Also, the comparative design of my study allowed me to control for any effects of the general physical setup of the casinos themselves (they were, of course, exact carbon copies). Differences between the two casinos, I concluded, could be traced to differences in the social, political, and economic contexts in which they were embedded. I thus extended my research focus beyond the confines of the casino floor.

First off, if workers experience labor as a game, it made sense to study firsthand those who make the rules: managers themselves. In South Africa, this was relatively easy, due to my role as a potential (though singularly incompetent) managerial "mole." I temporarily inhabited the managerial habitus by shadowing pit bosses and even working as one myself. I interned in the marketing and human resource departments and served as a personal assistant to the general manager. In Nevada, in contrast, I never did receive free rein to work as a pit boss or shadow inspectors. Collecting additional primary data on casino managers via interviews was thus essential for the comparison. At each of the four largest gaming firms in both countries, I interviewed corporate and property managers, around twenty interviews in each market and forty in all. My questions were fairly open-ended, focusing upon managers' work biographies and how they made decisions regarding the organization of the casino floor. I would also describe to managers in one jurisdiction the standard operating procedures of firms in the other.[5] By recording not just managers' stated rationales for why they do certain things but also their immediate reactions to existing alternative possibilities, I sought to capture their unique orientations to workers, consumers, and the state.

To round out the comparison of managerial decision making, I collected data on the utilization of technology and the demographics of workers. In South Africa, production practices are highly standardized (reflecting both the centralization of decision-making power within the firm and a common managerial habitus across firms), while data on the race and gender of workers are readily available from the Gambling Board (reporting such information, I argued herein, is a key tactic for publicly legitimating casinos). This is not the case in Nevada, where production practices vary across casinos, and demographic information on specific occupations is available from neither firms nor the state. I thus generated a random sample of twenty-eight casinos out of the population of 180 in Nevada's two main cities, Las Vegas and Reno. I visited each as a patron, visually surveying the casino floor to record the gender and racial composition of dealers and floor managers, the use of shuffling machines versus hand shuffling, and the use of shoes versus hand dealing.

Interviews with casino managers revealed that they act in regard not just to workers and consumers but also to the state. I thus sought to find out how state officials perceived their interests in a certain structuring of the industry, as well as how state discourse defined casinos and their effects upon "society." I interviewed ten regulators in each country and conducted content analysis of all relevant legal and policy documents. A third and final extension was in a temporal dimension. Given the current states of the gambling-industrial fields, what were their geneses and subsequent development? How were organizational structures produced, altered, or reproduced? This meant immersing myself in various archives, where I uncovered a wide range of sources such as the personal records of early regulators and managers, investigative government reports, and court cases. To fill in lacunae in the historical record, I conducted my own oral history interviews with veteran workers and managers. This was especially important in South Africa, where secondary source materials are scarce.

Conducting primary research on workers, managers, and regulators facilitated the aggregation of situational knowledge into social process. All groups face both material constraints (states seek solvency, firms produce profits, workers want a living wage) and the need to engage in symbolic labor (from establishing the legitimacy of the industry within the political field to managing the emotions of gamblers on the tables). The nature of social life as it plays out in the contemporary casino industry, as complex and varied as it may be, deserved a single, solid methodological commitment. The principle of reflexivity served me as a bedrock, both grounding my empirical findings and generating new understandings of the phenomenon for myself and for audiences both professional and public.

Notes

PREFACE

1. See John Meyer, Francisco Ramirez, and Yasemin Soysal, "World Expansion of Mass Education, 1870–1970," *Sociology of Education* 65, no. 2 (1992): 128–49.

2. Revenues are reported as real 2000 dollars. The remaining figures in this paragraph come from the following sources: Harold Vogel, *Entertainment Industry Economics: A Guide for Financial Analysis* (New York: Cambridge University Press, 2001), 26; Bear, Stearns and Co., *North American Gaming Almanac* (New York: Smith Barney, 2003), 6.

3. Eugene Martin Christiansen, "Alternative Growth," *International Gaming and Wagering Business* 27, no. 11 (2006): 22.

4. Lotteries, the other main form of contemporary commercial gambling, were legalized by U.S. and European states in the early twentieth century,

spreading to Africa, South America, and even socialist states. See William N. Thompson, "Casinos de Juego del Mundo: A Survey of World Gambling," *Annals of the American Academy of Political and Social Science* 556 (1998): 11–21.

5. Charles T. Clotfelter and Philip J. Cook, *Selling Hope: State Lotteries in America* (Cambridge, MA: Harvard University Press, 1989).

6. Ben Mezrich, *Bringing Down the House: How Six Students Took Vegas for Millions* (New York: Free Press, 2004).

7. Ed Reid and Ovid Demaris, *The Green Felt Jungle* (New York: Trident Press, 1963).

8. Stephen A. Herzenberg, John A. Alic and Howard Wial, *New Rules for a New Economy: Employment and Opportunity in Postindustrial America* (Ithaca, NY: Cornell University Press, 1998).

9. George Ritzer, *Explorations in the Sociology of Consumption: Fast Food, Credit Cards and Casinos* (Thousand Oaks, CA: Sage Publications, 2001); Jean Comaroff and John L. Comaroff, "Millennial Capitalism: First Thoughts on a Second Coming," *Public Culture* 12, no. 2 (2000): 291–343.

10. Estimates place employment in the American casino industry at over 600,000—twice the number of workers employed in motor vehicle assembly. See Terri C. Walker, *Casino and Gaming Market Research Handbook.* (Atlanta, GA: Terri C. Walker Consulting Inc., 2005), 4; Bureau of Labor Statistics, Career Guide to Industries (Washington DC: U.S. Department of Labor, 2007).

INTRODUCTION

1. Randall Collins, "The Passing of Intellectual Generations: Reflections on the Death of Erving Goffman," *Sociological Theory* 4, no. 1 (1986): 108.

2. Albert Bergesen, "Reflections on Erving Goffman," *Quarterly Journal of Ideology* 8, no. 3 (1984): 51–54.

3. In a posthumously published interview, Goffman stated, "If I had to be labeled at all, it would have been as a Hughesian urban ethnographer." See J. C. Verhoeven, "An Interview with Erving Goffman, 1980," *Research on Language and Social Interaction* 26, no. 3 (1993): 318.

4. Erving Goffman, *Asylums: Essays on the Social Situation of Mental Patients and Other Inmates* (Garden City, NY: Anchor Books, 1961).

5. Edward O. Thorp, *Beat the Dealer: A Winning Strategy for the Game of 21* (New York: Vintage Books, 1966).

6. Thomas Goffman, interview with author, October 2004.

7. Erving Goffman, *Strategic Interaction* (Philadelphia: University of Pennsylvania Press, 1969); Erving Goffman, *Interaction Ritual: Essays on Face-to-Face Behavior* (Garden City, NY: Anchor Books, 1967). It remains a mystery why Goff-

man did not publish further on his casino fieldwork. In 1977 he received a Guggenheim fellowship and moved to Las Vegas for a fresh round of research. At the time, he spoke with great excitement about his gambling book, and may even have composed a first draft. The book was never published, however, and so we are left with *Interaction Ritual*'s central essay, "Where the Action Is," as a rich appetizer for a main course that never arrived.

8. In this sense, they resembled the Balinese cockfighters famously described by Clifford Geertz. See "Deep Play: Notes on the Balinese Cockfight," in *The Interpretation of Cultures* (New York: Basic Books, 1972), 412–53.

9. Goffman, *Interaction Ritual*, 177.

10. Michael Burawoy, "Revisits: An Outline of a Theory of Reflexive Ethnography," *American Sociological Review* 68, no. 5 (2003): 645–79.

11. Because of the limited nature of Goffman's own published writing on casinos, I supplement his ethnographic evidence with memoirs and oral histories of casino dealers from the same period.

12. David Strow, "Vegas Unions Ponder Effort to Organize Dealers, Cashiers," *Las Vegas Sun*, November 3, 1999.

13. Verhoeven, "An Interview with Erving Goffman": 19.

14. For table games, the skill of the player will affect the hold. For slot machines, the hold percentage is constant and controlled by management, as players exercise no discretion in the outcome on any single slot play.

15. Many of these aspects of casino design are now standard in retail establishments such as department stores and malls. For a history of the spread of the science of casino design, see Bill Friedman, *Designing Casinos to Dominate the Competition* (Reno: University of Nevada Press, 2000).

16. Erving Goffman, "On Cooling the Mark Out: Some Aspects of Adaptation to Failure," *Psychiatry* 15 (1952): 451–63. That clients are not completely unaware of attempts to cool them out is revealed by a common joke, in which a cold gambler, after losing an entire bankroll before finishing the first complimentary drink, remarks, "This had better be the best screwdriver I've ever had. It cost me two hundred dollars."

17. The surveillance department is autonomous from the gambling divisions in order to serve as a check upon possible cheating conspiracies on the floor.

18. At the time of my fieldwork, an estimated 65 to 80 percent of all casino tables in the world were dedicated to the game. See Shufflemaster Inc., *2003 Annual Report* (Las Vegas, NV: Shufflemaster Inc., 2004).

19. This overview examines the phenomenology of the gambling act, not the question of why people choose to gamble in the first place. Freudians considered gambling a masochistic act of self-punishment; see Sigmund Freud, "Dostoevsky and Parricide," in *Writings on Art and Literature* (Stanford, CA: Stanford University Press, 1997), 234–55. Behaviorists in turn argue that gambling's allure

derives from the highs experienced during winning streaks: "A partial and random reinforcement schedule, as Skinner and others have clearly shown, is the most powerful behavioral conditioner" (see Jerome Skolnick, *House of Cards: Legalization and Control of Casino Gambling* [New York: Little, Brown and Company, 1978], 54).

20. Harold Vogel, *Entertainment Industry Economics*, 285. See also William R. Eadington, "The Casino Gaming Industry: A Study of Political Economy," *The Annals of the American Academy of Political and Social Science* 474 (1984): 23–35; Anthony N. Cabot and Robert C. Hannum, *Casino Practical Math* (Las Vegas, NV: Institute for the Study of Gambling and Commercial Gaming, 2001).

21. Kevin Heubusch, "Taking Chances on Casinos," *American Demographics* 19, no. 5 (1997): 35–40.

22. Harold S. Smith, *I Want to Quit Winners* (Englewood Cliffs, NJ: Prentice Hall, 1961), 56.

23. Skolnick, *House of Cards*, 54.

24. David Johnston, *Temples of Chance: How America Inc. Bought Out Murder Inc. to Win Control of the Casino Business* (New York: Doubleday, 1992), 7; Richard A. Epstein, *The Theory of Gambling and Statistical Logic* (New York: Academic Press, 1995).

25. The model outlined herein allows us to study gambling in line with classic analyses of the gift exchange. See Marcel Mauss, *The Gift: The Form and Reason for Exchange in Archaic Societies* (New York: Norton, 2000).

26. Pierre Bourdieu, *Outline of a Theory of Practice* (New York: Cambridge University Press, 1972), 5.

27. Burawoy's line of argumentation followed that of the industrial sociologist Donald Roy. See Donald F. Roy, "Efficiency and the Fix: Informal Intergroup Relations in a Piecework Machine Shop," *American Journal of Sociology* 60, no. 3 (1954): 255–66.

28. Michael Burawoy, *The Politics of Production: Factory Regimes under Capitalism and Socialism* (London: Verso, 1985); Ching Kwan Lee, *Gender and the South China Miracle: Two Worlds of Factory Women* (Berkeley: University of California Press, 1998); Leslie Salzinger, *Genders in Production: Making Workers in Mexico's Global Factories* (Berkeley: University of California Press, 2003).

29. Rachel Sherman, *Class Acts: Service and Inequality in Luxury Hotels* (Berkeley: University of California Press, 2006); Richard Lloyd, *Neo-Bohemia: Art and Commerce in the Postindustrial City* (New York: Routledge, 2006); Steven Lopez, "The Politics of Service Production: Route Sales Work in the Snack-Food Industry," in *Working in the Service Society*, ed. by Cameron Lynn MacDonald and Carmen Sirianni (Philadelphia: Temple University Press, 1996), 50–60.

30. Robin Leidner, *Fast Food, Fast Talk: Service Work and the Routinization of Everyday Life* (Berkeley: University of California Press, 1993); Susan Benson,

Counter Cultures (Chicago: University of Illinois Press,1986), 285; William F. Whyte, "The Social Structure of the Restaurant," *American Journal of Sociology* 54, no. 4 (1949): 302–10.

31. I am aware of no casinos in the world today that operate according to a commission system, whereby dealers retain a percentage of the winnings on their table, though this was not uncommon in the nineteenth century. See Henry Chafetz, *Play the Devil: A History of Gambling in the United States from 1492 to 1955* (New York: Clarkson N. Potter, 1960), 195.

32. Arlie Russell Hochschild, *The Managed Heart: Commercialization of Human Feeling* (Berkeley: University of California Press, 1983).

33. Michael Burawoy, *Manufacturing Consent: Changes in the Labor Process under Monopoly Capitalism* (Chicago: University of Chicago Press, 1979), 80.

34. Terry Austrin and Jackie West, "Skills and Surveillance in Casino Gaming: Work, Consumption and Regulation," *Work, Employment and Society* 19, no. 2 (2005): 305–26.

35. Goffman, *Interaction Ritual.*

36. Casinos may also use more than one deck of cards on a table; up to eight decks of 416 cards can be used. While a single-deck game requires a shuffling break every six to eight hands, an eight-deck game permits fifty to sixty hands before shuffling. Note, too, that an economy of scale regarding shuffling does exist such that it does not take the dealer eight times as long to randomize an eight-deck set of cards as it takes to randomize a single deck.

37. While early models could shuffle only one deck at a time, the first "continuous shuffler" was introduced in 2000. The shuffler randomly reinserts the cards just played during the previous hand into the current deck. Like its predecessors, the continuous shuffler practically eliminates the possibility that a dexterous or incompetent dealer could shuffle so as to not randomize the cards, but it has the added advantage of eliminating any opportunity for players to count cards.

38. Janet Plume, "Green Felt Jungle," *Casino Executive*, June 2001: 28–31.

39. Shufflemaster Inc., *2000 Annual Report* (Las Vegas, NV: Shufflemaster Inc., 2001).

40. This is termed a "natural metaphor" method of comparison. See Paul Drew and Anthony Wootton, *Erving Goffman: Exploring the Interaction Order* (Oxford, UK: Polity Press, 1988), 5.

41. David G. Schwartz, *Roll the Bones: The History of Gambling* (New York: Gotham, 2006).

42. Gerda Reith, *The Age of Chance: Gambling in Western Culture* (London: Routledge, 1999).

43. James Rutherford, "Vegas Comes to Manchester with LCI's First New-Style Casino," *International Gaming and Wagering Business* 27, no. 12 (2006): 6.

44. Robert Venturi, Denise Scott Brown and Steven Izenour, *Learning from Las Vegas* (Cambridge, MA: MIT Press, 1998).

45. Anthony M. Cabot, William Norman Thompson, Andrew Tottenham, and Carl Braunlich, *International Casino Law* (Reno, NV: Institute for the Study of Gambling and Commercial Gaming, 1999); David Barboza, "Asian Rival Moves Past Las Vegas," *New York Times,* January 24, 2007; Sytze Kingma, "Gambling and the Risk Society: The Liberalisation and Legitimation Crisis of Gambling in the Netherlands," *International Gambling Studies* 4, no. 1 (2004): 47–67; Douglas M. Walker, *The Economics of Casino Gambling* (New York: Springer, 2007); Global Betting and Gaming Consultants, *Global Gambling Comes of Age* (West Bromwich, UK.: Global Betting and Gaming Consultants, 2002); Paul Doocey, "A Yen for Gambling: Japan Leads the Wave of Emerging Asian Nations Considering Casino Expansion," *International Gambling and Wagering Business* 28, no. 6 (2007): 1.

46. Global Betting and Gaming Consultants, *Global Gambling Comes of Age,* 27.

47. Anthony W. Marx, *Making Race and Nation: A Comparison of South Africa, the United States and Brazil* (New York: Cambridge University Press, 1998); George M. Frederickson, *White Supremacy: A Comparative Study in American and South African History* (New York: Oxford University Press, 1981).

48. Some have even argued that early Nevada served as an "internal colony" within the United States. See Peter Wiley and Robert Gottlieb, *Empires in the Sun: The Rise of the New American West* (New York: G. P. Putnam's Sons, 1982). To take this "internal colony" analogy to its conclusion would entail comparing the importance of casinos to the apartheid project of ethnic isolation in South Africa with gambling's recent role in buttressing Native American "self-reliance." For a complete analysis, see Jeffrey J. Sallaz, "The Making of the Global Gambling Industry: An Application and Extension of Field Theory," *Theory and Society* 35, no. 3 (2006): 265–97.

49. In arguing that policy authors "constructed" the new nation's problems as economic, I do not imply that unemployment, state fiscal shortages, and the like were not pressing issues. But it could have been just as possible to frame the national needs as social ones, for instance, the amelioration of the world's highest inequality rate or the encouragement in the popular consciousness of an ideology of deferred gratitude. It is doubtful that, had those been the stated objectives, a corporate casino industry would have been the logical solution.

50. Gauteng Gambling Board, *Annual Report 2005* (Pretoria, South Africa: Gauteng Gambling Board, 2005).

51. In fact, because federal taxes on tip income are taken directly from workers' paychecks, on many weeks workers receive no wages at all and may even pay money back to the casino.

52. Erving Goffman, *Frame Analysis: An Essay on the Organization of Experience* (New York: Harper Colophon Books, 1974), 13.

53. Mauro F. Guillen, *Models of Management: Work, Authority, and Organization in a Comparative Perspective* (Chicago: University of Chicago Press, 1994), 37; Paul Hirsch, "Sociology without Social Structure: Neoinstitutional Theory Meets Brave New World," *American Journal of Sociology* 102, no. 6 (1997): 1693–701.

54. George E. Marcus labels this a multisited ethnography seeking "to bring [multiple] sites into the same frame of study and to posit their relationships on the basis of firsthand ethnographic research." See George E. Marcus, *Ethnography through Thick and Thin* (Princeton, NJ: Princeton University Press, 1998), 84. This method resembles that of "process tracing" as described by James Mahoney, "Strategies of Causal Inference in Small N Analysis," *Sociological Methods and Research* 28, no. 4 (2000): 387–424.

55. These two modes of governance corresponds to the distinction made by Hall and Soskice between liberal and coordinated market economies. See Peter A. Hall and David Soskice, *Varieties of Capitalism: The Institutional Foundations of Comparative Advantage* (New York: Oxford University Press, 2001).

56. These include the 1995 Labour Relations Act, the 1997 Basic Conditions of Employment Act, the 1999 Employment Equity Act, and the 1999 Skills Development Act. See Tom Lodge, *The Alliance of Power: Who Rules in South Africa?* (Harare, Zimbabwe: SAPES Books, 1999).

57. Las Vegas is frequently labeled the "New Detroit" because of the marked success of the Culinary Union in organizing support staff within the casino firms. See Hal K. Rothman and Mike Davis, eds., *The Grit beneath the Glitter: Tales from the Real Las Vegas* (Berkeley: University of California Press, 2002). Such accounts ignore the dark side of the union's success in organizing culinary and hotel staff: collaboration in a long history of rabid repression of unionization attempts by casino workers (i.e., those directly involved with the gambling transactions). The former's success can only be understood in light of the latter's failure. As reported in a 1980 exposé by the *Las Vegas Review Journal* and confirmed in my interviews with managers and union officials, a side agreement to the Culinary Union's contract with the Nevada Resort Association states that the unionization of maids, porters, etc. is granted only on condition that the union not only refrain from attempting to organize gambling employees, but offer no support to other unions trying to do so. See Jeanne M. Hall, "Secret Agreement Bars Dealers' Union," *Las Vegas Review Journal*, May 24, 1980.

CHAPTER ONE

1. Michel Foucault, *Discipline and Punish: The Birth of the Prison* (New York: Vintage Books, 1979), 171, 201.

2. Ibid., 177.

3. Nevada State Gaming Control Board, *Nevada Gaming Abstract 2006* (Carson City, NV: Nevada State Gaming Control Board, 2006).

4. Though I did not ask fellow students directly, it is highly likely that all possessed the proper documents to work in the United States. It is widely known that to obtain a dealer's license, an applicant must submit a variety of papers testifying to his or her biography and legal status. (This is not the case, however, for positions in housekeeping or food service.)

5. Matt Villano, "Between Win and Lose, the Casino Dealer," *New York Times*, August 12, 2007.

6. Devah Pager examines the effects of criminal records upon the employment prospects of American men in "The Mark of a Criminal Record," *American Journal of Sociology* 108, no. 5 (2003): 937–75.

7. Barbara F. Reskin and Patricia A. Roos, *Job Queues, Gender Queues: Explaining Women's Inroads into Male Occupations* (Philadelphia: Temple University Press, 1990).

8. Rothman and Davis, *The Grit beneath the Glitter*.

9. Pete Earley, *Super Casino: Inside the "New" Las Vegas* (New York: Bantam Books, 2000).

10. Elaine Draper, "Drug Testing in the Workplace: The Allure of Management Technologies," *The International Journal of Sociology and Social Policy* 18, nos. 5–6 (1998): 64–106.

CHAPTER TWO

1. All quoted material in this and the following paragraph comes from the Silver State Casino Employee Manual.

2. See H. Lee Barnes, *Dummy Up and Deal: Inside the Culture of Casino Dealing* (Las Vegas: University of Nevada Press, 2002), 64; Elaine Enarson, "Emotion Workers on the Production Line: The Feminizing of Casino Card Dealing," *NWSA Journal* 5, no. 2 (1993): 18–232; "Appeals Court Deals Former Casino Workers Losing Hand," *Las Vegas Review Journal*, June 7, 1992.

3. At the end of each sixty-minute dealing shift, the dealer drops his or her accumulated tips for that hour into the "toke box" located at the supervisor station. At the end of the shift, the toke committee—three dealers elected by their coworkers—collects the chips from each toke box, cashes them in, and divides them up for distribution to dealers.

4. Randall Collins, *Interaction Ritual Chains* (Princeton, NJ: Princeton University Press, 2004).

5. Michel De Certeau, *The Practice of Everyday Life* (Berkeley: University of California Press, 1984), 23 (emphasis in original).

6. The standard tip for a cocktail waitress is one dollar, while most slot machines accept only quarters or dollars.

7. This quote comes from an online discussion forum for Nevada dealers. See Scott Cameron, "How to Earn Tokes," *CasinoDealers.Net*, http://www.dicedealer.com/how_to_earn_tokes.htm (accessed January 6, 2007).

8. Ibid.

9. Lee Solkey, *Dummy Up and Deal* (Las Vegas, NV: GBC Press, 1980), 62–63.

10. For instance, a player should always split eights because the two-card hand—sixteen—is very bad (it is not high enough to win, yet will probably bust if you hit it), while two hands of eight played separately are good (you cannot bust when you hit them, and there is a good chance they will become eighteens. Yet you should never split two fives, for the same reasons. A ten is a strong hand, since it will not break and may become a twenty, while each hand of five is likely to bust.

11. Never split tens.

12. In this situation, the player should stay. If we assume that all unseen cards are tens, then an additional card—which I must take—will bust me. The player who takes a card here risks busting.

13. Kevin Kenyon, "Uphill Battle for New Concepts," *International Gaming and Wagering Business* 21, no. 1 (2000): 1.

14. Peter Michael Blau, *Power and Exchange in Social Life* (New York: J. Wiley, 1964); Alvin W. Gouldner, "The Norm of Reciprocity: A Preliminary Statement," *American Sociological Review* 25 (1960): 161–78.

15. When the dealer's up-card is an ace, the dealer must offer the players insurance. They may place a side bet to insure their original bet in case the dealer's down card is a ten (i.e., blackjack). It is a bad bet, and the smart player does not take it (though it constitutes another opportunity to differentially offer advice to players).

16. When the dealer's tray runs low on certain denominations of chips, the supervisor will call a security guard to bring more over from the cashier's cage. The dealer must stop the game for a few minutes in order to count the new chips and sign a receipt for the amount received.

17. Quoted in Barnes, *Dummy Up and Deal*, 44.

18. This joke was recounted in the memoirs of a long-time Nevada dealer; see Mike Newman, *Dealer's Special: Inside Look at the Casino Scene by a Working Casino Dealer* (Las Vegas: BGC Press, 1979), 18.

19. Christopher Taylor, "Visual Surveillance: Contemporary Sociological Issues" (PhD diss., University of Nevada, Las Vegas, 1997).

20. Quoted in Barnes, *Dummy Up and Deal*, 46–48.

21. Technologies of notification extend beyond the pit itself. Though I never encountered one, a "whale" is a player who gambles tens or hundreds of thou-

sands of dollars on each hand. When a whale sits down at a table, pit bosses immediately page the casino manager.

CHAPTER THREE

1. Men constitute about three-quarters of table game players at Gold City Casino.

2. The South African Commercial, Catering, and Allied Workers Union, itself an affiliate of COSATU.

3. Labour Relations Act, No. 66 of 1995, Schedule 8.

4. The housekeeping function at Gold City Casino was outsourced to a local company, which did not provide its staff with food privileges. An informal system had developed whereby dealers would "adopt" a maid or janitor and each donate to him or her one of their daily food serving allotments.

5. When workers and inspectors referred to top department management, they were generally referring to those above pit boss (i.e., those who worked in the department office and not on the casino floor). This included, in descending order, the casino manager (a white male), the tables manager (a white male), two assistant tables managers (two white males), and six shift managers (two white males, two white females, one black male, and one coloured [i.e., mixed-race] female).

6. In addition, there was a small room in the surveillance department where one senior officer monitored surveillance workers in the main camera room. For some reason, this senior officer also observed a monitor attached to a camera in the room itself, so that this watcher would watch himself watching others watch others.

CHAPTER FOUR

1. The hold percentage on blackjack games at Silver State Casino is around 10 percent; at Gold City Casino it is around 20 percent. I do not mean, however, to frame the two styles of play as "rational" (Nevada) versus "irrational" (South Africa). Both, in fact, are irrational, insofar as one purposefully partakes in a wager against the odds. We can, however, slightly twist Max Weber by positing as an ideal type the least irrational form of play (i.e., the one done strictly by "the book") against which to compare and then contrast the two systems of play. See *Economy and Society* (Berkeley: University of California Press, 1978).

2. I do not attempt to explain the genesis of these different "casino cultures." One obvious possibility is the "maturity" of the Nevadan casino market versus

the South African one. The former is more educated and has greater access to the huge amount of blackjack strategy literature available.

3. At first, I suspected that "playing behind" was a strategy used by novice players casting their lot with an experienced, skilled player to improve their chances of winning. It soon became clear, though, that this was not the case. New players on the table made no attempt to gauge the expertise of the players whom they bet behind, often placing bets behind several players.

4. As Ted Benton and Ian Craib argue, "The question of how an object, class of beings, or pattern of phenomena came into being is distinct from the question of how it now sustains itself or is sustained." See Benton and Craib, *Philosophy of Social Science: The Philosophical Foundations of Social Thought* (New York: Palgrave, 2001), 38.

5. In South Africa, as in the U.S. South, "boy" is used as a pejorative label for black men.

CHAPTER FIVE

1. Harry Braverman, *Labor and Monopoly Capital: The Degradation of Work in the Twentieth Century* (New York: Monthly Review Press, 1974). See also David M. Gordon, Richard Edwards, and Michael Reich, *Segmented Work, Divided Workers: The Historical Transformation of Labor in the United States* (New York: Cambridge University Press, 1982); Michael J. Piore and Charles F. Sabel, *The Second Industrial Divide: Possibilities for Prosperity* (New York: Basic Books, 1984).

2. Neil Fligstein and Roberto M. Fernandez, "Worker Power, Firm Power, and the Structure of Labor Markets," *The Sociological Quarterly* 29, no. 1 (1988): 5–28.

3. Erik Olin Wright, "Working-Class Power, Capitalist-Class Interests, and Class Compromise," *American Journal of Sociology* 105, no. 4 (2000): 957–1002. See also Beverly J. Silver, *Forces of Labor: Workers' Movements and Globalization since 1870* (New York: Cambridge University Press, 2003).

4. Bureau of Labor Statistics, *Regional and State Employment and Unemployment* (Washington, DC.: U.S. Department of Labor, 2008); Statistics South Africa, *Labour Force Survey* (Pretoria: Statistics South Africa, 2008). It must be noted that the large underground economy in South Africa renders direct comparisons of unemployment rates difficult. An estimated 12 percent of South Africans earn a livelihood through the informal economy.

5. For a critique of assimilation theory, see Michael Omi and Howard Winant, *Racial Formation in the United States: From the 1960s to the 1980s* (New York: Routledge, 1994).

6. In general, dealing labor is desexualized relative to other occupations in

the casino. Cocktail waitresses walk directly through crowds of male players, wear sexually provocative outfits, and handle small-denomination transactions about which the casino cares little. Female dealers, in contrast, have the table as a physical buffer between them and clients, wear the same tuxedo-style uniforms as do their male colleagues, and are empowered to discipline male players regarding security-related matters. See Molly George, "Interactions in Expert Service Work," *Journal of Contemporary Ethnography* 37, no. 1 (2008): 108–31.

7. Hochschild, *The Managed Heart*.

8. Leidner, *Fast Food, Fast Talk*, 127–8.

9. See Alan Tonelson, *The Race to the Bottom* (Boulder, CO: Westview Press, 2002); David Brady, Jason Beckfield, and Martin Seeleib-Kaiser, "Economic Globalization and the Welfare State in Affluent Democracies, 1975–2001," *American Sociological Review* 70, no. 6 (2005): 921–48; Steven C. McKay, *Satanic Mills or Silicon Islands? The Politics of High-tech Production in the Philippines* (Ithaca, NY: Cornell University Press, 2006).

10. Frederick Winslow Taylor, *Principles of Scientific Management* (New York: Harper and Brothers Publishers, 1911).

11. Herbert A. Simon, *Administrative Behavior: A Study of Decision-Making Processes in Administrative Organization* (New York: MacMillan, 1957); Robert Jackall, *Moral Mazes: The World of Corporate Managers* (New York: Oxford University Press, 1989).

12. Neil Fligstein, for instance, found that early education and work experiences produced unique conceptions of control in corporate executives, while Leslie Salzinger demonstrated that managers' gender identities shape their strategies for organizing work. See Fligstein, *The Transformation of Corporate Control* (Cambridge, MA: Harvard University Press, 1990); Salzinger, *Genders in Production*.

13. Pierre Bourdieu, *The Logic of Practice* (Stanford, CA: Stanford University Press, 1980), 53.

14. Pierre Bourdieu, *Distinction: A Social Critique of the Judgment of Taste* (Cambridge, MA: Harvard University Press, 1984), 170.

15. Ibid., 7; Pierre Bourdieu, *Masculine Domination* (Stanford, CA: Stanford University Press, 2001), 38.

16. Pierre Bourdieu, *The Social Structures of the Economy* (Malden, MA: Polity, 2005), 212; Loïc Wacquant, *Body and Soul: Notebooks of an Apprentice Boxer* (New York: Oxford University Press, 2004).

17. Pierre Bourdieu, *The State Nobility: Elite Schools in the Field of Power* (Stanford, CA: Stanford University Press, 1989), 264–78.

18. Along with economic, social, and symbolic capitals, cultural capital (especially educational credentials) is considered one of the fundamental forms of value in modern society. I found no evidence, however, that cultural capital

played a significant role in the casinos I studied. Neither workers nor managers were evaluated according to their possession of college degrees or their general linguistic competence.

19. This is the key point distinguishing my analysis of workers from my analysis of managers. For front-line service employees such as dealers, the intense organization of the labor process exerts a powerful pressure to adopt a particular disposition on the tables (entrepreneurialism in Nevada, effacement in South Africa). Prior life experiences are soon overwhelmed by the moment-to-moment exigencies of making a living. My own experiences illustrated the principle that "conduct relies less on habitus in situations that are highly codi-fied [and] regulated." (David Swartz, *Culture and Power: The Sociology of Pierre Bourdieu* [Chicago: University of Chicago Press, 1997], 113.) For workers, the spe-cific subjectivities required of work games are determinative. Role trumps biog-raphy.

20. This is in line with Weber's specification of traditional versus rational and charismatic forms of authority. See Weber, *Economy and Society.*

CHAPTER SIX

1. Charles Tilly's definition of trust—"placing valued outcomes at risk to oth-ers' malfeasance"—fits perfectly the relationship between casino managers and workers; See Charles Tilly, "Trust and Rule," *Theory and Society* 33 (2004): 4; Nis-sim Mizrachi, Israel Dorri and Renee R. Anspach, "Repertoires of Trust: The Practice of Trust in a Multinational Organization amid Political Conflict," *Amer-ican Sociological Review* 72 (2007): 143–65.

2. John M. Findlay, *People of Chance: Gambling in American Society from Jame-stown to Las Vegas* (New York: Oxford University Press, 1986).

3. Reith, *The Age of Chance.*

4. Schwartz, *Roll the Bones.*

5. As Cotton Mather wrote, "Lots, being mentioned in the sacred oracles of scripture as used only in weighty cases and as an acknowledgement of God sit-ting in judgment . . . cannot be made the tools and parts of our common sports." Quoted in Chafetz, *Play the Devil*, 14. See also G. Robert Blakey, *The Development of the Law of Gambling* (Washington, DC: National Institute of Law Enforcement and Criminal Justice, 1977).

6. Max Weber, *The Protestant Ethic and the Spirit of Capitalism* (New York: Rout-ledge Classics, 2006).

7. Chafetz, *Play the Devil*, 15.

8. Hank Messick and Burt Goldblatt, *The Only Game in Town: An Illustrated History of Gambling* (New York: Crowell, 1976).

9. Findlay, *People of Chance*, 70.

10. Blakey, *The Development of the Law of Gambling*, 84.

11. Ibid., 378; Findlay, *People of Chance*, 7.

12. Martin J. Sklar, *The Corporate Reconstruction of American Capitalism, 1890–1916: The Market, the Law, and Politics* (New York: Cambridge University Press, 1988); Joseph R. Gusfield, *Symbolic Crusade: Status Politics and the American Temperance Movement* (Chicago: University of Illinois Press, 1963).

13. Michael H. Bowers, *The Sagebrush State: Nevada's History, Government, and Politics* (Reno: University of Nevada Press, 2002), 14.

14. Nevada's non-Indian population, for example, was under 7,000.

15. Frankie Sue Del Papa, *Political History of Nevada* (Carson City, NV: State Press, 1990), 86.

16. Wiley and Gottlieb, *Empires in the Sun*, 192.

17. Bowers, *The Sagebrush State*, 119.

18. James W. Hulse, *The Silver State: Nevada's Heritage Reinterpreted* (Las Vegas: University of Nevada Press, 1991).

19. Gilman M. Ostrander, *Nevada: The Great Rotten Borough, 1859–1964* (New York: Alfred A. Knopf, 1966), 67.

20. Phillip I. Earl, "Veiling the Tiger: The Crusade against Gambling, 1859–1910," *Nevada Historical Society Quarterly* 29, no. 3 (1985): 179; Ralph J. Roske, "Gambling in Nevada: The Early Years, 1861–1931," *Nevada Historical Society Quarterly* 33, no. 1 (1990): 35.

21. Jerome E. Edwards, "From Back Alley to Main Street: Nevada's Acceptance of Gambling," *Nevada Historical Society Quarterly* 33, no. 1 (1990): 19; Hulse, *The Silver State*, 77.

22. C. Elizabeth Raymond, *George Wingfield: Owner and Operator of Nevada* (Reno: University of Nevada Press, 1992), 1.

23. S. Lotter, "The Odds against Gambling," *South African Criminal Justice* 7 (1994): 191. In neither country was gambling among indigenous peoples a significant concern to colonial governments.

24. Charles V. Hamilton et al. (ed.), *Beyond Racism: Race and Inequality in Brazil, South Africa, and the United States* (Boulder, CO: Lynne Rienner Publishers, 2001).

25. Charles Van Onselen, *Studies in the Social and Economic History of the Witwatersrand, 1886–1914: I. New Babylon* (New York: Longman, 1982).

26. John Vorster, *Parliamentary Debates of South Africa*, House of Assembly, April 30, 1965, column 5145.

27. John Vorster, *Parliamentary Debates of South Africa*, House of Assembly, March 26, 1965, column 3558.

28. Mr. Visse, *Parliamentary Debates of South Africa*, House of Assembly, March 26, 1965, column 3567.

29. See Ray Joseph, "The Games People Play . . . and Casino Boss Died Playing Them," *Sunday Times* (Johannesburg), April 24, 1977; June Bearzi, "Illicit Gambling Dens Flourishing in Hillbrow," *Star* (Johannesburg), November 29, 1980; Rosemary Northcott, "Jo'burg's Gambling Cold War Heats Up," *Citizen* (Johannesburg), September 20, 1977.

30. Belinda Bozzoli, *Women of Phokeng: Consciousness, Life Strategy, and Migrancy in South Africa, 1900–1983* (Johannesburg: Raven Press, 1991); Henry Livingston Dugmore, "Becoming Coloured: Class, Culture and Segregation in Johannesburg's Malay Location, 1918–1939" (PhD diss., University of the Witwatersrand, 1993); Laura Longmore, "A Study of Fahfee," *South African Journal of Science* 52 (1956): 275–82.

31. Anthony Lemon, *The Geography of Change in South Africa* (New York: John Wiley and Sons, 1995), 3.

32. Laurine Platzky and Cheryl Walker, *The Surplus People: Forced Removals in South Africa* (Johannesburg: Raven Press, 1985); Gillian Hart, *Disabling Globalization: Places of Power in Post-apartheid South Africa* (Berkeley: University of California Press, 2002).

33. Jeffrey Butler, Robert I. Rotberg, and John Adams, *The Black Homelands of South Africa: The Political Economy of Development in Bophuthatswana and KwaZulu* (Berkeley: University of California Press, 1977); T. Dunbar Moodie and Vivienne Ndatshe, *Going for Gold: Men, Mines and Migration* (Berkeley: University of California Press, 1994).

34. Martin Legassick and Harold Wolpe, "The Bantustans and Capital Accumulation in South Africa," *Review of African Political Economy* 7 (1977): 87–107.

35. Stanley B. Greenberg, *Legitimating the Illegitimate: States, Markets and Resistance in South Africa* (Berkeley: University of California Press, 1987); Ivan Evans, *Bureaucracy and Race: Native Administration in South Africa* (Berkeley: University of California Press, 1997); Robert Ross, *A Concise History of South Africa* (New York: Cambridge University Press, 1999).

36. Shula Marks, *The Ambiguities of Dependence in South Africa: Class, Nationalism and the State in Twentieth-Century Natal* (Baltimore: Johns Hopkins University Press, 1986).

37. Gay Seidman, "Is South Africa Different? Sociological Comparisons and Theoretical Contributions from the Land of Apartheid," *Annual Review of Sociology* 25 (1999): 425; Mahmood Mamdani, *Citizen and Subject: Contemporary Africa and the Legacy of Late Colonialism* (Princeton, NJ: Princeton University Press, 1996), 90–96

38. Bernard Makhosezwe Magubane, *The Political Economy of Race and Class in South Africa* (New York: Monthly Review Press, 1979); Stanley B. Greenberg, *Race and State in Capitalist Development: South Africa in Comparative Perspective* (Johannesburg: Raven Press, 1980).

39. Michael Burawoy, "The Functions and Reproduction of Migrant Labor: Comparative Material from Southern Africa and the United States," *American Journal of Sociology* 81 (1976): 1049–87; Michael Burawoy, "The Capitalist State in South Africa: Marxist and Sociological Perspectives on Race and Class," *Political Power and Social Theory* 2 (1981): 279–335.

40. Harold Wolpe, "Capitalism and Cheap Labour-Power in South Africa: From Segregation to Apartheid," *Economy and Society* 1, no. 4 (1972): 425–56.

41. Ross, *A Concise History of South Africa*, 144–6; A. J. Christopher, *The Atlas of Changing South Africa* (New York: Routledge, 2001), 10.

42. Butler et al., *The Black Homelands of South Africa*, 5; Frederickson, *White Supremacy*, 244.

43. Herbert Adam, *Modernizing Racial Domination* (Berkeley: University of California Press, 1971); Edward Webster and Glenn Adler, "Toward a Class Compromise in South Africa's 'Double Transition': Bargained Liberalization and the Consolidation of Democracy," *Politics and Society* 27, no. 3 (1999): 347–85.

44. Hart, *Disabling Globalization*.

45. Eric Hobsbawm and Terence Ranger, *The Invention of Tradition* (New York: Cambridge University Press, 1983).

46. Greenberg, *Legitimating the Illegitimate*.

47. See Jonathon Crush and Paul Wellings, "Southern Africa and the Pleasure Periphery," *Journal of Modern Africa Studies* 21 (1983): 676.

48. Robert D. Faiss, *Gaming Regulation and Gaming Law in Nevada* (Reno: University of Nevada Oral History Program, Reno, 2006), 66.

49. Jack Sheehan, *The Players: The Men Who Made Las Vegas* (Reno: University of Nevada Press, 1997), 4–6.

50. Eric N. Moody, "The Early Years of Casino Gambling in Nevada, 1931–1945," (PhD diss., University of Nevada, Las Vegas, 1997), 123.

51. During the 1930s, the number of casinos licensed in Reno increased from twenty-four to forty-two; in Las Vegas, from four to twenty.

52. Oscar Lewis, *Sagebrush Casinos: The Story of Legal Gambling in Nevada* (New York: DoubleDay, 1953), 12.

53. Silvio Petricciani, *The Evolution of Gaming in Nevada: The Twenties to the Eighties* (Reno: University of Nevada Oral History Program, 1982), 94.

54. While the historical evidence is scarce, it seems that casino owners' discrimination toward the two other main racial groups in early twentieth-century Nevada—Native Americans and the Chinese—was not as vociferous as it was toward African Americans. See Eugene Moehring, *Resort City in the Sunbelt: Las Vegas, 1930–1970* (Reno: University of Nevada Press, 1989), 174.

55. Moody, "The Early Years of Casino Gambling in Nevada," 132. Important federal projects in these years included the Hoover Dam, Nellis Air Force Base and Basic Magnesium Plant.

56. John Cahlan, *Fifty Years in Journalism and Community Development* (Reno: University of Nevada Oral History Program, 1987), 226.

57. "Definite Policy Outlined Last Night at Meeting," *Las Vegas Evening Review and Journal,* April 10, 1931.

58. Dwayne Kling, ed., *Every Light Was On: Bill Harrah and His Clubs Remembered* (Reno: University of Nevada Oral History Program, 1999).

59. Mark Gottdiener, *The Theming of America: American Dreams, Media Fantasies, and Themed Environments* (Boulder, CO: Westview Press, 2000), 105.

60. David G. Schwartz, *Suburban Xanadu: The Casino Resort on the Las Vegas Strip and Beyond* (New York: Routledge, 2003).

61. Skolnick, *House of Cards,* 37–50.

62. Mark H. Haller, "The Changing Structure of American Gambling in the Twentieth Century," *Journal of Social Issues* 35, no. 3 (1979): 87–114.

63. Gary Provost, *High Stakes: Inside the New Las Vegas* (New York: Truman Talley Books, 1994), 185; Hal Rothman, *Neon Metropolis: How Las Vegas Started the Twenty-First Century* (New York: Routledge, 2002), 14.

64. Schwartz, *Suburban Xanadu,* 103–7.

65. Individual syndicate financing reached its limits in the 1950s, and leaders turned to illicit funding from the Teamsters Union Pension Fund (over 60 percent of which was invested in hotels by 1963).

66. Moody, "The Early Years of Casino Gambling in Nevada," 437.

67. Robbins E. Cahill, *Recollections of Work in State Politics, Government, Taxation, Gaming Control, Clark County Administration, and the Nevada Resort Association* (Reno: University of Nevada Oral History Program, 1977), 279–84.

68. John R. Goodwin, *Gaming Control Law: The Nevada Model* (Columbus, OH: Publishing Horizons, 1985), 82.

69. Cahill, *Recollections of Work,* 279–84.

70. Lewis, *Sagebrush Casinos.*

71. All figures on revenues are found in the state's annual Gaming Abstracts, available from the State Gaming Control Board in Carson City. Numbers on the composition of the general fund are found in the state's annual Executive Budget in Brief.

72. Skolnick, *House of Cards,* 161; Ronald A. Farrell and Carole Case, *The Black Book and the Mob: The Untold Story of the Control of Nevada's Casinos* (Madison: University of Wisconsin Press, 1995).

73. Skolnick, *House of Cards,* 309.

74. Schwartz, *Suburban Xanadu,* 83.

75. Moody, "The Early Years of Casino Gambling in Nevada," 355–62.

76. Earley, *Super Casino,* 51.

77. Moehring, *Resort City in the Sunbelt,* 176.

78. Ken Robbins, "Dealer License Ban Amendment Defeated," *Las Vegas*

Review Journal, February 24, 1959; "Dealer Signup Bill Defeated as 'Unworkable,'" *Las Vegas Review Journal*, March 24, 1959.

79. Ed Vogel, "Panel Upholds At-will Firings," *Las Vegas Review Journal*, May 31, 1991.

80. As codified in NRS 613.250, specifying that one cannot be denied employment for refusing to join a labor organization, and NRS 613.270, which states that unions cannot "compel" workers to go on strike.

81. Edward A. Olsen, *My Career as a Journalist in Oregon, Indiana and Nevada, with Nevada Gaming Control, and at the University of Nevada* (Reno: University of Nevada Oral History Program, 1972), 457.

82. Christopher, *The Atlas of Changing South Africa*, 95.

83. Author interview with former official in the South African Department of Justice.

84. Jeremy Baskin, *Casinos and Development in Southern Africa: A Case Study of Mzamba-Transkei* (Umtata, Transkei: Institute for Management and Development Studies, 1983), 2.

85. Leonard Thompson, *The Political Mythology of Apartheid* (New Haven, CT: Yale University Press, 1985).

86. Crush and Wellings, "Southern Africa and the Pleasure Periphery," 694.

87. For instance, Bophuthatswana's 1984 Industrial Conciliation Act No. 8 banned South African unions.

88. Sun International was first listed on the Johannesburg Stock Exchange in 1981.

89. Human Sciences Research Council, *The Effects of a Hotel Complex on Immediate Social Environment: An Explanatory Study* (Pretoria: South Africa Institute for Sociological, Demographic and Criminological Research, 1980), 3.2.7.

90. While some prostitutes worked independently, most liaisons appear to have been organized by hotel staff.

91. Of course, corruption was not unique to the casino industry, as has been demonstrated by a series of post-apartheid investigations, such as the 1996 Heath Commission Report and the 1992 Skweyiya Commission Reports.

92. Alan Greenblo, "The Mangope Connection," *Sunday Times* (Johannesburg), October 26, 1997; see also Thabo Kobokoane, "Gambling on an Unrealistic Flow of Money," *Sunday Times* (Johannesburg), December 4, 1998.

93. Commission of Enquiry into the Department of Works and Energy, *Third Report with Particular Reference to Gambling Rights and Related Matters* (Transkei: Government Press, 1988). Interestingly, in private correspondence between casino officials and Matanzima, bribes were referred to as "lobola"—the payment made by a male suitor to a woman's family in exchange for marriage rights.

94. Greenblo, "The Mangope Connection."

95. Kling, *Every Light Was On,* 7–8.

96. Raymond, *George Wingfield,* 13; Findlay, *People of Chance,* 91.

97. Robert K. DeArment, *Knights of the Green Cloth: The Saga of the Frontier Gamblers* (Norman: University of Oklahoma Press, 1990), 26.

98. Petricciani, *The Evolution of Gaming in Nevada,* 303.

99. Robert A. Ring, *Recollections of Life in California, Nevada Gaming, and Reno and Lake Tahoe Business and Civic Affairs* (Reno: University of Nevada Oral History Program, 1972), 78.

100. Petricciani, *The Evolution of Gaming in Nevada,* 336.

101. Kling, *Every Light Was On,* 337–38.

102. Warren Nelson, *Gaming from the Old Days to Computers* (Reno: University of Nevada Oral History Program, 1978), 27–33.

103. Phyllis Darling, "Dealer's Choice," in *Nevada: Official Bicentennial Book,* ed. Stanley W. Paher (Las Vegas: Nevada Publications, 1976), 366–67.

104. William F. Harrah, *My Recollections of the Hotel-Casino Industry and as an Auto-Collecting Enthusiast* (Reno: University of Nevada Oral History Program, 1978), 140–41.

105. 1939 Statutes of Nevada, Assembly Bill 72.

106. Lester Ben "Benny" Binion, *Some Recollections of a Texas and Las Vegas Gaming Operator* (Reno: University of Nevada Oral History Program, 1973), 34. For further accounts of "frontier justice" for cheating dealers, see Reid and Demaris, *The Green Felt Jungle,* 52.

107. Ring, *Recollections of Life,* 79; Petricciani, *The Evolution of Gaming in Nevada,* 316.

108. Nelson, *Gaming from the Old Days to Computers,* 56.

109. Cahill, *Recollections of Work,* 947.

110. Bill Friedman, *Casino Management* (Secaucus, NJ: Lyle Stuart, 1982), 50.

111. Marcia A. McDowell, *Techniques of Casino Surveillance* (Las Vegas, NV: Candlelight Books, 1995).

112. Schwartz, *Suburban Xanadu,* 112.

113. See Petricciani, *The Evolution of Gaming,* 249; Kling, *Every Light Was On,* 43; Ring, *Recollections of Life,* 82. It is believed that Erving Goffman first broke into the Las Vegas casino scene via a distant personal connection to Moe Dalitz, a notorious Cleveland syndicate boss. See Yves Winkin, "The Casino as a Total Institution: Erving Goffman in Las Vegas" (paper presented at the annual meeting for the Society for the Study of Symbolic Interactionism, Chicago, Illinois, February 6, 1999).

114. Solkey, *Dummy Up and Deal,* 46–47; Dean M. Macomber, "Management Policy and Practices in Modern Casino Operations," *The Annals of the American Academy of Political and Social Science* 474 (1984): 80–90.

115. Andrew Michael Nyre, "Union Jackpot: Culinary Workers Local 226, Las

Vegas, Nevada, 1970–2000" (master's thesis, California State University at Fullerton, 2001), 32; Luberta Johnson, *Civil Rights Efforts in Las Vegas: 1940s to 1960s* (Reno: University of Nevada Oral History Program, 1988), 61–65.

116. Newman, *Dealer's Special*, 17; Alan Balboni, *Beyond the Mafia: Italian Americans and the Development of Las Vegas* (Las Vegas: University of Nevada Press, 1996).

117. In fact, when shoes were first made available in the 1970s, casinos successfully deflected an attempt by the state gaming board to make their use mandatory on the tables. Casino bosses preferred that their dealers be able to shuffle by hand. See Olsen, *My Career*, 302.

118. Quoted in Schwartz, *Suburban Xanadu*, 96.

119. George Ackerlof, "Labor Contracts as Partial Gift Exchanges," *Quarterly Journal of Economics* 97, no. 2 (1982): 543–69.

120. Kling, *Every Light Was On*, 303.

121. Solkey, *Dummy Up and Deal*, 55. Casino owners also appealed unsuccessfully to the National Labor Relations Board for a ruling that casino dealers were not eligible for unionization. See "Gaming Union Aides Blast New Casino Workers Law," *Las Vegas Review Journal*, February 24, 1966.

122. Edward Webster and Karl Von Holdt, *Beyond the Apartheid Workplace* (Durban: University of Kwazulu Natal Press, 2005); Edna Bonacich, "Capitalism and Race Relations in South Africa," *Political Power and Social Theory* 2 (1981): 239–77.

123. Macomber, "Management Policy and Practices."

CHAPTER SEVEN

1. James W. Hulse, *Forty Years in the Wilderness: Impressions of Nevada, 1940–1980* (Las Vegas: University of Nevada Press, 1986), 68.

2. Nevada Gaming Commission, *Triennial Report of the Nevada Gaming Commission and State Gaming Control Board* (Carson City, NV: Nevada Gaming Commission, 1962), 7.

3. Jerome E. Edwards, "From Back Alley to Main Street: Nevada's Acceptance of Gambling," *Nevada Historical Society Quarterly* 33, no. 1 (1990): 22.

4. Stanley Cohen, *Folk Devils and Moral Panics: The Creation of the Mods and the Rockers* (London: Macgibbon and Kee, 1972); Thomas A. Reppetto, *Bringing Down the Mob: The War against the American Mafia* (New York: Henry Holt and Company, 2006).

5. As quoted in William Howard Moore, *The Kefauver Committee and the Politics of Crime, 1950–1952* (Columbia: University of Missouri Press, 1974), 43.

6. Earley, *Super Casino*, 57.

7. Moore, *The Kefauver Committee and the Politics of Crime,* 49.

8. Jerome E. Edwards, *Pat McCarran: Political Boss of Nevada* (Reno: University of Nevada Press, 1982), 149.

9. Estes Kefauver, *Crime in America* (Garden City, NY: Doubleday, 1951), 14.

10. Albert J. Bergeson, "Political Witch-Hunts: The Sacred and the Subversive in Cross-National Perspective," *American Sociological Review* 42 (1977): 220–33.

11. Kefauver, *Crime in America,* 229–34.

12. Cahill, *Recollections of Work,* 300, 344, 763.

13. Kefauver, *Crime in America,* 233.

14. G. Robert Blakey, *The Development of the Law of Gambling* (Washington, DC: National Institute of Law Enforcement and Criminal Justice, 1977), 571.

15. Moehring, *Resort City in the Sunbelt,* 89.

16. William J. Moore, *An Interview with William J. Moore* (Reno: University of Nevada Oral History Program, 1981), 70.

17. Skolnick, *House of Cards,* 118.

18. *State Ex Rel. Grimes v. Board of Commissioners of City of Las Vegas,* 1 Nev. P.2d 570 (1931).

19. Cahill, *Recollections of Work,* 280.

20. Lionel, Sawyer, and Collins, *Nevada Gaming Law* (Las Vegas, NV: Lionel, Sawyer and Collins, 2000), 15.

21. *Nevada Tax Commission v. Hicks,* 73 Nev. 115, 310 P.2d 852 (1957).

22. Ibid.

23. Quoted in Hulse, *Forty Years in the Wilderness,* 75.

24. Nevada Gaming Commission, *Triennial Report,* 9

25. Lionel, Sawyer, and Collins, *Nevada Gaming Law,* 57.

26. Olsen, *My Career as a Journalist,* 270.

27. John J. Galliher and John R. Cross, *Morals Legislation without Morality: The Case of Nevada* (New Brunswick, NJ: Rutgers University Press, 1983).

28. Skolnick, *House of Cards,* 154.

29. Farrell and Case, *The Black Book and the Mob.*

30. Schwartz, *Suburban Xanadu,* 82.

31. Sheehan, *The Players,* 15–17; Balboni, *Beyond the Mafia,* 28.

32. Cahill, *Recollections of Work,* 591; see also Hulse, *Forty Years in the Wilderness,* 80.

33. Robert F. Kennedy, *The Enemy Within* (New York: Popular Library, 1960).

34. Quoted in Skolnick, *House of Cards,* 125.

35. Ibid.

36. Skolnick, *House of Cards,* 131.

37. Sheehan, *The Players,* 13.

38. Quoted in Hulse, *Forty Years in the Wilderness,* 80–82.

39. Skolnick, *House of Cards,* 144.

40. Monica Prasad, *The Politics of Free Markets: The Rise of Neoliberal Economic Policies in Britain, France, Germany, and the United States* (Chicago: University of Chicago Press, 2006).

41. Eadington, "The Casino Gaming Industry," 23–35; Schwartz, *Suburban Xanadu*, 163.

42. Michael Drosnin, *Citizen Hughes* (New York: Holt, Rinehart and Winston, 1985).

43. Sheehan, *The Players*, 142–43.

44. Rothman, *Neon Metropolis*, 22.

45. Wiley and Gottlieb, *Empires in the Sun*, 207; Schwartz, *Suburban Xanadu*, 163.

46. Rothman, *Neon Metropolis*, 24.

47. Farrell and Case, *The Black Book and the Mob*, 239.

48. Commission on the Review of the National Policy toward Gambling, *Gambling in America: Final Report* (Washington, DC: U.S. Government Printing Office, 1976), 80, 102; see also Peter Reuter, "Easy Sport: Research and Relevance," *Journal of Social Issues* 35, no. 3 (1979): 166–82.

49. Moehring, *Resort City in the Sunbelt*, 176.

50. For insider accounts of the movement to desegregate casinos, see James B. McMillan, *Fighting Back: A Life in the Struggle for Civil Rights* (Reno: University of Nevada Oral History Program, 1997); Johnson, *Civil Rights Efforts in Las Vegas*.

51. Moehring, *Resort City in the Sunbelt*, 186.

52. Grant Sawyer, *Hang Tough! Grant Sawyer: An Activist in the Governor's Mansion* (Reno: University of Nevada Oral History Program, 1993), 102.

53. Nevada Attorney General, *Official Opinions of the Attorney General #143*, March 8, 1960; see also "Gaming Board Cannot Forbid Discrimination," *Las Vegas Review Journal*, March 11, 1960; Sawyer, *Hang Tough*, 102–104. The Gaming Commission publicly reaffirmed its refusal to make equitable employment practices a precondition of a license privilege in 1976 and 1998. See "Hilton's Minority Hiring Policy Hit," *Las Vegas Review Journal*, August 20, 1976; Howard Stutz, "Imperial Palace Bias Charges Turned Over to Equal Rights Panel," *Las Vegas Review Journal*, December 14, 1998.

54. Hulse, *Forty Years in the Wilderness*, 92.

55. Sawyer, *Hang Tough*, 97, 103; see also Clyde H. Mathews Jr., *Oral Autobiography of a Modern-Day Baptist Minister* (Reno: University of Nevada Oral History Program, 1969); Elmer R. Rusco, "Racial Discrimination in Nevada: A Continuing Problem," *Governmental Research Newsletter* 11, no. 5 (1973): 9.

56. Sawyer, *Hang Tough*, 98.

57. Cahill, *Recollections of Work*, 1395.

58. McMillan, *Fighting Back*, 128.

59. Nevada Equal Rights Commission, *Biennial Report* (Carson City, NV:

Nevada Equal Rights Commission, 1969); Claytee D. White, "The Roles of African American Women in the Las Vegas Gaming Industry, 1940–1980" (master's thesis, University of Nevada Las Vegas, 1997).

60. Clarence Ray, *Black Politics and Gaming in Las Vegas, 1920s to 1980s* (Reno: University of Nevada Oral History Program, 1991), 95.

61. Moehring, *Resort City in the Sunbelt,* 190.

62. Rusco, "Racial Discrimination in Nevada," 9.

63. Figures compiled from quarterly reports submitted per the 1971 Consent Decree.

64. Paul Burstein, *Discrimination, Jobs, and Politics: The Struggle for Equal Opportunity in the United States since the New Deal* (Chicago: University of Chicago Press, 1985).

65. John D. Skrentny, *The Minority Rights Revolution* (Cambridge, MA: Harvard University Press, 2002), 8.

66. Civil Rights Act of 1964, 42 USC. 2000e; Complaint, Civil Action 1645, U.S. District Court Las Vegas, filed June 4, 1971; hereafter, "Complaint."

67. Complaint, 7.

68. Ibid., 6.

69. Consent Decree, Civil Action 1645, Las Vegas District Court, filed June 4, 1971, p. 3; hereafter, "Consent Decree."

70. Cahill, *Recollections of Work,* 1383–88.

71. Ibid., 1388 (emphasis in original).

72. Consent Decree.

73. Ibid., 6, 14.

74. Ibid., 9.

75. Ibid., 15.

76. Ibid., 10, 19.

77. Letter from United States Department of Justice to Elmer R. Rusco, February 25, 1972, Box T-123, Special Collections, University of Nevada, Las Vegas.

78. These estimates derive from my interviews with former workers and managers at several homeland casinos, as well as two labor force surveys performed in 1994. See William D. Gallaway, "The Association between Job Satisfaction and Service Quality" (MBA thesis, University of the Witwatersrand, 1995), 52.

79. *Big Brother* is a reality TV game show in which ten people are sequestered in a house while a series of cameras record their every move. Each week the television audience votes to cast out one contestant.

80. Black casino floor managers throughout South Africa today are disproportionately female, an expression probably of the better ability with which women could play this game of feigned ignorance in the homeland casinos (or at least of management's perception of women workers as less distrustful).

81. See Norman West, "MP Crosses Party Line in Casino Controversy," *Sunday Times* (Johannesburg), March 3, 1993.

82. See for example "Jo'burg's Gambling Cold War Heats Up," *Citizen* (Johannesburg), September 20, 1977; "Police Take R1-M Haul in Gambling Den Raids," *Citizen* (Johannesburg), March 21, 1987.

83. Marcia Klein, "Revenue from Fast Growing Casino Industry Nears R200m a Month," *Sunday Times* (Johannesburg), September 8, 1992; Ciaran Ryan, "Boom Time at Gaming Clubs," *Sunday Times* (Johannesburg), July 12, 1992.

84. "Casinos Have Had Their Chips as Government Pounces," *Citizen* (Johannesburg), January 30, 1993.

85. This information is drawn from my interviews with a former official in the South African Police Service and a lawyer with the Gambling Association of South Africa. See also Hendrik Brand, *Gambling Laws of South Africa* (Johannesburg: Juta and Company, 1997).

86. Author interview with former official in the South African Department of Justice. See also David Capel, "Gambling Giants Prepare for War," *Star* (Johannesburg), June 14, 1997; "Sol Speaks Out as Casino War Reaches Climax," *Sunday Times* (Johannesburg), October 4, 1992.

87. "Government Plans to Plug Loopholes in the Gambling Act," *Sunday Times* (Johannesburg), May 3, 1992.

88. M. A. Hendrickse, *Parliamentary Debates of South Africa*, Joint Meeting of House and Senate, October 14, 1992, column 12193; "Who's Rolling the Dice?" *Financial Mail* (Johannesburg), June 5, 1992.

89. Adam Ashforth, *The Politics of Official Discourse in South Africa* (Oxford, UK: Clarendon Press, 1990), 3; T. R. H. Davenport, *The Transfer of Power in South Africa* (Cape Town: University of Toronto Press, 1998), 73.

90. James Allen Howard, *Commission of Inquiry into Lotteries, Sports Pools, Fund-Raising Activities and Certain Matters Related to Gambling: Report* (Pretoria: Government Printer, 1993), 103; hereafter, "Howard Report."

91. Howard Report, 105–12.

92. Ciaran Ryan, "Casino Proposals Draw Fire from Kerzner's Rival," *Sunday Times* (Johannesburg), October 12, 1993.

93. James Allen Howard (chair, Howard Commission), interview with author, August 2001; Sie Strauss (member, Howard Commission), interviews with author, August 2001 and May 2002.

94. D. J. Dalling, *Parliamentary Debates of South Africa*, Joint Meeting of House and Senate, October 14, 1992, column 12254; N. A. Sisulu, *Parliamentary Debates of South Africa*, Proceedings of the National Assembly, June 18, 1996, column 3144; David Breier, "Clampdown Could Prove to Be Pointless," *Sunday Star* (Johannesburg), June 7, 1993; "Stacking the Deck," *Financial Mail* (Johannesburg), April 30, 1993.

95. Davenport, *The Transfer of Power,* 56. For a detailed recounting of negotiations over gambling during the GNU, see Alec Erwin, "Regulating the Gambling Industry in South Africa: Address by the Minister of Trade and Industry" (presentation at the Second South African Gambling Conference, Pretoria, 2002).

96. Fismer, a former NP parliamentarian, had switched allegiance to the ANC.

97. Hazel Friedman, "Russian Roulette and the RDP," *Weekly Mail and Guardian* (Johannesburg), March 1, 1996.

98. Chris Fismer, interviews with author, July and November 2002.

99. Social scientists writing on the South African state since the fall of apartheid have documented a "conservative" or "neoliberal" shift in the ANC's economic and social doctrine since it came to power; see Patrick Bond, *Elite Transition: From Apartheid to Neoliberalism in South Africa* (Pietermaritzburg: University of Natal Press, 2000); Jonathon Michie and Vishnu Padayachee, *The Political Economy of South Africa's Transition* (New York: Dryden Press, 1997).

100. Hein Marais, *South Africa: Limits to Change: The Political Economy of Transformation* (Cape Town: University of Cape Town Press, 1998).

101. Chris Fismer, *Parliamentary Debates of South Africa,* Proceedings of the National Assembly, June 18, 1996, column 3118.

102. Edward West, "ANC Shows Its Hand on Gambling," *Business Day* (Johannesburg), February 28, 1994.

103. Chris Fismer, *Parliamentary Debates of South Africa,* Proceedings of the National Senate, June 3, 1996, column 1677.

104. See Human Sciences Research Council, *An Independent Socio-economic Assessment of the Conditions and Contents of Afrisun Mpumalanga's Bid for a Casino License in Mpumalanga* (Witbank: Witbank Academics, 1996). A 1999 national survey found that four years after legalization, only 28 percent of South Africans felt positive about gambling in South Africa. See Human Sciences Research Council, *The Social Impact of Gambling in South Africa* (Pretoria: National Gambling Board of South Africa, 2000).

105. Seidman, "Is South Africa Different?" 433.

106. Webster and Adler, "Toward a Class Compromise," 347–85.

107. Nicholas Wiehahn, interviews with author, July 2001 and May 2002.

108. South Africa's major labor unions were conspicuously silent at this phase of the policy production process. They may have simply deferred to the ANC on the question of casino policy, but many, including COSATU itself, were being courted by aspiring casino licensees with offers of equity participation in new casino projects. See "COSATU in Secret Gambling Talks with Sol," *Weekly Mail and Guardian* (Johannesburg), August 5, 1994; "Unions, Ozz and Civics Bid for Randburg Casino License," *Business Report* (Johannesburg), June 17, 1997.

109. South Africa Federation for Mental Health, representation to Wiehahn Commission. Similar proposals were made by the S.A. Institute of Fundraising, Association of Racing Clubs of Southern Africa, Christian Reformed Church of Benoni, and Community Chest of Durban.

110. Sun International, "Structuring the Gaming Industry in the Public Interest," submission to the Wiehahn Commission.

111. Pendant Casino Operators, South Africa, submission to Wiehahn Commission. Similar submissions were made by the Gaming Association of South Africa, Karos Hotels Ltd., and Casino Club of Cape Town.

112. Nicholas Everhardus Wiehahn, *The Complete Wiehahn Report on Gambling in South Africa* (Pretoria: Beta Printers, 1995); hereafter, "Wiehahn Report."

113. Vicki Abt, James Smith, and Eugene Martin Christianson, *The Business of Risk: Commercial Gambling in Mainstream America* (Lawrence: University of Kansas Press, 1985).

114. Wiehahn Report, 2, 3, 135.

115. The question of lotteries and other forms of betting were dealt with in the report as well. All were legalized and privatized.

116. Wiehahn Report, 5, 59–62.

117. Ibid., 73.

118. Ibid., 196, 203.

119. Ibid., 3, 4, 68, 75.

120. Ibid., 95–97.

121. Deborah Fine, "Gambling Association Challenges Gauteng Act," *Star* (Johannesburg), July 17, 1996. See also Bonile Ngqiyaza, "Hundreds Protest against Clamp on Casinos," *Business Day* (Johannesburg) August 7, 1996.

122. Wiehahn Report, 101–3.

123. Claire Keeton, "SA Starts to Count the Cost of Get-Rich-Quick Epidemic," *Business Report* (Johannesburg), April 17, 2001.

CHAPTER EIGHT

1. Rob Sanders and Ray Knight, "Corporate Culture," *Casino Executive* 7, no. 1 (2001): 28.

2. Macomber, "Management Policy and Practices," 81.

3. Skolnick, *House of Cards,* 174. Nevada's regulatory philosophy is summarized in its Public Policy Concerning Gaming: "The gaming industry is vitally important to the economy of the state and the general welfare of its inhabitants. . . . Gaming is dependent upon public confidence and trust that . . . gaming is free from criminal and corruptive elements" (Nevada Revised Statutes 463.0129).

4. Balboni, *Beyond the Mafia*, 70–71.

5. Quoted in Balboni, *Beyond the Mafia*, 64.

6. Schwartz, *Suburban Xanadu*, 113, 148.

7. Mark J. Roe, *Strong Managers, Weak Owners: The Political Roots of American Capitalism* (Princeton, NJ: Princeton University Press, 1994).

8. The 1971 figures derive from the initial worker demographic reports filed by the Nevada casinos per the Consent Decree. They are on file at the National Archives and Records Administration, Pacific Region, case file CV-S-71–1645 (hereafter, "NARA"). The current figures derive from a visual survey performed by the author of all dealers and gaming tables at a random sample of 28 casinos in Nevada (details available in the appendix).

9. Transcript of proceedings held before Magistrate Joseph L. Ward, Las Vegas District Court, March 26, 1975, NARA.

10. See, for example, letter dated July 2, 1974 from June Wooliver, Assistant Regional Attorney for the EEOC, to Burton M. Cohen, President and General Manager of the Thunderbird Hotel, NARA.

11. "Plaintiff's Interrogatories," U.S. District Court, Las Vegas, July 2, 1974, NARA.

12. "Motion for Protective Order," Lionel, Sawyer, Collins, and Wartman, attorneys for Nevada Resort Association et al., U.S. District Court, Las Vegas, August 5, 1974, NARA.

13. Ibid.

14. "Motion for Protective Order," Gibson, Dunn, and Crutcher, attorneys for Hughes Tool Co., U.S. District Court, Las Vegas, August 29, 1974, NARA.

15. "Many Black Hotel Workers Charge Loss of Jobs Due to Color of Their Skin," *Las Vegas Sun*, February 19, 1979.

16. Figures and interview quotes in this paragraph derive from interviews with two lawyers with the EEOC in December 2003.

17. In 2005, the EEOC announced plans to build a field office in Las Vegas.

18. Statistics on charges available at the EEOC website, http://www.eeoc.gov/.

19. Shannon Harper and Barbara Reskin, "Affirmative Action at School and on the Job," *Annual Review of Sociology* 31 (2005): 357–79.

20. Data derive from the aforementioned survey of dealers in Nevada.

21. There is a sizable literature documenting U.S. employers' preferences for immigrant workers over native-born, and especially African Americans, for entry-level jobs. See Roger Waldinger and Michael I. Lichter, *How the Other Half Works: Immigration and the Social Organization of Labor* (Berkeley: University of California Press, 2003). By comparing identical industries and occupations in two countries, I hope to make clear that the American experience is premised

upon a particular mode of state regulation that neglects claims by native-born workers for employment equity.

22. GLS Research, *Las Vegas Visitor Profile* (Las Vegas, NV: Las Vegas Convention and Visitors Authority, 2006).

23. See Mia Tuan, *Forever Foreigners or Honorary Whites? The Asian Ethnic Experience Today* (New Brunswick, NJ: Rutgers University Press: 1998).

24. "Desperation for Dealers: Help Wanted," *Las Vegas Review Journal*, July 16, 2000.

25. Quoted in Earley, *Super Casino*, 391.

26. Enarson, "Emotion Workers," 225; Barney Vinson, *Las Vegas: Behind the Tables* (Grand Rapids, MI: Gollehon, 1986).

27. "Industry Blacklist Feared," *Las Vegas Review Journal*, June 7, 1992.

28. The most significant challenge to Nevada casinos' autonomy to fire at will was a lawsuit brought against the Hilton Corporation in 1983 by 37 dealers claiming to have been wrongfully terminated because of their age. After a series of appeals, the U.S. 9th Circuit Court of Appeals ruled that Nevada's fire at will doctrine exonerated the casino. See "Appeals Court Deals Former Casino Workers Losing Hand," *Las Vegas Review Journal*, May 5, 1992.

29. Data derive from aforementioned survey of blackjack tables in Nevada.

30. See John M. Brubaker, *The Eye in the Sky: A Casino Surveillance Reference for Management, Directors, and other Casino Executive Personnel* (Special Collections Library, University of Nevada, Las Vegas, 2002); Taylor, "Visual Surveillance."

31. I was able to document unsuccessful unionization drives among casino dealers in the following years: 1949, 1964, 1965, 1968, 1974, 1977 (through the Teamsters), 1982 (again through the Teamsters), 1991 (through SACE and NCDA), 1993 (through the United Steel Workers of America), and 2001 (through the Transport Workers Union). Countless others undoubtedly occurred but did not make their way into press accounts.

32. A 1993 survey of Nevada dealers found that 88 percent had worked for two or more casinos during their career. See Donna R. Burrows, "The Woman 21 Dealer in Las Vegas: An Examination of Her Special Place in the Gaming Industry," (master's thesis, California Coast University, 1993).

33. Phyllis Smith, "Oral History," in *Every Light Was On: Bill Harrah and His Clubs Remembered*, ed. Dwayne Kling (Reno: University of Nevada Oral History Program, 1999), 34–35.

34. Chris Barron, "The Casino Kings," *Sunday Times* (Johannesburg), November 15, 1998; A. Koz, "South Africa's New Flush of Royalty," *Star* (Johannesburg), June 17, 1998.

35. Department of Finance and Economic Affairs, *The Role of Gambling in the Economic Development of Gauteng: Strategic Considerations and Policy Positions* (Pretoria: Gauteng Provincial Government, 1997), 4.

36. This document is available through the Gauteng Gambling Board, 1256 Heuwel Avenue, Centurion 0157.

37. Several European casino firms also received casino licenses in South Africa, though none have a significant presence in the national market.

38. Author interview with Gauteng Gambling Board official, August 2001.

39. David Gleason, "Gauteng Gaming Fiasco Continues," *Mail and Guardian* (Johannesburg), July 9, 1999; Cecelia Russell, "'All Above Board' in Casino License Scramble," *Star* (Johannesburg), March 23, 1999; Charley Woodgate, "Bid for R2-bn Soweto Casino Complex Adds Fuel to Casino License Race," *Star* (Johannesburg), July 5, 1996.

40. See, for example, Department of Finance and Economic Affairs, *License Evaluation Criteria* (Pretoria: Gauteng Provincial Government, 1997).

41. This and all quotes in this section are drawn from Gauteng Gambling Board, "Memorandum: Application for Casino Licenses" (Pretoria: Gauteng Gambling Board, 1997).

42. Celean Jacobson, "New Voice in Gauteng Casino Uproar," *Sunday Times* (Johannesburg), January 24, 1999.

43. Gauteng Gambling Board, "Draft Minutes of the Meeting Held with the Provincial Executive," February 5, 1998.

44. This document was provided to me by Empowerment Inc. on the condition that I not reveal the true identity of the firm.

45. Everett C. Hughes, *The Sociological Eye: Selected Papers* (Chicago: University of Chicago Press, 1971), 87.

46. Webster and Von Holdt, *Beyond the Apartheid Workplace*.

47. A similar phenomenon was discovered by Burawoy during his research on the copper mines in newly independent Zambia. There, too, expatriate managers blamed the state's new quota system for all of the enterprise's ills: "'Zambianization' was a once-and-for-all, irrefutable explanation for all that went wrong." See Michael Burawoy, *The Colour of Class on the Copper Mines: From African Advancement to Zambianization* (Manchester, UK: Manchester University Press, 1972), 38.

CONCLUSION

1. The state's per capita spending on education, public welfare, and health and human services annually ranks among the lowest in the United States. See Wilbur S. Shepperson, *East of Eden, West of Zion: Essays on Nevada* (Reno: University of Nevada Press, 1989).

2. Richard Lewis Siegel, "Nevada among the States: Converging Public Policies," *Nevada Historical Society Quarterly* 43, no. 3 (2000): 214–62.

3. John W. Meyer, John Boli, George Thomas, and Francisco O. Ramirez, "World Society and the Nation State," *American Journal of Sociology* 103, no. 1 (1997): 164. See also George Ritzer, *The McDonaldization of Society* (Thousand Oaks, CA: Pine Forge Press, 1993).

4. Colin Crouch and Wolfgang Streeck, eds. *Political Economy of Modern Capitalism: Mapping Convergence and Divergence* (London: Sage, 1997).

5. Weber, *The Protestant Ethic*.

6. Alfred Chandler, *The Visible Hand: The Managerial Revolution in American Business* (Cambridge, MA: Harvard University Press. 1977).

7. Ritzer, *The McDonaldization of Society*.

8. Other studies document ongoing differences in the organization of states, societies, and economies. One strand of thought within this divergence perspective posits that the integration of the global economy will lead countries to specialize in order to best utilize their comparative advantages. Rather than a race to the bottom, these theorists argue, all nations will "find a unique place for themselves under the sun of the global economy"; see Mauro F. Guillen, *The Limits of Convergence: Globalization and Organizational Change in Argentina, South Korea and Spain* (Princeton, NJ: Princeton University Press, 2001). A second variation of the divergence perspective, the "varieties of capitalism" approach, attributes ongoing national differences to historical patterns of authority and domination in society, especially the balance of power among labor, capital, and the state. See Hall and Soskice, *Varieties of Capitalism*.

9. Meyer et al., "World Society and the Nation State," 164.

10. Paul J. DiMaggio and Walter W. Powell, "The Iron Cage Revisited: Institutional Isomorphism and Collective Rationality in Organizational Fields," *American Sociological Review* 48, no. 2 (1983): 147–60.

11. See James Ferguson, *The Anti-Politics Machine: "Development," Depoliticization and Bureaucratic Power in Lesotho* (Minneapolis: University of Minnesota Press, 1994); Joseph E. Stiglitz, *Globalization and Its Discontents* (New York: W.W. Norton and Company, 2003).

12. William N. Thompson, "Nevada Goes Global: The Foreign Gaming Rule and the Spread of Casinos," in *The Grit beneath the Glitter: Tales from the Real Las Vegas,* ed. Hal K. Rothman and Mike Davis (Berkeley: University of California Press, 2002), 347–62.

13. DiMaggio and Powell, "The Iron Cage Revisited," 151.

14. Meyer et al., "World Society and the Nation State."

15. Ibid., 150–51.

16. See, for example, Clem Brooks and Jeff Manza, "Social Policy Responsiveness in Developed Democracies," *American Sociological Review* 71, no. 3 (2006): 474–94.

17. DiMaggio and Powell, "The Iron Cage Revisited," 152.

18. John Dombrink and William N. Thompson, *The Last Resort: Success and Failure in Campaigns for Casinos* (Las Vegas: University of Nevada Press, 1990); Heubusch, "Taking Chances on Casinos," 35–40; Ilan Greenberg, "A Sleepy City on the Steppe Fears Hordes of High Rollers," *New York Times*, January 23, 2007, A3.

19. Gusfield, *Symbolic Crusade.*

20. Joseph A. Schumpeter, "The Crisis of the Tax State," in *The Economics and Sociology of Capitalism*, ed. Richard Swedberg (Princeton, NJ: Princeton University Press, 1991), 99–140; Isaac William Martin, *The Permanent Tax Revolt: How the Property Tax Transformed American Politics* (Stanford, CA: Stanford University Press, 2008).

21. Marion Fourcade-Gourinchas and Sarah L. Babb, "The Rebirth of the Liberal Creed: Paths to Neoliberalism in Four Countries," *American Journal of Sociology* 108, no. 3 (2002): 533–79.

22. John Hannigan, *Fantasy City: Pleasure and Profit in the Postmodern Metropolis* (New York: Routledge, 1999).

23. Nicole Woolsey Biggart, "Labor and Leisure," in *The Handbook of Economic Sociology*, ed. Neil J. Smelser and Richard Swedberg (Princeton, NJ: Princeton University Press, 1994), 672; Vogel, *Entertainment Industry Economics*, 21.

24. Average hours worked per week, for instance, declined markedly across industrialized nations in the twentieth century, with the notable exception of the United States. See Thorstein Veblen, *The Theory of the Leisure Class* (New York: Mentor, 1953); John Kenneth Galbraith, *The Affluent Society* (Cambridge, MA: Riverside Press, 1998), 243–54; David Evans and Richard Schmalensee, *Paying with Plastic: The Digital Revolution in Buying and Borrowing* (Cambridge, MA: MIT Press, 2000); Juliet B. Schor, *The Overspent American: Upscaling, Downshifting and the New Consumer* (New York: Basic Books, 1998).

25. William R. Eadington, "Economic Development and the Introduction of Casinos: Myths and Realities," *Economic Development Review* 13, no. 4 (1995): 51–54.

26. Walker, *Casino and Gaming Market Research Handbook*, 15.

27. As the *New York Times* reported, "The sums are so alluring that some officials worry that their states are becoming as addicted as problem gamblers. 'We're drunk on gambling revenues,' said . . . House majority leader in the Delaware General Assembly." See Fox Butterfield, "As Gambling Grows, States Depend on Their Cut to Bolster Revenues," *New York Times*, March 31, 2005, A24.

28. Walker, *Casino and Gaming Market Research Handbook*, 7.

29. Eadington, "Economic Development and the Introduction of Casinos"; Robert Goodman, *The Luck Business: The Devastating Consequences and Broken Promises of America's Gambling Explosion* (New York: Free Press, 1995); Ken Bel-

son, "Buffalo Looks for Work but Debates Casino's Value," *New York Times*, February 2, 2007.

30. Marcus, *Ethnography through Thick and Thin*, 14.

31. Meyer et al., "World Society and the Nation State," 152.

32. Erving Goffman, *The Presentation of Self in Everyday Life* (New York: Doubleday, 1959), 166.

33. Collins, *Interaction Ritual Chains*.

34. Mary Douglas, *Purity and Danger* (London: Routledge and Kegan Paul, 1966), 158.

35. Erving Goffman, *Stigma: Notes on the Management of Spoiled Identity* (Englewood Cliffs, NJ: Prentice Hall, 1963), 127, emphasis mine.

APPENDIX

1. Bourdieu, *The Logic of Practice*.

2. Eileen M. Otis, "Beyond the Industrial Paradigm: Market-Embedded Labor and the Gender Organization of Global Service Work in China," *American Sociological Review* 73 (2008): 15–36.

3. Michael Burawoy, "The Extended Case Method," *Sociological Theory* 16, no. 1 (1998): 4–33.

4. Ibid., 14.

5. Joseph J. Tobin, David Y.H. Yu and Dana H. Davidson, *Preschool in Three Cultures: Japan, China and the United States* (New Haven, CT: Yale University Press, 1986).

Bibliography

PRIMARY SOURCES

Newspapers and Periodicals

Business Day (Johannesburg). 1994–1996.
Business Report (Johannesburg). 1997–2001.
Casino Executive. 2001.
Citizen (Johannesburg). 1977–1993.
Financial Mail (Johannesburg). 1992–1993.
International Gaming and Wagering Business. 2000–2007.
Las Vegas Evening Review and Journal. 1931.
Las Vegas Review Journal. 1959–2000.
Las Vegas Sun. 1979–1999.
New York Times. 2005–2007.

Star (Johannesburg). 1980–1999.
Sunday Times (Johannesburg). 1977–1999.
Weekly Mail and Guardian (Johannesburg). 1994–1996.

Interviews and Oral Accounts

Binion, Lester Ben "Benny." *Some Recollections of a Texas and Las Vegas Gaming Operator.* Reno: University of Nevada Oral History Program, 1973.

Cahill, Robbins E. *Recollections of Work in State Politics, Government, Taxation, Gaming Control, Clark County Administration, and the Nevada Resort Association.* Reno: University of Nevada Oral History Program, 1977.

Cahlan, John. *Fifty Years in Journalism and Community Development.* Reno: University of Nevada Oral History Program, 1987.

Faiss, Robert D. *Gaming Regulation and Gaming Law in Nevada.* Reno: University of Nevada Oral History Program, 2006.

Fismer, Chris (interview by author).

Goffman, Thomas (interview by author).

Harrah, William F. *My Recollections of the Hotel-Casino Industry and as an Auto-Collecting Enthusiast.* Reno: University of Nevada Oral History Program, 1978.

Howard, James Allen (interview by author).

Johnson, Luberta. *Civil Rights Efforts in Las Vegas: 1940s to 1960s.* Reno: University of Nevada Oral History Program, 1988.

Mathews, Clyde H., Jr. *Oral Autobiography of a Modern-Day Baptist Minister.* Reno: University of Nevada Oral History Program, 1969.

McMillan, James F. *Fighting Back: A Life in the Struggle for Civil Rights.* Reno: University of Nevada Oral History Program, 1997.

Moore, William J. *An Interview with William J. Moore.* Reno: University of Nevada Oral History Program, 1981.

Nelson, Warren. *Gaming from the Old Days to Computers.* Reno: University of Nevada Oral History Program, 1978.

Olsen, Edward A. *My Career as a Journalist in Oregon, Indiana and Nevada, with Nevada Gaming Control, and at the University of Nevada.* Reno: University of Nevada Oral History Program, 1972.

Petricciani, Silvio. *The Evolution of Gaming in Nevada: The Twenties to the Eighties.* Reno: University of Nevada Oral History Program, 1982.

Ray, Clarence. *Black Politics and Gaming in Las Vegas, 1920s to 1980s.* Reno: University of Nevada Oral History Program, 1991.

Ring, Robert A. *Recollections of Life in California, Nevada Gaming, and Reno and Lake Tahoe Business and Civic Affairs.* Reno: University of Nevada Oral History Program, 1972.

Rossi, Joe (interview by author).

Sawyer, Grant. *Hang Tough! Grant Sawyer: An Activist in the Governor's Mansion.* Reno: University of Nevada Oral History Program, 1993.

Smith, Phyllis. "Oral History." In *Every Light Was On: Bill Harrah and His Clubs Remembered,* edited by Dwayne Kling, 34–35. Reno: University of Nevada Oral History Program, 1999.

Strauss, Sie (interview by author).

Wiehahn, Nicholas (interview by author).

Industry Sources

Bear, Stearns and Co. *North American Gaming Almanac.* New York: Smith Barney, 2003.

Brubaker, John M. *The Eye in the Sky: A Casino Surveillance Reference for Management, Directors and other Casino Executive Personnel.* Special Collections Library, University of Nevada, Las Vegas, 2002.

Cameron, Scott. "How to Earn Tokes," CasinoDealers.Net, www.dicedealer. com/how_to_earn_tokes.htm (accessed January 6, 2007).

Global Betting and Gaming Consultants. *Global Gambling Comes of Age: 2nd Annual Review of the Global Betting and Gaming Market.* West Bromwich, UK: Global Betting and Gaming Consultants, 2002.

GLS Research. *Las Vegas Visitor Profile.* Las Vegas, NV: Las Vegas Convention and Visitors Authority, 2006.

Human Sciences Research Council. *The Effects of a Hotel Complex on Immediate Social Environment: An Explanatory Study.* Pretoria: South Africa Institute for Sociological, Demographic and Criminological Research, 1980.

McDowell, Marcia A. *Techniques of Casino Surveillance.* Las Vegas, NV: Candlelight Books, 1995.

Shufflemaster Inc. *Annual Report.* 2001–04.

Sun International (Bophuthatswana) Limited. *Annual Report.* 1986–92.

Sun International (South Africa) Limited. *Annual Report.* 1997–2005.

Walker, Terri C. *Casino and Gaming Market Research Handbook.* Atlanta, GA: Terri C. Walker Consulting Inc., 2005.

Government Sources

SOUTH AFRICA

Commission of Enquiry into the Department of Works and Energy. *Third Report with Particular Reference to Gambling Rights and Related Matters.* Transkei, South Africa: Government Press, 1988.

Department of Finance and Economic Affairs. *License Evaluation Criteria.* Pretoria, South Africa: Gauteng Provincial Government, 1997.

———. *The Role of Gambling in the Economic Development of Gauteng: Strategic*

Considerations and Policy Positions. Pretoria, South Africa: Gauteng Provincial Government, 1997.

Erwin, Alec. "Regulating the Gambling Industry in South Africa: Address by the Minister of Trade and Industry." Presentation at the Second South African Gambling Conference, Pretoria, South Africa, 2002.

Gauteng Gambling Board. "Memorandum: Application for Casino Licenses." Pretoria, South Africa: Gauteng Gambling Board,1997.

———. "Draft Minutes of the Meeting Held with the Provincial Executive." February 5, 1998.

———. *Annual Report 2005*. Pretoria, South Africa: Gauteng Gambling Board, 2005.

Howard, James Allen. *Commission of Inquiry into Lotteries, Sports Pools, Fund-Raising Activities and Certain Matters Related to Gambling: Report*. Pretoria, South Africa: Government Printer, 1993.

Human Sciences Research Council. *An Independent Socio-economic Assessment of the Conditions and Contents of Afrisun Mpumalanga's Bid for a Casino License in Mpumalanga*. Witbank, South Africa: Witbank Academics, 1996.

———. *The Social Impact of Gambling in South Africa*. Pretoria, South Africa: National Gambling Board, 2000.

Parliamentary Debates of South Africa. 1965–1996.

Statistics South Africa. *Labour Force Survey*. Pretoria, South Africa: 2008.

Wiehahn, Nicholas Everhardus. *The Complete Wiehahn Report on Gambling in South Africa*. Pretoria, South Africa: Beta Printers, 1995.

Wiehahn Report on Gambling in South Africa: Public Submissions. 1995.

UNITED STATES

Blakey, G. Robert. *The Development of the Law of Gambling*. Washington, DC: National Institute of Law Enforcement and Criminal Justice, 1977.

Bureau of Labor Statistics. *Career Guide to Industries*. Washington, DC: U.S. Department of Labor, 2007.

———. *Regional and State Employment and Unemployment*. Washington, DC: U.S. Department of Labor, 2008.

Commission on the Review of the National Policy toward Gambling. *Gambling in America: Final Report*. Washington, DC: U.S. Government Printing Office, 1976.

Complaint, Civil Action 1645, U.S. District Court Las Vegas, filed June 4, 1971.

Consent Decree, Civil Action 1645, U.S. District Court Las Vegas, filed June 4, 1971.

Consent Decree. Casino Quarterly Labor Reports. National Archives and Records Administration, Pacific Region, Case file CV-S-71–1645. 1972–2005.

Nevada Attorney General. *Official Opinions of the Attorney General #143*, March 8, 1960.

Nevada Equal Rights Commission. *Biennial Report*. Carson City, NV: Government Press, 1969.

Nevada Gaming Commission. *Triennial Report of the Nevada Gaming Commission and State Gaming Control Board*. Carson City, NV: Nevada Gaming Commission, 1962.

Nevada Gaming Control Board. *Nevada Gaming Abstract 2006*. Carson City, NV: Nevada State Gaming Control Board, 2006.

Nevada Tax Commission v. Hicks, 73 Nev. 115, 310 P.2d 852 (1957).

State Ex Rel. Grimes v. Board of Commissioners of City of Las Vegas, 1 Nev. P.2d 570 (1931).

SECONDARY SOURCES

Abt, Vicki, James Smith, and Eugene Martin Christianson. *The Business of Risk: Commercial Gambling in Mainstream America*. Lawrence: University of Kansas Press, 1985.

Ackerlof, George. "Labor Contracts as Partial Gift Exchanges." *Quarterly Journal of Economics* 97, no. 2 (1982): 543–69.

Adam, Herbert. *Modernizing Racial Domination*. Berkeley: University of California Press, 1971.

Ashforth, Adam. *The Politics of Official Discourse in South Africa*. Oxford, UK: Clarendon Press, 1990.

Austrin, Terry, and Jackie West. "Skills and Surveillance in Casino Gaming: Work, Consumption and Regulation." *Work, Employment and Society* 19, no. 2 (2005): 305–26.

Balboni, Alan. *Beyond the Mafia: Italian Americans and the Development of Las Vegas*. Las Vegas: University of Nevada Press, 1996.

Barnes, H. Lee. *Dummy Up and Deal: Inside the Culture of Casino Dealing*. Las Vegas: University of Nevada Press, 2002.

Baskin, Jeremy. *Casinos and Development in Southern Africa: A Case Study of Mzamba-Transkei*. Umtata, South Africa: Institute for Management and Development Studies, 1983.

Benson, Susan. *Counter Cultures*. Chicago: University of Illinois Press, 1986.

Benton, Ted, and Ian Craib. *Philosophy of Social Science: The Philosophical Foundations of Social Thought*. New York: Palgrave, 2001.

Bergesen, Albert J. "Political Witch-Hunts: The Sacred and the Subversive in Cross-National Perspective." *American Sociological Review* 42 (1977): 220–33.

————. "Reflections on Erving Goffman." *Quarterly Journal of Ideology* 8, no. 3 (1984): 51–54.

Biggart, Nicole Woolsey. "Labor and Leisure." In *The Handbook of Economic Sociology*, edited by Neil J. Smelser and Richard Swedberg, 672–90. Princeton, NJ: Princeton University Press, 1994.

Blau, Peter Michael. *Power and Exchange in Social Life.* New York: J. Wiley, 1964.

Bonacich, Edna. "Capitalism and Race Relations in South Africa." *Political Power and Social Theory* 2 (1981): 239–77.

Bond, Patrick. *Elite Transition: From Apartheid to Neoliberalism in South Africa.* Pietermaritzburg, South Africa: University of Natal Press, 2000.

Bourdieu, Pierre. *Outline of a Theory of Practice.* New York: Cambridge University Press, 1972.

————. *The Logic of Practice.* Stanford, CA: Stanford University Press, 1980.

————. *Distinction: A Social Critique of the Judgment of Taste.* Cambridge, MA: Harvard University Press, 1984.

————. *The State Nobility: Elite Schools in the Field of Power.* Stanford, CA: Stanford University Press, 1989.

————. *Masculine Domination.* Stanford, CA: Stanford University Press, 2001.

————. *The Social Structures of the Economy.* Malden, MA: Polity, 2005.

Bowers, Michael H. *The Sagebrush State: Nevada's History, Government, and Politics.* Reno: University of Nevada Press, 2002.

Bozzoli, Belinda. *Women of Phokeng: Consciousness, Life Strategy, and Migrancy in South Africa, 1900–1983.* Johannesburg: Raven Press, 1991.

Brady, David, Jason Beckfield, and Martin Seeleib-Kaiser. "Economic Globalization and the Welfare State in Affluent Democracies, 1975–2001." *American Sociological Review* 70, no. 6 (2005): 921–48.

Brand, Hendrik. *Gambling Laws of South Africa.* Johannesburg: Juta and Company, 1997.

Braverman, Harry. *Labor and Monopoly Capital: The Degradation of Work in the Twentieth Century.* New York: Monthly Review Press, 1974.

Brooks, Clem, and Jeff Manza. "Social Policy Responsiveness in Developed Democracies." *American Sociological Review* 71, no. 3 (2006): 474–94.

Burawoy, Michael. *The Colour of Class on the Copper Mines: From African Advancement to Zambianization.* Manchester, UK: Manchester University Press, 1972.

————. "The Functions and Reproduction of Migrant Labor: Comparative Material from Southern Africa and the United States." *American Journal of Sociology* 81 (1976): 1049–87.

————. *Manufacturing Consent: Changes in the Labor Process under Monopoly Capitalism.* Chicago: University of Chicago Press, 1979.

———. "The Capitalist State in South Africa: Marxist and Sociological Perspectives on Race and Class." *Political Power and Social Theory* 2 (1981): 279–335.

———. *The Politics of Production: Factory Regimes under Capitalism and Socialism*. London: Verso, 1985.

———. "The Extended Case Method." *Sociological Theory* 16, no. 1 (1998): 4–33.

———. "Revisits: An Outline of a Theory of Reflexive Ethnography." *American Sociological Review* 68, no. 5 (2003): 645–79.

Burrows, Donna R. "The Woman 21 Dealer in Las Vegas: An Examination of Her Special Place in the Gaming Industry." Master's thesis, California Coast University, 1993.

Burstein, Paul. *Discrimination, Jobs, and Politics: The Struggle for Equal Employment Opportunity in the United States since the New Deal*. Chicago: University of Chicago Press, 1985.

Butler, Jeffrey, Robert I. Rotberg, and John Adams. *The Black Homelands of South Africa: The Political Economy of Development in Bophuthatswana and KwaZulu*. Berkeley: University of California Press, 1977.

Cabot, Anthony N., and Robert C. Hannum. *Casino Practical Math*. Las Vegas, NV: Institute for the Study of Gambling and Commercial Gaming, 2001.

Cabot, Anthony N., William Norman Thompson, Andrew Tottenham, and Carl Braunlich. *International Casino Law*. Reno, NV: Institute for the Study of Gambling and Commercial Gaming, 1999.

Chafetz, Henry. *Play the Devil: A History of Gambling in the United States from 1492 to 1955*. New York: Clarkson N. Potter, 1960.

Chandler, Alfred. *The Visible Hand: The Managerial Revolution in American Business*. Cambridge, MA: Harvard University Press, 1977.

Christopher, A. J. *The Atlas of Changing South Africa*. New York: Routledge, 2001.

Clotfelter, Charles T., and Philip J. Cook. *Selling Hope: State Lotteries in America*. Cambridge, MA: Harvard University Press, 1989.

Cohen, Stanley. *Folk Devils and Moral Panics: The Creation of the Mods and the Rockers*. London: Macgibbon and Kee, 1972.

Collins, Randall. "The Passing of Intellectual Generations: Reflections on the Death of Erving Goffman." *Sociological Theory* 4, no. 1 (1986): 106–13.

———. *Interaction Ritual Chains*. Princeton, NJ: Princeton University Press, 2004.

Comaroff, Jean, and John L. Comaroff. "Millennial Capitalism: First Thoughts on a Second Coming." *Public Culture* 12, no. 2 (2000): 291–343.

Crouch, Colin, and Wolfgang Streeck, eds. *Political Economy of Modern Capitalism: Mapping Convergence and Divergence*. London: Sage, 1997.

Crush, Jonathon, and Charles Amber. *Liquor and Labor in Southern Africa*. Athens: Ohio University Press, 1992.

Crush, Jonathon, and Paul Wellings. "Southern Africa and the Pleasure Periphery." *Journal of Modern Africa Studies* 21 (1983): 673–98.

Darling, Phyllis. "Dealer's Choice." In *Nevada: Official Bicentennial Book*, edited by Stanley W. Paher, 366–67. Las Vegas, NV: Nevada Publications, 1976.

Davenport, T. R. H. *The Transfer of Power in South Africa*. Cape Town, South Africa: University of Toronto Press, 1998.

De Certeau, Michel. *The Practice of Everyday Life*. Berkeley: University of California Press, 1984.

DeArment, Robert K. *Knights of the Green Cloth: The Saga of the Frontier Gamblers*. Norman: University of Oklahoma Press, 1990.

Del Papa, Frankie Sue. *Political History of Nevada*. Carson City, NV: State Press, 1990.

DiMaggio, Paul J., and Walter W. Powell. "The Iron Cage Revisited: Institutional Isomorphism and Collective Rationality in Organizational Fields." *American Sociological Review* 48, no. 2 (1983): 147–60.

Dombrink, John, and William N. Thompson. *The Last Resort: Success and Failure in Campaigns for Casinos*. Las Vegas: University of Nevada Press, 1990.

Douglas, Mary. *Purity and Danger*. London: Routledge and Kegan Paul, 1966.

Draper, Elaine. "Drug Testing in the Workplace: The Allure of Management Technologies." *The International Journal of Sociology and Social Policy* 18, nos. 5–6 (1998): 64–106.

Drew, Paul, and Anthony Wootton. *Erving Goffman: Exploring the Interaction Order*. Oxford, UK: Polity Press, 1988.

Drosnin, Michael. *Citizen Hughes*. New York: Holt, Rinehart and Winston, 1985.

Dugmore, Henry Livingston. "Becoming Coloured: Class, Culture and Segregation in Johannesburg's Malay Location, 1918–1939." PhD diss., University of the Witwatersrand, 1993.

Eadington, William R. "The Casino Gaming Industry: A Study of Political Economy." *The Annals of the American Academy of Political and Social Science* 474 (1984): 23–35.

———. "Economic Development and the Introduction of Casinos: Myths and Realities." *Economic Development Review* 13, no. 4 (1995): 51–54.

Earl, Phillip I. "Veiling the Tiger: The Crusade against Gambling, 1859–1910." *Nevada Historical Society Quarterly* 29, no. 3 (1985): 175–204.

Earley, Pete. *Super Casino: Inside the "New" Las Vegas*. New York: Bantam Books, 2000.

Edwards, Jerome E. *Pat McCarran: Political Boss of Nevada*. Reno: University of Nevada Press, 1982.

———. "From Back Alley to Main Street: Nevada's Acceptance of Gambling." *Nevada Historical Society Quarterly* 33, no. 1 (1990): 16–27.

Enarson, Elaine. "Emotion Workers on the Production Line: The Feminizing of Casino Card Dealing." *NWSA Journal* 5, no. 2 (1993): 218–32.

Epstein, Richard A. *The Theory of Gambling and Statistical Logic.* New York: Academic Press, 1995.

Evans, David, and Richard Schmalensee. *Paying with Plastic: The Digital Revolution in Buying and Borrowing.* Cambridge, MA: MIT Press, 2000.

Evans, Ivan. *Bureaucracy and Race: Native Administration in South Africa.* Berkeley: University of California Press, 1997.

Farrell, Ronald A., and Carole Case. *The Black Book and the Mob: The Untold Story of the Control of Nevada's Casinos.* Madison: University of Wisconsin Press, 1995.

Ferguson, James. *The Anti-Politics Machine: "Development," Depoliticization and Bureaucratic Power in Lesotho.* Minneapolis: University of Minnesota Press, 1994.

Findlay, John M. *People of Chance: Gambling in American Society from Jamestown to Las Vegas.* New York: Oxford University Press, 1986.

Fligstein, Neil. *The Transformation of Corporate Control.* Cambridge, MA: Harvard University Press, 1990.

Fligstein, Neil, and Roberto M. Fernandez. "Worker Power, Firm Power, and the Structure of Labor Markets." *The Sociological Quarterly* 29, no. 1 (1988): 5–28.

Foucault, Michel. *Discipline and Punish: The Birth of the Prison.* New York: Vintage Books, 1979.

Fourcade-Gourinchas, Marion, and Sarah L. Babb. "The Rebirth of the Liberal Creed: Paths to Neoliberalism in Four Countries." *American Journal of Sociology* 108, no. 3 (2002): 533–79.

Frederickson, George M. *White Supremacy: A Comparative Study in American and South African History.* New York: Oxford University Press, 1981.

Freud, Sigmund. "Dostoevsky and Parricide." In *Writings on Art and Literature,* 234–55. Stanford, CA: Stanford University Press, 1997.

Friedman, Bill. *Casino Management.* Secaucus, NJ: Lyle Stuart, 1982.

———. *Designing Casinos to Dominate the Competition.* Reno: University of Nevada Press, 2000.

Galbraith, John Kenneth. *The Affluent Society.* Cambridge, MA: Riverside Press, 1998.

Gallaway, William D. "The Association between Job Satisfaction and Service Quality." MBA thesis, University of the Witwatersrand, 1995.

Galliher, John J., and John R. Cross. *Morals Legislation without Morality: The Case of Nevada.* New Brunswick, NJ: Rutgers University Press, 1983.

Geertz, Clifford. "Deep Play: Notes on the Balinese Cockfight." In *The Interpretation of Cultures,* 412–53. New York: Basic Books, 1972.

George, Molly. "Interactions in Expert Service Work." *Journal of Contemporary Ethnography* 37, no. 1 (2008): 108–31.

Global Betting and Gaming Consultants. *Global Gambling Comes of Age: 2nd Annual Review of the Global Betting and Gaming Market.* West Bromwich, UK: Global Betting and Gaming Consultants, 2002.

Goffman, Erving. "On Cooling the Mark Out: Some Aspects of Adaptation to Failure." *Psychiatry* 15 (1952): 451–63.

———. *The Presentation of Self in Everyday Life.* New York: Doubleday, 1959.

———. *Asylums: Essays on the Social Situation of Mental Patients and Other Inmates.* Garden City, NY: Anchor Books, 1961.

———. *Stigma: Notes on the Management of Spoiled Identity.* Englewood Cliffs, NJ: Prentice Hall, 1963.

———. *Interaction Ritual: Essays on Face-to-Face Behavior.* Garden City, NY: Anchor Books, 1967.

———. *Strategic Interaction.* Philadelphia: University of Pennsylvania Press, 1969.

———. *Frame Analysis: An Essay on the Organization of Experience.* New York: Harper Colophon Books, 1974.

Goodman, Robert. *The Luck Business: The Devastating Consequences and Broken Promises of America's Gambling Explosion.* New York: Free Press, 1995.

Goodwin, John R. *Gaming Control Law: The Nevada Model.* Columbus, OH: Publishing Horizons, 1985.

Gordon, David M., Richard Edwards, and Michael Reich. *Segmented Work, Divided Workers: The Historical Transformation of Labor in the United States.* New York: Cambridge University Press, 1982.

Gottdiener, Mark. *The Theming of America: American Dreams, Media Fantasies, and Themed Environments.* Boulder, CO: Westview Press, 2000.

Gouldner, Alvin W. "The Norm of Reciprocity: A Preliminary Statement." *American Sociological Review* 25 (1960): 161–78.

Greenberg, Stanley B. *Race and State in Capitalist Development: South Africa in Comparative Perspective.* Johannesburg: Raven Press, 1980.

———. *Legitimating the Illegitimate: States, Markets and Resistance in South Africa.* Berkeley: University of California Press, 1987.

Guillen, Mauro F. *Models of Management: Work, Authority, and Organization in a Comparative Perspective.* Chicago: University of Chicago Press, 1994.

———. *The Limits of Convergence: Globalization and Organizational Change in Argentina, South Korea and Spain.* Princeton, NJ: Princeton University Press, 2001.

Gusfield, Joseph R. *Symbolic Crusade: Status Politics and the American Temperance Movement.* Chicago: University of Illinois Press, 1963.

Hall, Peter A., and David Soskice. *Varieties of Capitalism: The Institutional Foundations of Comparative Advantage.* New York: Oxford University Press, 2001.

Haller, Mark H. "The Changing Structure of American Gambling in the Twentieth Century." *Journal of Social Issues* 35, no. 3 (1979): 87–114.

Hamilton, Charles V., Lynn Huntley, Neville Alexander, Antonio Sergio Alfredo Guimaraes, and Wilmot James, eds. *Beyond Racism: Race and Inequality in Brazil, South Africa, and the United States.* Boulder, CO: Lynne Rienner Publishers, 2001.

Hannigan, John. *Fantasy City: Pleasure and Profit in the Postmodern Metropolis.* New York: Routledge, 1999.

Harper, Shannon, and Barbara Reskin. "Affirmative Action at School and on the Job." *Annual Review of Sociology* 31 (2005): 357–79.

Hart, Gillian. *Disabling Globalization: Places of Power in Post-apartheid South Africa.* Berkeley: University of California Press, 2002.

Herzenberg, Stephen A., John A. Alic, and Howard Wial. *New Rules for a New Economy: Employment and Opportunity in Postindustrial America.* Ithaca, NY: Cornell University Press, 1998.

Heubusch, Kevin. "Taking Chances on Casinos." *American Demographics* 19, no. 5 (1997): 35–40.

Hirsch, Paul. "Sociology without Social Structure: Neoinstitutional Theory Meets *Brave New World.*" *American Journal of Sociology* 102, no. 6 (1997): 1693–701.

Hobsbawm, Eric, and Terence Ranger. *The Invention of Tradition.* New York: Cambridge University Press, 1983.

Hochschild, Arlie Russell. *The Managed Heart: Commercialization of Human Feeling.* Berkeley: University of California Press, 1983.

Hughes, Everett C. *The Sociological Eye: Selected Papers.* Chicago: University of Chicago Press, 1971.

Hulse, James W. *Forty Years in the Wilderness: Impressions of Nevada, 1940–1980.* Las Vegas: University of Nevada Press, 1986.

———. *The Silver State: Nevada's Heritage Reinterpreted.* Las Vegas: University of Nevada Press, 1991.

Jackall, Robert. *Moral Mazes: The World of Corporate Managers.* New York: Oxford University Press, 1989.

Johnston, David. *Temples of Chance: How America Inc. Bought Out Murder Inc. to Win Control of the Casino Business.* New York: Doubleday, 1992.

Kefauver, Estes. *Crime in America.* Garden City, NY: Doubleday, 1951.

Kennedy, Robert F. *The Enemy Within.* New York: Popular Library, 1960.

Kingma, Sytze. "Gambling and the Risk Society: The Liberalisation and Legitimation Crisis of Gambling in the Netherlands." *International Gambling Studies* 4, no. 1 (2004): 47–67.

Kling, Dwane, ed. *Every Light Was On: Bill Harrah and His Clubs Remembered.* Reno: University of Nevada Oral History Program, 1999.

———. *A Family Affair: Harold's Club and the Smiths Remembered.* Reno: University of Nevada Oral History Program, 2003.

Lee, Ching Kwan. *Gender and the South China Miracle: Two Worlds of Factory Women.* Berkeley: University of California Press, 1998.

Legassick, Martin, and Harold Wolpe. "The Bantustans and Capital Accumulation in South Africa." *Review of African Political Economy* 7 (1977): 87–107.

Leidner, Robin. *Fast Food, Fast Talk: Service Work and the Routinization of Everyday Life.* Berkeley: University of California Press, 1993.

Lemon, Anthony. *The Geography of Change in South Africa.* New York: John Wiley and Sons, 1995.

Lewis, Oscar. *Sagebrush Casinos: The Story of Legal Gambling in Nevada.* New York: DoubleDay, 1953.

Lionel, Sawyer, and Collins. *Nevada Gaming Law.* Las Vegas, NV: Lionel, Sawyer, and Collins, 2000.

Lloyd, Richard. *Neo-Bohemia: Art and Commerce in the Postindustrial City.* New York: Routledge, 2006.

Lodge, Tom. *The Alliance of Power: Who Rules in South Africa?* Harare, Zimbabwe: SAPES Books, 1999.

Longmore, Laura. "A Study of Fahfee." *South African Journal of Science* 52 (1956): 275–82.

Lopez, Steven. "The Politics of Service Production: Route Sales Work in the Snack-Food Industry." In *Working in the Service Society,* edited by Cameron Lynn MacDonald and Carmen Sirianni, 50–73. Philadelphia: Temple University Press, 1996.

Lotter, S. "The Odds against Gambling." *South African Criminal Justice* 7 (1994): 189–99.

Macomber, Dean M. "Management Policy and Practices in Modern Casino Operations." *The Annals of the American Academy of Political and Social Science* 474 (1984): 80–90.

Magubane, Bernard Makhosezwe. *The Political Economy of Race and Class in South Africa.* New York: Monthly Review Press, 1979.

Mahoney, James. "Strategies of Causal Inference in Small N Analysis." *Sociological Methods and Research* 28, no. 4 (2000): 387–424.

Mamdani, Mahmood. *Citizen and Subject: Contemporary Africa and the Legacy of Late Colonialism.* Princeton, NJ: Princeton University Press, 1996.

Marais, Hein. *South Africa: Limits to Change: The Political Economy of Transformation.* Cape Town, South Africa: University of Cape Town Press, 1998.

Marcus, George E. *Ethnography through Thick and Thin.* Princeton, NJ: Princeton University Press, 1998.

Marks, Shula. *The Ambiguities of Dependence in South Africa: Class, Nationalism and the State in Twentieth-Century Natal.* Baltimore: Johns Hopkins University Press, 1986.

Martin, Isaac William. *The Permanent Tax Revolt: How the Property Tax Transformed American Politics.* Stanford, CA: Stanford University Press, 2008.

Marx, Anthony W. *Making Race and Nation: A Comparison of South Africa, the United States and Brazil.* New York: Cambridge University Press, 1998.

Mauss, Marcel. *The Gift: The Form and Reason for Exchange in Archaic Societies.* New York: Norton, 2000.

McKay, Steven C. *Satanic Mills or Silicon Islands? The Politics of High-tech Production in the Philippines.* Ithaca, NY: Cornell University Press, 2006.

Messick, Hank, and Burt Goldblatt. *The Only Game in Town: An Illustrated History of Gambling.* New York: Crowell, 1976.

Meyer, John W., John Boli, George Thomas, and Francisco O. Ramirez. "World Society and the Nation State." *American Journal of Sociology* 103, no. 1 (1997): 144–81.

Meyer, John, Francisco Ramirez, and Yasemin Soysal. "World Expansion of Mass Education, 1870–1970." *Sociology of Education* 65, no. 2 (1992): 128–49.

Mezrich, Ben. *Bringing Down the House: How Six Students Took Vegas for Millions.* New York: Free Press, 2004.

Michie, Jonathon, and Vishnu Padayachee. *The Political Economy of South Africa's Transition.* New York: Dryden Press, 1997.

Mizrachi, Nissim, Israel Dorri, and Renee R. Anspach. "Repertoires of Trust: The Practice of Trust in a Multinational Organization amid Political Conflict." *American Sociological Review* 72 (2007): 143–65.

Moehring, Eugene. *Resort City in the Sunbelt: Las Vegas, 1930–1970.* Reno: University of Nevada Press, 1989.

Moodie, T. Dunbar, and Vivienne Ndatshe. *Going for Gold: Men, Mines and Migration.* Berkeley: University of California Press, 1994.

Moody, Eric N. "The Early Years of Casino Gambling in Nevada, 1931–1945." PhD diss., University of Nevada, Las Vegas, 1997.

Moore, William Howard. *The Kefauver Committee and the Politics of Crime, 1950–1952.* Columbia: University of Missouri Press, 1974.

Newman, Mike. *Dealer's Special: Inside Look at the Casino Scene by a Working Casino Dealer.* Las Vegas, NV: BGC Press, 1979.

Nyre, Andrew Michael. "Union Jackpot: Culinary Workers Local 226, Las Vegas, Nevada, 1970–2000." Master's thesis, California State University at Fullerton, 2001.

Omi, Michael, and Howard Winant. *Racial Formation in the United States: From the 1960s to the 1980s.* New York: Routledge, 1994.

Ostrander, Gilman M. *Nevada: The Great Rotten Borough, 1859–1964*. New York: Alfred A. Knopf, 1966.

Otis, Eileen M. "Beyond the Industrial Paradigm: Market-Embedded Labor and the Gender Organization of Global Service Work in China." *American Sociological Review* 73 (2008): 15–36.

Pager, Devah. "The Mark of a Criminal Record." *American Journal of Sociology* 108, no. 5 (2003): 937–75.

Piore, Michael J., and Charles F. Sabel. *The Second Industrial Divide: Possibilities for Prosperity*. New York: Basic Books, 1984.

Platzky, Laurine, and Cheryl Walker. *The Surplus People: Forced Removals in South Africa*. Johannesburg: Raven Press, 1985.

Prasad, Monica. *The Politics of Free Markets: The Rise of Neoliberal Economic Policies in Britain, France, Germany, and the United States*. Chicago: University of Chicago Press, 2006.

Provost, Gary. *High Stakes: Inside the New Las Vegas*. New York: Truman Talley Books, 1994.

Raymond, C. Elizabeth. *George Wingfield: Owner and Operator of Nevada*. Reno: University of Nevada Press, 1992.

Reid, Ed, and Ovid Demaris. *The Green Felt Jungle*. New York: Trident Press, 1963.

Reith, Gerda. *The Age of Chance: Gambling in Western Culture*. London: Routledge, 1999.

Reppetto, Thomas A. *Bringing Down the Mob: The War against the American Mafia*. New York: Henry Holt and Company, 2006.

Reskin, Barbara F., and Patricia A. Roos. *Job Queues, Gender Queues: Explaining Women's Inroads into Male Occupations*. Philadelphia: Temple University Press, 1990.

Reuter, Peter. "Easy Sport: Research and Relevance." *Journal of Social Issues* 35, no. 3 (1979): 166–82.

Ritzer, George. *The McDonaldization of Society*. Thousand Oaks, CA: Pine Forge Press, 1993.

———. *Explorations in the Sociology of Consumption: Fast Food, Credit Cards and Casinos*. Thousand Oaks, CA: Sage Publications, 2001.

Roe, Mark J. *Strong Managers, Weak Owners: The Political Roots of American Capitalism*. Princeton, NJ: Princeton University Press, 1994.

Roske, Ralph J. "Gambling in Nevada: The Early Years, 1861–1931." *Nevada Historical Society Quarterly* 33, no. 1 (1990): 28–40.

Ross, Robert. *A Concise History of South Africa*. New York: Cambridge University Press, 1999.

Rothman, Hal. *Neon Metropolis: How Las Vegas Started the Twenty-First Century*. New York: Routledge, 2002.

Rothman, Hal K., and Mike Davis, eds. *The Grit beneath the Glitter: Tales from the Real Las Vegas*. Berkeley: University of California Press, 2002.

Roy, Donald F. "Efficiency and the Fix: Informal Intergroup Relations in a Piecework Machine Shop." *American Journal of Sociology* 60, no. 3 (1954): 255–66.

Rusco, Elmer R. "Racial Discrimination in Nevada: A Continuing Problem." *Governmental Research Newsletter* 11, no. 5 (1973): 1.

Sallaz, Jeffrey J. "The Making of the Global Gambling Industry: An Application and Extension of Field Theory." *Theory and Society* 35, no. 3 (2006): 265–97.

Salzinger, Leslie. *Genders in Production: Making Workers in Mexico's Global Factories*. Berkeley: University of California Press, 2003.

Schor, Juliet B. *The Overspent American: Upscaling, Downshifting and the New Consumer*. New York: Basic Books, 1998.

Schumpeter, Joseph A. "The Crisis of the Tax State." In *The Economics and Sociology of Capitalism*, edited by Richard Swedberg, 99–140. Princeton, NJ: Princeton University Press, 1991.

Schwartz, David G. *Suburban Xanadu: The Casino Resort on the Las Vegas Strip and Beyond*. New York: Routledge, 2003.

———. *Roll the Bones: The History of Gambling*. New York: Gotham, 2006.

Seidman, Gay. "Is South Africa Different? Sociological Comparisons and Theoretical Contributions from the Land of Apartheid." *Annual Review of Sociology* 25 (1999): 419–40.

Sheehan, Jack. *The Players: The Men Who Made Las Vegas*. Reno: University of Nevada Press, 1997.

Shepperson, Wilbur S. *East of Eden, West of Zion: Essays on Nevada*. Reno: University of Nevada Press, 1989.

Sherman, Rachel. *Class Acts: Service and Inequality in Luxury Hotels*. Berkeley: University of California Press, 2006.

Siegel, Richard Lewis. "Nevada among the States: Converging Public Policies." *Nevada Historical Society Quarterly* 43, no. 3 (2000): 214–62.

Silver, Beverly J. *Forces of Labor: Workers' Movements and Globalization since 1870*. New York: Cambridge University Press, 2003.

Simon, Herbert A. *Administrative Behavior: A Study of Decision-Making Processes in Administrative Organization*. New York: MacMillan, 1957.

Sklar, Martin J. *The Corporate Reconstruction of American Capitalism, 1890–1916: The Market, the Law, and Politics*. New York: Cambridge University Press, 1988.

Skolnick, Jerome. *House of Cards: Legalization and Control of Casino Gambling*. New York: Little, Brown and Company, 1978.

Skrentny, John D. *The Minority Rights Revolution*. Cambridge, MA: Harvard University Press, 2002.

Smith, Harold S. *I Want to Quit Winners*. Englewood Cliffs, NJ: Prentice Hall, 1961.

Solkey, Lee. *Dummy Up and Deal*. Las Vegas, NV: GBC Press, 1980.

Stiglitz, Joseph E. *Globalization and Its Discontents*. New York: W. W. Norton and Company, 2003.

Swartz, David. *Culture and Power: The Sociology of Pierre Bourdieu*. Chicago: University of Chicago Press, 1997.

Taylor, Christopher. "Visual Surveillance: Contemporary Sociological Issues." PhD diss., University of Nevada, Las Vegas, 1997.

Taylor, Frederick Winslow. *Principles of Scientific Management*. New York: Harper and Brothers Publishers, 1911.

Thompson, Leonard. *The Political Mythology of Apartheid*. New Haven, CT: Yale University Press, 1985.

Thompson, William N. "Casinos de Juego del Mundo: A Survey of World Gambling." *Annals of the American Academy of Political and Social Science* 556 (1998): 11–21.

———. "Nevada Goes Global: The Foreign Gaming Rule and the Spread of Casinos." In *The Grit beneath the Glitter: Tales from the Real Las Vegas*, edited by Hal K. Rothman and Mike Davis, 347–62. Berkeley: University of California Press, 2002.

Thorp, Edward O. *Beat the Dealer: A Winning Strategy for the Game of 21*. New York: Vintage Books, 1966.

Tilly, Charles. "Trust and Rule." *Theory and Society* 33 (2004): 1–30.

Tobin, Joseph J., David Y. H. Yu, and Dana H. Davidson. *Preschool in Three Cultures: Japan, China and the United States*. New Haven, CT: Yale University Press, 1986.

Tonelson, Alan. *The Race to the Bottom*. Boulder, CO: Westview Press, 2002.

Tuan, Mia. *Forever Foreigners or Honorary Whites? The Asian Ethnic Experience Today*. New Brunswick, NJ: Rutgers University Press: 1998.

Van Onselen, Charles. *Studies in the Social and Economic History of the Witwatersrand, 1886–1914: I. New Babylon*. New York: Longman, 1982.

Veblen, Thorstein. *The Theory of the Leisure Class*. New York: Mentor, 1953.

Venturi, Robert, Denise Scott Brown, and Steven Izenour. *Learning from Las Vegas*. Cambridge, MA: MIT Press, 1998.

Verhoeven, J. C. "An Interview with Erving Goffman, 1980." *Research on Language and Social Interaction* 26, no. 3 (1993): 317–48.

Vinson, Barney. *Las Vegas: Behind the Tables*. Grand Rapids, MI: Gollehon, 1986.

Vogel, Harold. *Entertainment Industry Economics: A Guide for Financial Analysis*. New York: Cambridge University Press, 2001.

Wacquant, Loïc. *Body and Soul: Notebooks of an Apprentice Boxer*. New York: Oxford University Press, 2004.

Waldinger, Roger, and Michael I. Lichter. *How the Other Half Works: Immigration and the Social Organization of Labor.* Berkeley: University of California Press, 2003.

Walker, Douglas M. *The Economics of Casino Gambling.* New York: Springer, 2007.

Weber, Max. *Economy and Society.* Berkeley: University of California Press, 1978.

———. *The Protestant Ethic and the Spirit of Capitalism.* New York: Routledge Classics, 2006.

Webster, Edward, and Glenn Adler. "Toward a Class Compromise in South Africa's 'Double Transition': Bargained Liberalization and the Consolidation of Democracy." *Politics and Society* 27, no. 3 (1999): 347–85.

Webster, Edward, and Karl Von Holdt. *Beyond the Apartheid Workplace.* Durban, South Africa: University of Kwazulu Natal Press, 2005.

White, Claytee D. "The Roles of African American Women in the Las Vegas Gaming Industry, 1940–1980." Master's thesis, University of Nevada, Las Vegas, 1997.

Whyte, William F. "The Social Structure of the Restaurant." *American Journal of Sociology* 54, no. 4 (1949): 302–10.

Wiley, Peter, and Robert Gottlieb. *Empires in the Sun: The Rise of the New American West.* New York: G. P. Putnam's Sons, 1982.

Winkin, Yves. "The Casino as a Total Institution: Erving Goffman in Las Vegas." Paper presented at the annual meeting for the Society for the Study of Symbolic Interactionism, Chicago, Illinois, February 6, 1999.

Wolpe, Harold. "Capitalism and Cheap Labour-Power in South Africa: From Segregation to Apartheid." *Economy and Society* 1, no. 4 (1972): 425–56.

Wright, Erik Olin. "Working-Class Power, Capitalist-Class Interests, and Class Compromise." *American Journal of Sociology* 105, no. 4 (2000): 957–1002.

Index

Italicized page numbers indicate tables and illustrations.

apartheid era: casino corporations linked to, 72, 76, 106–7; end of, 180; gambling as right denied in, 193; illicit urban casino industry in, xvi, 72, 126–27, 185–87, 193–94, 195; labor regime in, 144–45; labor transition after, 117, 119–20, 180–84; legislation creating, 135–36; prohibition and, 132–35; tips allowed during, 119, 149, 155–56, 159–61. *See also* casino industry in homelands; homeland states (including Lesotho and Swaziland)

architecture of casinos: carpet joint type of, 139–40; exotic themes, 146; goals of, 6; proposed in Gauteng casino bids, 219–20; as retail model, 263n15; sawdust house type of, 138, 139; Silver State as model, 73

Arizona: casinos outlawed in, 130

Arness, Dianne, 51

art unions (lotteries), 132–33. *See also* lotteries and raffles

Ashforth, Adam, 186

Asian immigrants: as dealers and floor managers, 34, 45, 63, 207, 207–8, 245; discrimination against, 276n54; as players, 75

Atlantic City (N.J.): legalization of casinos in, 201–2

Balboni, Albert, 201

Bank Crowd, The, 131

Basic Conditions of Employment Act (South Africa, 1997), 267n56

BEE (Black Economic Empowerment) plan (South Africa), 73. *See also* black empowerment requirement

Bentham, Jeremy, 29

Benton, Ted, 271n4

betting patterns: for avoiding blame for cold table, 101; "the book" (basic strategy), 94; changes in, 8–9; doubling and chasing strategies, 9–10; "playing behind" strategy, 95–96, 271n3

Bible, 128

Binion, Ben "Benny," 152

Black Economic Empowerment plan (BEE, South Africa), 73

black empowerment requirement: casino legalization linked to, 189–95; casino reports and commission audits of, 226–29; licenses based on potential for, 220–22;

no-tipping policy in context of, 232–33; obstacles to, 223–26

blackjack and blackjack tables: bird's-eye view of, 7; busting in, 7, 269n12; classic vs. "6 to 5," 214; dealer's influence of outcomes, 44, 49, 52–57; denying credit for "hot," 97–99; design developments of, 54–55; determination stage, 14; dig vs. hustle in, 66–67; displacing blame for "cold," 100–106; as fiefdoms of floor managers, 3, 25, 63–64; house advantage on, 2; in Nevada vs. South Africa, 243–44; number of decks per, 265n36; open boxes and fate of, 95–96, 103; popularity of, 7, 263n18; roulette compared with, 92; in service production regime model, 11–12; side bets on, 54–55, 269n15; slowing play on, 233; small talk at, 44; squaring off, 12–13; strategy in, 42, 52–53. *See also* betting patterns; card-counting technique; dealing techniques; players; shuffling cards

blacklisting of workers, 2, 210

blacks (South Africa): as "back of house" workers, 156–57; casino license bid of, 221–22; as croupiers, 180–83; legal protections absent for, 183–84. *See also* apartheid era; black empowerment requirement; homeland states (including Lesotho and Swaziland); PDIs (previously disadvantaged individuals); race and ethnicity; racial discrimination

Boer War (1899–1902), 133–34

Botha, P.W., 135, 186

Bourdieu, Pierre, 24, 114, 122–23

boy: use of term, 107, 176, 215, 271n5

Braverman, Harry, 115

bribes: for dealers, 56, 105, 152; for regulators and legislators, 131, 147–48, 180, 278n93

Burawoy, Michael, 6, 11, 22, 114, 289n47. *See also* service production regimes

busting: definition of, 7, 269n12

Buthelezi, Sfiso, 195

cabana republics, 135–37

Cahill, Robbins E., 141–42

California: casinos outlawed in, 130; WWII growth of, 139

cameras. *See* surveillance

Cape Town: lotteries (art unions) of, 135–36

276n55; gambling revenues for, *17, 19,* 141–
42, *164,* 167; as "internal colony," 266n48;
legalization of casinos in, 16, 17–18, 130,
132, 149, 163; non-Indian population of,
274n14; One Sound State policy, 235–36;
parallels of South Africa with, 17–19; Public Policy Concerning Gaming of, 286n3;
1950s-era casino in, 15; "sharpers" in, 151;
unemployment rate of, 116. *See also* casino
industry in Nevada; dealers in Nevada;
Las Vegas; legislation in Nevada; mid-
level managers in Nevada; pit bosses,
floor managers, and inspectors in Nevada;
Reno; Silver State Casino (pseud.)
Nevada Gaming Commission and Control
Board: author's contact with, 254; Consent
Decree and, 203; desegregation and, 176,
282n53; establishment of, 169; Hughes's
casino purchase and, 172–73; legitimacy
of casinos fostered by, 201; policy of, sum-
marized, 286n3
Nevada model: characteristics of, 235–36;
diffusion of, 237–38; limits of, 239–40. *See
also* casino industry in Nevada
Nevada Progressive Party, 131–32
Nevada Resort Association (NRA): on blacklists, 210; complaint against EEOC, 205;
Culinary Union's deal with, 267n57; on
desegregation, 174; Justice Department
complaint against, 177–79
Nevada Supreme Court, 167–68
New Jersey: legalization of casinos in, 201–2
Newman, Mike, 269n18
New Orleans: first stand-alone casino at, 129
New York Times, 291n27
NIMBY (not in my backyard) syndrome,
239–40
nonprofit organizations (South Africa):
gambling for good causes of, 15, 128–29;
on gambling policy and empowerment,
189–90; license refused for, 218; lotteries
of, banned, 133; opposed to gambling, 192
NP. *See* National Party (NP, South Africa)
NRA. *See* Nevada Resort Association (NRA)

Obama, Barack, 248, 249
Olympics (1960), 174
owners and proprietors: clean type of, 199–
203; competent type of, 216–26; criminal

backgrounds of, 163–64; early oversight
by, 149–50; labor issues and, 143, 171–72,
188–96; legal case of, 167–68; loyalty to,
151–53; marginal status of, 126, 137–38;
race of, 145; racial discrimination by, 138–
40; removed by regulators, 121. *See also*
corporate managers; corporations (gaming); crime syndicates

Pager, Devah, 268n6
panopticon: effacement strategies in, 72, 93–
96; Gold City as, 72, 80–88; as preventing
and producing infractions, 234; Silver State
as not, 29, 41, 69; surveillance central to,
72, 76, 80, 83–88; survival in, 106–7. *See
also* despotic service regimes; total
institution
Pass Law Act (South Africa, 1952), 136
PDIs (previously disadvantaged individuals): as croupiers, 73–75, 86, 106–7; definitions of, 18, 75, 228; empowerment of, 192–
94; licenses based on jobs for, 221–22;
managers' distrust of, 229–31; paradox of
experience as, 72; as pit bosses and floor
managers, 80, 82–83; quotas for, 82, 223–
25; white females as, 224. *See also* black
empowerment requirement; blacks (South
Africa)
pit bosses, floor managers, and inspectors in
homelands: labor practices of, 157, 159–61
pit bosses, floor managers, and inspectors in
Nevada: appearance of, 63; author's work
as, 22; autonomy of dealers regulated by,
62–64; continuity on floor for, 210–16;
decentralized context of, 199, 201–3;
demographics of, 63, *207;* fiefdoms of, 3,
25, 63–64; hiring decisions of, 37–38, 209–
10; players classified by, 20, 62, 63–69; on
player's motivation, 9; role of, 6–7, 62, 63;
in syndicate casinos, 140, 153–54; table
assignments by, 43; tip system under, 20,
65–66; warnings from, 53; "whale" noted
by, 269–70n21. *See also* juice system; mid-
level managers in Nevada
pit bosses, floor managers, and inspectors
in South Africa: black females as, 283n80;
blacks excluded from, 183; demographics
of, 80; as deskilled tokens, 72, 80; empowerment policy and, 224–25; estranged from

Text: 10/14 Palatino
Display: Univers Condensed Light 47 and Bauer Bodoni
Compositor: BookMatters, Berkeley
Indexer: Margie Towery
Printer & Binder: Sheridan Books, Inc.